Conversations with Robert Morgan

Literary Conversations Series
Monika Gehlawat
General Editor

Conversations with Robert Morgan

Edited by Randall Wilhelm and Jesse Graves

University Press of Mississippi / Jackson

The University Press of Mississippi is the scholarly publishing agency of
the Mississippi Institutions of Higher Learning: Alcorn State University,
Delta State University, Jackson State University, Mississippi State University,
Mississippi University for Women, Mississippi Valley State University,
University of Mississippi, and University of Southern Mississippi.

www.upress.state.ms.us

The University Press of Mississippi is a member
of the Association of University Presses.

First printing 2019
∞

Library of Congress Cataloging-in-Publication Data available

ISBN 9781496825711 (hardcover)
ISBN 9781496825728 (paperback)
ISBN 9781496825735 (epub single)
ISBN 9781496825742 (epub institutional)
ISBN 9781496825759 (pdf single)
ISBN 9781496825766 (pdf institutional)

British Library Cataloging-in-Publication Data available

Books by Robert Morgan

Zirconia Poems. Northwood Narrows, NH: Lillabulero Press, 1969.

The Voice in the Crosshairs. Ithaca, NY: Angelfish Press, 1971.

Red Owl. New York: W. W. Norton, 1972.

Land Diving. Baton Rouge: Louisiana State UP, 1976.

Trunk & Thicket. Fort Collins, CO: L'Epervier Press. 1978.

Groundwork. Frankfort, KY: Gnomon Press, 1979.

Bronze Age. Emory, VA: Iron Mountain Press, 1981.

At the Edge of the Orchard Country. Middletown, CT: Wesleyan UP, 1987.

The Blue Valleys. Atlanta: Peachtree Publishers, 1989.

Sigodlin. Middletown, CT: Wesleyan UP, 1990.

Green River: New and Selected Poems. Middletown, CT: Wesleyan UP, 1991.

The Mountains Won't Remember Us. Atlanta: Peachtree Publishers, 1992.

Good Measure: Essays, Interviews, and Notes on Poetry. Baton Rouge: Louisiana State UP, 1993.

The Hinterlands. Chapel Hill, NC: Algonquin Books, 1994.

The Truest Pleasure. Chapel Hill, NC: Algonquin Books, 1995.

Wild Peavines. Frankfort, KY: Gnomon Press, 1999.

The Balm of Gilead Tree: New and Selected Stories. Frankfort, KY: Gnomon Press, 1999.

Gap Creek: The Story of a Marriage. Chapel Hill, NC: Algonquin Books, 1999.

Topsoil Road: Poems. Baton Rouge: Louisiana State UP, 2000.

This Rock. Chapel Hill, NC: Algonquin Books, 2001.

Brave Enemies: A Novel of the American Revolution. Chapel Hill, NC: Algonquin Books, 2003.

The Strange Attractor: New and Selected Poems. Baton Rouge: Louisiana State UP, 2004.

Boone: A Biography. Chapel Hill, NC: Algonquin Books, 2007.

October Crossing. Frankfort, KY: Broadstone Books, 2009.

Terroir. New York: Penguin, 2011.

Lions of the West. Chapel Hill, NC: Algonquin Books, 2011.

The Road from Gap Creek. Chapel Hill, NC: Algonquin Books, 2013.

Dark Energy. New York: Penguin, 2015.

Chasing the North Star. Chapel Hill, NC: Algonquin Books, 2016.

As Rain Turns to Snow. Frankfort, KY: Broadstone, 2017.

Contents

Introduction

As interviewers and readers have discovered over the course of his career, a conversation with Robert Morgan is always illuminating about art, history, and the ways in which we live in this world. In Morgan's earliest recorded interview, with East Tennessee poet Jeff Daniel Marion, for instance, a simple question about sense of place unspools into a historical account of Thomas Edison's purchase of zircon mines in the 1890s. Morgan tells of the occurrence taking place "two miles east of our place" in Green River, North Carolina, so Edison could create filaments for the new electric bulbs lighting cities and towns across the country. The telling blends into a discussion of science, poetic imagery, and metaphor, and then characteristically expands into Morgan's larger vision of life and the cosmos:

> The image of a filament has always fascinated me, slender structures that through resistance to the current candesce and illuminate. Of course it takes just the right amount of resistance to the flow of things, in poems and in life; too much and the whole system burns out, too little and there's no heat generated. That and dams, which also obstruct the natural flow and transform it into power, channeling trillions of raindrops say, harvesting both sun and gravity.

Morgan's early and abiding interest in science, particularly the myriad and subtle connections between human and nonhuman worlds, is perhaps an unusual topic to find in conversations with a poet, fiction writer, and historian, but such is the case when talking with Robert Morgan, as many interviews in this volume make clear. Speaking with Rebecca Godwin in 2017, for instance, Morgan recalls how fundamental science has been to the development of his imagination: "From an early age I loved the articles in the *National Geographic* about science and technology. Through those articles on nuclear energy, rockets, astronomy, geology, I found a thrilling connection to a much larger world, ancient, futuristic, and timeless. Science promised new ideas, beyond the limited world I knew." In other interviews Morgan tells how this interest—"I wanted to be a rocket scientist!" he enthusiastically recalls to Tessa Joseph—led him to leave home for college [Emory University at Oxford] at the age of sixteen, without graduating high school. Morgan then transferred to North Carolina State and took classes in advanced calculus, differential equations, physics, and mechanics with an eye on the developing NASA moon program. But, in a story that builds to legendary status through the interviews, when prohibited by his advisor from registering for an advanced course in mathematics, Morgan instead took a creative writing class—and forever changed the direction of his life. As he tells Godwin with a dash of wry humor, "I went off to college to study science and mathematics, then got sidetracked by writing."

Morgan's sidetrack eventually became a career path that has led to the production of thirty books of poetry, short fiction, novels, essays, and histories, with more work to come. While Morgan's verse often transcends earthly bounds, as nearly every interview in this collection makes clear Morgan's creative world is firmly rooted in his childhood experiences in a subsistence farm in the mountains of western North Carolina. As Morgan tells Marion in the collection's first interview,

> I spent the first sixteen years of my life on our farm near Zirconia. There's about a square mile of land there I know every foot of. It was bought by my great-great-grandfather back in 1840. . . . I was privileged to tramp and play on all of it. I think my sense of place is very local indeed, not a culture, not a region, just one community. Since moving away I have found myself comparing everything I've seen to that archetypal acreage, soil, plants, climate, stream beds, as well as people.

In the following interviews, spanning more than forty years, Morgan's comments reveal him to be, in Tessa Joseph's words, "an interviewer's dream: articulate, erudite, patient, warm, and above all, a great teller of stories." Significant strands emerge in the early interviews, and are further developed in later discussions, such as the importance of family, the power of storytelling, and the mysteries of nature and religion, themes that run throughout Morgan's work in poetry and prose. In many of the interviews Morgan talks about the strong personalities of his parents who were both gifted storytellers and shared a fascination with the natural and spiritual worlds. Morgan tells Suzanne Booker about his mother's interest "in natural things, in looking for herbs and flowers, in the names of medicinal roots and barks, and she often pointed out hummingbirds and nests, tiny things. I think I share that love of the miniscule, the intricate and intimate." Morgan also tells interviewers about his father, an avid reader and towering figure who dominated familial and communal conversations "in the field, at prayer meeting, around the fireplace . . . a brilliant talker, who I'm sure turned me toward an early love of language."

The influence of religion, especially in Morgan's early life in the mountains, arises in many of the conversations about family and community. In several interviews Morgan discusses his father's Pentecostal fervor, his taking part in services in private homes that involved the laying on of hands, shouting, speaking in tongues, and other rituals. For the young Morgan, these experiences were both terrifying and fascinating, and as he confesses to one interviewer, "out of it I think I acquired a resistance to the orthodox and established, a distrust of formality, a taste for the rebellious and New Testament ecstatic." But these experiences also irrevocably shaped his poetic vision, as he tells William Harmon:

> I don't think there's any real doubt that it's relevant that I grew up in a fundamentalist church and heard the language of the Bible and the language of preachers; and perhaps more important was being among people who thought of things in spiritual terms—moral and spiritual terms. I can't imagine poetry without some sense of worlds beyond the merely physical; perhaps poetry is the unifier, seeing at once the spiritual and the physical.

Morgan's move away from North Carolina in 1971 to Cornell University in Ithaca, New York—in what would become a permanent, award-winning Ivy League teaching career—offers surprising insights about his development as a writer. In an interview for the *Iron Mountain Review*, Morgan recalls the irony of the geographical transition regarding what would become his primary subject matter. In writing the poems for his second collection *Red Owl* (1972), Morgan had considering himself as globally cosmopolitan, "in the company of Baudelaire in Paris and Pasternak in Moscow and Gary Snyder in Berkeley. I had not thought that much about the region. It was only after I had left it that I got increasingly interested in the history and geography and geology of the southern mountains. And I'm not sure I would have ever written as much about the place if I had stayed down here."

The early years at Cornell also forced Morgan to rethink his use of poetic voice and form, an aesthetic dilemma he discusses with several interviewers. In one exchange, Morgan confesses "I'd lived so much in isolation, and worked at perfecting a compact kind of poem surrounded by silence, and rarely discussed writing with anyone except by letter. Suddenly I was working in a community where everyone seemed to be a writer, talking to dozens of students every day about their poetry. It was disorienting to say the least." As a result, Morgan's poems became more conversational, "longer in wavelength and plot. As I taught and talked more, the poems began to talk more. But I didn't want to dilute the symbolic and emotional content for the sake of fluency. . . . The issue is poetic power, not manner." As Morgan recalls, this dilemma proved a near impasse for his poetry writing in 1973: "I wanted concision and atomic density, but found I talked too easily."

Morgan's "rediscovery" of traditional forms, ballad meter, rhymed endings, and syllabics offered solutions to this dilemma and allowed him to recover—like the filament metaphor of Edison's light bulb—the necessary resistance for his poetic lines. In *Land Diving* (1976), Morgan moves away from the object poem to a larger canvas, incorporating narratives and history, folktales and science, monologue and traditional forms. In melding his "easy talk" to the lattice of formal structures, Morgan's poems became longer and deeper, integrating more levels of language and experience into the verse that had been so spare before. The freedom was intoxicating for Morgan, as he experimented with an array of poetic techniques and forms, including the feverish, incantatory poems in *Trunk & Thicket* (1978), before launching a steady progression of masterful collections, *Groundwork* (1979), *Bronze Age* (1981), *At the Edge of the Orchard Country* (1987), *Sigodlin* (1990), and *Green River: New and Selected Poems* (1991). The narrative thrust charged Morgan's poems with a new vitality and depth as he discusses in many interviews. For Morgan, "Only action matters. And poetry is action, is embodiment of idea and figure. Poetry is story, motion, not gloss or explication." Morgan returned to fiction writing during the late 1980s, a practice he began as a college student, and employed aspects of craft and subject matter culled from his experiences writing poetry.

While poetry remains the subject of the later interviews as well, Morgan's fiction writing increasingly becomes a topic of discussion. Within a ten-year span, Morgan produced three short story collections, *The Blue Valleys* (1989), *The Mountains Won't Remember Us* (1992), and *The Balm of Gilead Tree* (1999); one collection of novellas, *The Hinterlands* (1994); and his first novel, *The Truest Pleasure* (1996). While Morgan's fiction writing may have surprised readers of his poetry, as he tells Patrick and Resa Crane Bizarro, "What I really wanted to do—when I was eighteen and nineteen . . . was to be a novelist, more than anything in the world." Bridging the two genres is Morgan's fascination with the historical past—familial, local, regional, national, and global. The narratives in these collections range across historical eras and events from Native American and frontier struggles to national

military conflicts such as the American Revolution and Civil War, to twentieth-century global conflicts such as World Wars I and II and Cold War
paranoia, to more recent cultural and societal changes that have forever
altered the mountains of Appalachia.

Although Morgan rarely takes a story from life and merely "transcribes
it," one incident speaks to an odd synchronicity at work in the mountains.
As he tells Donald Anderson:

> I have a story in [*The Mountains Won't Remember Us*], a story called "The
> Bullnoser," where a character is burying industrial chemicals on the property.
> Now I just made this up. One of my cousins said, "How did you know?" and then
> she named another cousin who had been burying waste from the G. E. plant on
> his property, and I said, "I didn't know." So, life is a page of fiction.

Morgan frequently discusses the crucial role of voice in his fiction, and
in the rollicking Peter Josyph interview, how important voice is for accurate representation of southern speech in the film production of Cormac
McCarthy's *The Gardener's Son* (1976). The adoption of the first-person
narrator, especially Morgan's use of the female voice, provided his breakthrough in writing fiction and has become a hallmark of his narrative aes-
thetics. As he tells one interviewer, "When I started letting these people tell
their own stories—in their own words—the narratives came alive in a new
way." The process was not only aesthetic, but psychological. As he confesses
to Sandra Ballard in a 2004 interview: "I discovered I could be another person if I could hear the voice," especially when "you live with the voice for
months, even years." Responding in depth to one question, Morgan talks
about the "balancing act" of representing "authentic" speech:

> You can't transcribe the way people talk—you just want to give a flavor of the way
> they speak, and you want to make it accessible, clear to any reader. At the same
> time, you want to make the voice seem plausible and authentic, so you're always
> doing this balancing act—keeping the inflections, the special things of the dialect,
> and at the same time trying to make it clear so it's the story that's coming through
> and readers are not saying, "Oh, these people talk funny."

The blending of the female voice with narratives of familial and regional
history formed a productive shape for Morgan's storytelling that followed. In
works such as *Gap Creek* (1999), *Brave Enemies* (2001), *The Road from Gap
Creek* (2013), and *Chasing the North Star* (2016), Morgan continued working

in the female voice that spoke through historical stories. Without question, Morgan's biggest commercial success came with his *Gap Creek: A Story of a Marriage*, which became a national bestseller, an Oprah Book Club selection, and as he tells Peter Josyph, thrilled his publisher [Algonquin]: "Before this, the most copies they had sold of a book was 150,000. The day Oprah made the announcement, they had orders for 650,000 copies overnight." The narrator of *Gap Creek* is Julie Harmon, based on Morgan's maternal grandmother, and whose voice Morgan "knew and remembered." As he tells Jesse Graves in the volume's deepest conversation, Julie's speech affected many readers because of its emotional accuracy: "Any number of people have come up to me and said, 'You know, I didn't think that anybody could ever recreate the voice of my grandmother, but you nailed it.'"

In many interviews, Morgan discusses the historical aspects of his fiction, informed by acute attention to detail and event, as a form natural to his storytelling imagination. Speaking with Donald Anderson, for instance, Morgan tells of the connection between his family stories and the historical bent that infuses his fiction:

> I've always felt very close to the past. . . . [My father] knew an awful lot about the history of America and of the South and of the area where I was raised. From the time I was a kid, I was very much aware of the Native American past in the mountains, and I would look for arrowheads. . . . My dad had been a hunter and a trapper when he was young. I have an uncle who still is a trapper, even though he's eighty-six years old. . . . Where I was raised there was lots of talk of deer and bear and panthers and people went out on trap lines in wintertime. . . . I suppose I feel a connection to the frontier past that most people do not.

Working in historical fiction ultimately led Morgan to take up the historian's pen and the mantle of biographer, writing the award-winning *Boone: A Biography* (2007) and *Lions of the West: Heroes of the Westward Expansion* (2011), a facet of Morgan's work discussed in interviews with D. G. Martin and Rebecca Godwin.

Morgan's conversation with former mentee and close friend Jesse Graves discusses, among many topics, Morgan's connections to "the more mysterious" aspects of nature and human existence. Discussing his essay "Nature Is a Stranger Yet," whose title echoes the poem by Emily Dickinson, Morgan converses with Graves about the inexhaustibility of the world, the wonders that can never be known in plants or ecosystems, in science and astrophysics, in family and friends. The more one knows, the less one knows, he tells

Graves: "Dickinson was absolutely right that while you may learn more and more and more and more about anything, it actually becomes more and more mysterious, for you then have a better sense of what you don't know. So the more you know, the larger your ignorance—your sense of ignorance—becomes. That's one of my favorite passages in her poetry and, in fact, in all American poetry." In speaking about his fiction writing, Morgan returns to the theme of mystery, telling Graves "there is no such thing as a good story that goes where you expect it to go . . . every good story has a surprise, a turn."

Morgan's practice as a professor of creative writing and the value of MFA programs is a topic several interviewers pursue. In one exchange, Morgan is bluntly candid: "You don't really teach anybody to write. You teach them, maybe, to be critics of their writing, or to have greater confidence in their abilities. The teachers that had the most influence on me were the people who taught me to believe in what I could do. If you approach it from that angle, I think you can actually do some good." In a 1997 interview with Robert West, Morgan reflects on his own experiences working for the *Carolina Quarterly* as a graduate student at UNC-Chapel Hill, where he published a story by "Ray[mond] Carver." Morgan tells West "there is no such thing as teaching writing as a skill without a subject," so he encourages young writers to work "from family, or philosophical ideas, or love, or emotional trauma." In several interviews, he stresses the importance of moving through stereotypical characters and plots to find emotional veracity, telling his students "they will know they are getting somewhere when an idea, a scene, is so painful they can just barely bring themselves to write about it. A writer has to touch quick, and draw blood."

Reading through Morgan's interviews in this collection provides insightful and indispensable details about the life of the writer, including his creative methods and work habits: "I keep farmer's hours. I get up early and go to bed early," he tells one interviewer. Readers will also discover conversations about Morgan's literary influences, his experiments with poetic and fictional craft, his connection to the natural world and the larger cosmos, his family experiences in times of war, and his observations about literature that reveal an astonishing depth and range of knowledge without parallel. In one interview Morgan denies a question about his rumored photographic memory, humbly admitting that he forgets some incidents but then recounts what he usually does not remember. Such humility is one of many reasons these interviews ring with exceptional candor, clarity, and eloquence. The mind of Morgan is a vibrant space to become immersed in, full of mystery and contemplation, dazzling with insight, humor, and a hard-earned wisdom, giving good measure by delivering more than one may imagine.

The editors would like to thank the following for their encouragement, support, and help in bringing this volume to fruition. Obviously, this book would not have been possible without the kindness and generosity of Robert Morgan, whose friendship, guidance, and wisdom throughout the development of this project has been indispensable. We also thank our editorial supervisor at University Press of Mississippi, Mary Heath, and acquisitions editor Katie Keene, as well as all of our contributors and publishing venues that worked with us so graciously. Gratitude as well for graduate student assistants Randi Adams at Western Carolina University, and Rieppe Moore and Lacy Snapp at East Tennessee State University, whose help in preparation of this manuscript proved invaluable.

RW

Chronology

1944   Robert Ray Morgan born October 3 in Hendersonville, North Carolina, to Clyde and Fanny Morgan. Raised on family farm in Green River, North Carolina.

1961   Attends Emory-at-Oxford College, Emory University, at Oxford, Georgia, 1961–62, without graduating high school at age sixteen.

1962   Attends North Carolina State University, 1962–63, studying applied mathematics and aerospace engineering.

1966   Graduates University of North Carolina at Chapel Hill, where classmates included writers Russell Banks and William Matthews. Attends 1963–66, and studies mathematics, then English. Marries Nancy Keith Bullock, August 6.

1967   Son Benjamin born, July 12.

1968   Receives MFA in Creative Writing from UNC-Greensboro, where Fred Chappell was one of his professors. Instructor in English, Salem College, 1968–69. National Endowment for the Arts Fellowship.

1969   *Zirconia Poems* (Northwood Narrows, NH: Lillabulero Press). Works as self-employed writer, farmer, housepainter, 1969–71.

1971   *The Voice in the Crosshairs* (Ithaca, NY: Angelfish Press). Lecturer in English, Cornell University, 1971–73.

1972   *Red Owl* (New York: W. W. Norton).

1973   Becomes assistant professor of English, Cornell University, 1973–78.

1974   National Endowment for the Arts Fellowship. Daughter Laurel born, July 14.

1976   *Land Diving* (Baton Rouge: Louisiana State UP).

1978   *Trunk & Thicket* (Fort Collins, CO: L'Epervier Press). Promoted to associate professor of English, Cornell University, 1978–84. Daughter Nancy Kathryn born, January 16.

1979   *Groundwork* (Frankfort, KY: Gnomon Press). Eunice Tietjens Prize from *Poetry*.

1981   *Bronze Age* (Emory, VA: Iron Mountain Press).

1982   National Endowment for the Arts Fellowship.

1984   Promoted to professor of English, Cornell University, 1984–92.
1986   Hawthornden Fellow in Poetry, International Writers Retreat. Hawthornden Castle, Scotland.
1987   *At the Edge of the Orchard Country* (Middletown, CT: Wesleyan UP). National Endowment for the Arts Fellowship.
1988   Jacaranda Review Fiction Prize. Guggenheim Fellowship, 1988–89.
1989   *The Blue Valleys* (Atlanta: Peachtree Publishers). *The Blue Valleys* nominated for First Fiction Award, American Academy of Arts and Letters Fellowship at Rockefeller Bellagio Center. Amon Liner Prize, *Greensboro Review.*
1990   *Sigodlin* (Middletown, CT: Wesleyan UP).
1991   *Green River: New and Selected Poems* (Middletown, CT: Wesleyan UP). North Carolina Award in Literature. James G. Hanes Poetry Prize from Fellowship of Southern Writers.
1992   *The Mountains Won't Remember Us* (Atlanta: Peachtree Publishers). Becomes Kappa Alpha Professor of English, Cornell University.
1993   *Good Measure: Essays, Interviews, and Notes on Poetry* (Baton Rouge: Louisiana State UP).
1994   *The Hinterlands* (Chapel Hill, NC: Algonquin Books).
1995   *The Truest Pleasure* (Chapel Hill, NC: Algonquin Books). *The Truest Pleasure* selected as New York Times Notable Book 1995; first runner-up for the Southern Book Critics Circle award; listed by *Publishers Weekly* as Outstanding Book.
1996   *Wild Peavines* (Frankfort, KY: Gnomon Press).
1997   "The Balm of Gilead Tree" selected for O. Henry Awards.
1998   McGee Visiting Writer, Davidson College, spring 1998.
1999   *Gap Creek* (Chapel Hill, NC: Algonquin Books). *The Balm of Gilead Tree: New and Selected Stories* (Frankfort, KY: Gnomon Press).
2000   *Topsoil Road* (Baton Rouge: Louisiana State UP). Distinguished Visiting Professor, Appalachian State University, fall 2000. *Gap Creek* receives Southern Book Critics Circle Award and Appalachian Book of the Year Award; selected for the Oprah Book Club and became a New York Times Bestseller and Notable Book of the Year.
2001   *This Rock* (Chapel Hill, NC: Algonquin Books).
2003   *Brave Enemies* (Chapel Hill, NC: Algonquin Books). Visiting writer, Furman University, winter 2003. Blackburn Visiting Writer, Duke University, spring 2003. Appalachian Heritage Award, Shepherd University. Inducted into Fellowship of Southern Writers.

2004   *The Strange Attractor: New and Selected Poems* (Baton Rouge: Louisiana State UP). Visiting professor, Duke University, spring 2004. Writer in residence, Furman University, winter 2004.

2005   Whichard Professor, East Carolina University, spring 2005.

2006   Receives honorary doctor of letters degree, UNC-Chapel Hill.

2007   *Boone: A Biography* (Chapel Hill, NC: Algonquin Books). Rivers-Coffey Distinguished Visiting Writer, Appalachian State University, fall 2007. R. Hunt Parker Award, North Carolina Literary and Historical Association. Academy Award in Literature, American Academy of Arts and Letters.

2008   Thomas Wolfe Prize, UNC-Chapel Hill. Kentucky Book Award for *Boone*.

2009   *October Crossing* (Frankfort, KY: Broadstone Books).

2010   Inducted into the North Carolina Literary Hall of Fame.

2011   *Terroir* (New York: Penguin). *Lions of the West* (Chapel Hill, NC: Algonquin Books). Hobson Award, Chowan University.

2013   *The Road from Gap Creek* (Chapel Hill, NC: Algonquin Books). "Singing" Billy Walker Award, University of South Carolina. The DAR History Award Medal.

2014   *Mockingbird: A Poem* (Frankfort, KY: Broadstone Books). The Thomas Wolfe Memorial Literary Award. The East Tennessee Civil War Alliance John Cullum Drama Prize.

2015   *Dark Energy* (New York: Penguin). The Southern Book Award for Nonfiction.

2016   *Chasing the North Star* (Chapel Hill, NC: Algonquin Books).

2017   *As Rain Turns to Snow, and Other Stories* (Frankfort, KY: Broadstone Books). Southern Book Award for Historical Fiction for *Chasing the North Star*.

Conversations with Robert Morgan

Interview with Robert Morgan

Jeff Daniel Marion / 1976

From *The Small Farm*, no. 3 (1976): 40–43. Reprinted by permission.

Jeff Daniel Marion: Are there specific individuals who have been important guides for you in your writing? Individuals who have opened you to possibilities?

Robert Morgan: I suppose the most honest answer would be to start off and say yes, many teachers and friends have of course had a great deal of influence on me and my writing, but that more than any literary work or personality the force and presence of my parents in the beginning have shaped the kind of poetry I write and would like to write.

In many ways their influence was always something contradictory and for that reason invigorating. I have discovered since I left home that mountain families are much closer than the average American family. I had no way or need to know that when I was growing up, but it's true. The family is really the only social organization in the mountains, and all the relationships almost are family relationships. But there were such differences within the family. For instance, there was and is the presence of my father, a well-read man with little formal education, a brilliant talker, who I'm sure turned me toward an early love of language. He always dominated conversations, in the field, at prayer meeting, around the fireplace. I've seen him stand by the road and talk to a friend stopped in his car for hours. I would have to go beg him to come so we could eat. He and his family leaned away from the Southern Baptists toward the Pentecostal Holiness church, and he often took part in the services of various splinter groups in private homes, shouting and speaking in tongues. I was both terrified and fascinated by all this, and out of it I think I acquired a resistance to the orthodox and established, a distrust of formality, a taste for the rebellious and New Testament ecstatic. My father is a huge man, ill at ease in public society, preferring to be off with a friend or two working and talking.

Contrastingly, my mother, though not really a quiet person, taught me a sense of delight in the small and ordinary. It is that I have developed most in my poems, what I have often referred to as the "Chinese mountaineer" sensibility, a calm and lucid feeling for things in their objective fullness. . . . My mother, who has had a very hard life, much death and long sickness in her family, and who always worked to help support us, has a tremendous strength and reserve and even tranquility that I find awesome.

Beyond the early relationships I find the strictly literary influences seem relatively small. But I would like to add that the poetry and fiction of Fred Chappell, and his encouragement, have had a great impact on later years. His novel *The Inkling* is a minor classic, well known in France and England, though not as much in America. He is a great teacher, with something of the same genius Pound had for spotting talent and drawing it out. When I went off to college I remember feeling pretty much lost among the upper-middle-class types I met there. But Fred was from my part of the state, and talked the way I did. More than anyone he taught me the craft of words. I have several letters that he wrote from Florence in 1968 about poems I was sending him, which I treasure.

JDM: How would you define your sense of place?
RM: I spent the first sixteen years of my life on our farm near Zirconia. There's about a square mile of land there I know every foot of. It was bought by my great-great-grandfather back in 1840 and though now divided into remnants among the descendants (some of it has been sold out of family), I was privileged to tramp and play on all of it. I think my sense of place is very local indeed, not a culture, not a region, just one community. Since moving away I have found myself comparing everything I've seen to that archetypal acreage, soil, plants, climate, stream beds, as well as people. This strong attachment to one particular piece of ground is both an advantage and a liability in our times. There is that solidity there, a home, a place to go back to no matter what happens. But that very tie can make you uneasy and a little alien in the other places you're bound to move to in our nomadic times. It took years for me to learn to write about other places and people. I'm still working on it. In America today there's a great fluidity and uncertainty that I find creative. I feel part of that too, and sometimes think I can see more clearly than my friends who grew up in the suburbs.

One feature I keep returning to about the area around Zirconia is the mining. All over our property there are pits and depressions where my ancestors dug for zircons or explored for lead, or mica, or gold. The tiny stream below our barn called Kimble Branch yields a trace of gold, and during the Civil War it was panned repeatedly. In the 1890s Edison and a mineralogist named Hidden opened a large zircon mine two miles east of our place and hired locals to work it. They hauled away tons of low-grade gems to make zirconium for their filaments. (I had relatives named Edison Staton and Hidden Freeman). The image of a filament has always fascinated me, slender structures that through resistance to the current candesce and illuminate. Of course it takes just the right amount of resistance to the flow of things, in poems and in life; too much and the whole system burns out, too little and there's no heat generated. That and dams, which also obstruct the natural flow and transform it into power, channeling trillions of raindrops say, harvesting both sun and gravity.

It might be interesting to mention that electricity was just coming to our valley when I was a child. I remember well the old kerosene lamps that are now back in fashion. The hintervalleys of our creek were not lighted until about the time I left for college. My friends around Cornell often tease me that I'm really eighty years old, instead of thirty, having lived through technological development that in the rest of the country stretches roughly over the period since World War I. Before I was eight my father had neither car nor pickup and we hauled corn out of the field with the horse and wagon, and used them to gather creek rock for our new house.

One of the less pleasant legacies of the Blue Ridge is the painful sense of insularity and alienation the mountain people feel, or did then, even a sense of inferiority to the rest of the country. In my county this was heightened by the presence of many wealthy lowlanders in the nearby Flat Rock area, going back to the 1820s, who summered in the mountains and sometimes hired my relatives for menial jobs. And in my time by the thousands of tourists that drove in from Florida and the rest of the Deep South. Nothing can make you feel more backward than hundreds of Miami Cadillacs among the pickups of your hometown, and the smart-talking language of the slickers trying to get your produce cheap.

I understand that one of the great problems of such cities as Cincinnati and Chicago now is the influx of people from Appalachia. It is a national tragedy that these people have been economically forced off their land into urban hell. No good will ever come from their exile in the ghettos.

JDM: Do you feel you are a voice for a particular place?

RM: It would be pretentious of me to say that I feel I am the voice of any area or people. On the other hand if I'm any good as a writer it will be because I speak what others know and feel but don't say. A poet if he's really great becomes the spokesman for his whole race or nation. What I worry about is saying it my way; if that's done well enough it aligns with what others see and would say too. I have tried to create verbal spaces in which other *things* and animals, not just people, can be heard. Maybe what I've tried to voice most is how natural things and manmade things decay and endure: institutions, artifacts, the dirt. For a long while I've been working at a little poem called "Tear Bottle," where I compare my writing to a nutshell of brine, "Wept by the saints of my childhood for law / and changes."

JDM: What sort of obligations or commitments does this sense of place bring?

RM: I think a certain loyalty to the mud and trash around us can help the poet deal with the narcissism and prosiness rampant in so much verse we see these days.

There is something releasing about moving through language outside yourself into unlikely places and vantages. Dealing directly with the briar patch and gullies of waste can divert the ego, triggering, at least for me, a rush of imagination. My prime obligation is to communicate that surge of feeling that comes when the ordinary stuff around is seen anew.

Interview with Robert Morgan

Suzanne Booker / 1985

From *Carolina Quarterly* 37, no. 3 (Spring 1985): 13–22. Reprinted by
permission of Suzanne Booker-Canfield.

Suzanne Booker: Since this issue is devoted to North Carolina writers, and
since your southern Appalachian heritage contributes so forcefully to your
themes and subjects, would you tell me more about growing up in Zirconia?
Robert Morgan: I'm not sure how important the place where one grows
up is to poetry, except as setting, background. It's after all the quality of the
writing, the art, and the vision, that make poetry interesting, not the scen-
ery and locale, not even the subject matter. But one of the particular things
about growing up when I did in Henderson County, North Carolina, was
that I was able to see a community change rapidly and forever. I was raised
on a farm that had been in the family since 1840, and very few of my cousins
or uncles had ever left the valley, except to work temporarily on construction
jobs, or to go into the army. It was a life that revolved around farming and
family and church. You were related by blood to almost everyone you knew.

But at the same time you were aware of the isolation, partly because
so many tourists were coming to western North Carolina even then. The
wealthy of Charleston and Atlanta had used Henderson County as a summer resort since the 1820s, and there was that strange juxtaposition of the
local people with the low country rich.

So there was a great contrast of sophistication and poverty side by side.
Paradox and change are always enriching to the imagination. Perhaps I was
lucky in that way. But I never felt quite at home in Zirconia, even as a child.
Industry was moving in from the North, and new families were buying land
and sending their children to the schools. It was scary and exciting . . .

What is impossible to communicate to my contemporaries in the worlds
of universities and poetry is the awesome sense of remoteness and difference you have growing up in a little cove in the Blue Ridge Mountains.

When I've tried to write about that sense of *outsideness* I've been accused of exaggerating, of bragging. What is most literal and accurate in my writing has often been taken to be fantastic. I have a friend who's the heir to a considerable corporate fortune, who has often said to me, "Of course you're from the middle class just like the rest of us." And I always smile and nod. It astonishes me when reviewers question, not my art, but my veracity. It's as though they're upholding the very difference I was trying to communicate.

SB: Why are there so many good poets in North Carolina?

RM: It's a fairly recent thing: the North Carolina writers we have early in the century, Thomas Wolfe and Paul Green, had fabulous reputations. I was astonished the other day to think of Paul Green and just how famous he was. He's pretty much forgotten now, but he won a Pulitzer Prize in 1927 when he was in his early thirties. Thomas Wolfe was the most famous writer in America in 1930, and the Playmakers had presented all his first plays in Chapel Hill. Then for a long time you don't have much happening in North Carolina, until the sixties when people like Reynolds Price and Doris Betts, John Ehle and Fred Chappell, came along. It was just in the last decade and a half that there were many poets from North Carolina; it's astonishing and thrilling. I certainly don't know the explanation for it. Yet what impresses me is the variety: everybody from Jonathan Williams, representing a very individual sort of Black Mountain style of poetry, to A. R. Ammons, another highly individual style. Fred Chappell, Bill Harmon (he's certainly his own kind of poet), me, James Applewhite, Michael McFee, Betty Adcock, and I've left out a half a dozen people publishing nationally. It must have something to do with the way North Carolina has been a collision place for cultures; it's South, but it's upper-middle South. In the sixties when I was in college it was a place changing so rapidly, and I think that is always good for poetry.

SB: You've cited your parents as also important in shaping the kind of poetry you write.

RM: Of course, it goes without saying, in these post-Freudian times, that everyone is deeply influenced by his parents. We're just what our mothers made us, one of my colleagues keeps saying. But as I get older I realize more and more what strong personalities my parents were and are. Though without benefit of formal education they are both readers, my mother of fiction and my father of history and the *National Geographic* magazine. Both have always read constantly in the Bible, and they read to my sister and me every night when we were little. I used to listen to Evangeline's lesson—she was three years older than me—and by the time I was six I could read all her books. Because I was born in October I couldn't attend school until almost seven, but my mother taught me at home and I knew arithmetic and reading well before the first grade.

My mother was always interested in natural things, in looking for herbs and flowers, in the names of medicinal roots and barks, and she often pointed out hummingbirds and nests, tiny things. I think I share that love of the miniscule, the intricate and intimate. Her mother, who I remember a little, had known the names of all wild things and passed much of her memory on to her. My mother worked in cotton mills, beauty shops in town, and in an electrical plant, but she never lost her delight, even passion, for gardening. When young she had memorized poems from textbooks and magazines and she used to recite them.

My father is the talker in the family. Where I'm the introvert, he's the extrovert. His mother and father had belonged to the Pentecostal Holiness movement of the 1890s, and he himself used to attend Holiness revivals. When young, I remember being extremely frightened of him and others speaking in tongues, shouting, and I remember being especially terrified of the phrase "baptism of fire." It sounded too much like Hell to me. And I was often afraid the Rapture would come and I'd be left with the sinners and the moon turned to blood. But I think I must have acquired some taste for the white-hot rhetoric of the New Testament, and for the ecstatic aspects of religion. I've always been moved by such ceremonies as the laying on of hands, foot washing, baptism.

But mostly I remember the great relief when the service was over, and we could go back out into the sunlight and the sweet breeze among the pines. There seemed a wonderful poise in nature, as it merely went about its business, with no interest or designs on us. How friendly the stars seemed over the dark mountains after the sweat of a prayer meeting. I have never enjoyed gatherings, whether lectures, classes, poetry readings. They seem to violate the essential and integral *aloneness* of poetry. Poetry at its best is the expression of the community, but through and to the solitary individual. In a similar way the doctrinal disputes I listened to as a child gave me a distaste for controversy and debate I've never been able to outgrow. Poetry does not argue; it affirms and embodies, or it is nothing.

SB: When you left Zirconia to go to college, you studied science, then math. What prompted the switch to English at Chapel Hill? Was it at this point that you knew you wanted to be a writer?

RM: All through my teens I wanted to be a writer. I had the example of Carl Sandburg just down the road in Flat Rock. A friend of mine had a brother at Harvard who sent us a paperback of *Crime and Punishment*. And there was a woman who drove the bookmobile who gave me *War and Peace* and Dickens. I read constantly, and I wanted to write. But I also wanted to be a composer, and studied piano, and books on harmony and technique, and banged on our old piano into the night, after working in the fields during the day. I wanted to be a philosopher also, and read Nietzsche, Sartre, Kant, Shaw, and about anything I could get my hands on. Colin Wilson's *The Outsider* came out about that time, and I read that too, and thought about "existentialism."

I first went away to college at the age of sixteen, without graduating from high school, to Emory at Oxford, thinking of chemistry and medicine. But while there I got increasingly interested in calculus and the space program. John Glenn had just orbited the earth. At Emory I was at the top of my class in calculus, and I think it was vanity more than anything else that drove me toward mathematics. I was good, but not really that good. I made A's, but I would never have been a creative mathematician.

The year at NC State studying applied math and engineering was one of the most confused and exciting of my life. I found I could do my schoolwork in minimal time, so I really spent my days browsing in library and bookstore, walking in the city of Raleigh, going to the museum there, and to movies. I'd never been allowed to go to movies as a child, but I made up for it at college, attending every free flick, every foreign film, and every new release that came to Raleigh and Chapel Hill. I was so disturbed about what I wanted to do that I must have walked every block in the city of Raleigh. There was a lot of building going on then at NC State and in Raleigh, and the whole landscape seemed to be pits and heaps of red clay, new-poured cement, new expressways. I walked far into the suburbs and outskirts, stopping in diners and strange little restaurants. I was entirely on my own; I had no friends. One gray November afternoon I saw *Lolita* in a fleabag theater on the northwest side of the city, my first encounter with Nabokov.

In the spring of 1963 I wanted to take an advanced course in differential equations, but my advisor would not let me since I'd never made up a deficiency in solid geometry. So I registered for Creative Writing instead. The class was taught by Guy Owen, who was a generous and charming teacher. I wrote both poems and stories, but he encouraged the stories especially. The poems were terrible. I borrowed my roommate's typewriter and pecked away all spring, forgetting thermodynamics and partial differential equations, trying to remember exactly how my great-aunt had spoken, and the smells of old houses heated by cooking stoves and fireplaces.

Even so, I wasn't ready to leave math entirely behind. When I transferred to UNC in 1963 I wanted to study both pure mathematics and comparative literature, if I remember correctly. So I took courses in Tolstoy and Dostoyevsky as well as algebra and analysis. Chapel Hill seemed gentle and humane after the military atmosphere of NC State. I'll never forget how courteous everyone, from librarians to department secretaries, seemed. My two years as an undergraduate at Carolina were heady and invigorating. I met writers and actors, filmmakers and painters, worked on the *Carolina Quarterly*, saw hundreds of movies, studied the history of art, knew political activists and civil rights activists, beatniks who had lived in the East Village and Tangier. Around the *Quarterly*, I got to know people with prep-school educations who knew far more about poetry than I. They talked about Yeats and Lowell and Berryman, and I began to listen.

I'd been writing poetry all along, but the first I did with any quality at all was in the late summer of 1964. I was working in the GE plant in Hendersonville, and looked out from the loading dock after a rain and saw a great shaft of sun coming through the overcast. I realized I wanted to describe that as a timber holding up and bracing the clouds. For days I wrote and rewrote, trying to get the verb and gesture of that image right. After returning to Chapel Hill I wrote a little piece inspired by Sibelius's "Swan of Tuonela." That was the first thing that I ever did where I felt the sound was right. Guy Owen printed it in the *Southern Poetry Review* the next spring.

One of the finest things that happened to me at Chapel Hill was meeting Jessie Rehder, a wonderful teacher and encourager. It was she who invited me to work for Honors in writing, and to do that I had to become an English major. I abandoned math forever, though I'd finished most of the coursework for that degree, and wrote stories and poems, pieces of novels, film scripts, and plays, during my senior year. In the fall of 1964, I felt that I too could write poetry, maybe, by being true to the world of experience beyond the ego, and true to the plainest, most honest voice. I heard a lucid, modern measure I wanted to learn to use, lean as Webern, subtle as Bartok, crisp as Pound's *Cathay*. I wrote scores of poems in 1964–65 trying to realize that voice. Mostly they didn't work out, but I felt privileged to be that close to something that seemed authentic.

SB: What's the relationship between your teaching and your writing? Do certain things change as an outgrowth of your teaching and research?

RM: Apparently my teaching began to change after I started teaching at Cornell. I'd lived so much in isolation, and worked at perfecting a compact kind of poem surrounded by silence, and rarely discussed writing with anyone except by letter. Suddenly I was working in a community where everyone seemed to be a writer, talking to dozens of students every day about their poetry. It was disorienting to say the least. But stimulating also, to find others interested in the same technical and poetic and historical questions I'd been working through.

My poems began to get more conversational, longer in wavelength and plot. As I taught and talked more, the poems began to talk more. But I didn't want to dilute the symbolic and emotional content for the sake of fluency. I've always been suspicious of the emphasis on "American speech" as any sort of artistic justification. The issue is poetic power, not manner. It was mostly this dilemma that almost brought my poetry writing to a halt in 1973, the year after *Red Owl* was published. I wanted concision and atomic density, but found I talked too easily. It was a dead end I didn't solve until a year later, when I began writing in rhymed forms. By focusing on end rhymes of the elaborate a b c c b a stanza or the chant royal I felt I'd recovered the necessary resistance for lines, and could go ahead. It was in that period that most of the *Land Diving* poems were written. That book means the most to me because in some ways it cost me the most. I found I was able to incorporate narratives and history, folktales and science, monologue and traditional forms into my writing, and that gave me a gratifying sense of control and freedom. I could write poems longer than a page, and integrate more levels of language and experience. I was no longer restricted to the tension of the free verse line I'd worked to learn in the decade before. I tried writing a poem of over a hundred pages, from which I salvaged the fragments that later became *Trunk & Thicket*. It was just sheer good luck that a number of things came together for me around that time, from my reading of Smart's *Jubilate Agno*, and discovering the textures of Geoffrey Hill's poetry, and beginning to fumble around with my own memories and childhood, with stories my grandfather and father had told, and a new coming to terms with the rhetoric of the New Testament, which I had forgotten since childhood. The poems of that period are probably uneven, but through them I found abilities I didn't know I had.

SB: In *Trunk & Thicket* you write about the instability and impotence of language. How do you reconcile this skepticism about language with your idealism and optimism about the function of poetry?

RM: In the passage you are referring to I mean my difficulties with speech more than with language itself. I have a light stammer, especially when excited or embarrassed. And I've always had a terror of having to *explain*. For every explaining seems to lead to yet another crux. There seems no end to formulation and argumentation. I often have an overwhelming sense of the futility of explaining anything. Only action matters. And poetry is action, is embodiment of idea and figure. Poetry is story, motion, not gloss or explication.

But I do have a skepticism about language too. It so rarely does what we want it to. The first step to becoming a writer is to learn to distrust words and the obvious combinations. You really have to hate the "poetic" effects to get anywhere as a poet. The more you know about language the more you see that it is all cliché, just a set of conventions. Every phrase wears out quickly. So you work against the erosion of freshness, that abrasion of use, not only by newness of diction and texture, but by voice and gesture. No word in itself is poetic for long, except by incorporating into the movement of voice, of imagination. It is not so much what is *said* as what is evoked, is enacted, by language that is important. A favorite quote is from Hollis Summers: "The point of a story is always the point beside the point." Peripheral vision is the important vision.

SB: Your cadence frequently resembles that of hymns. To what extent has music influenced the rhythm of your lines?
RM: Well, hymn meter is ballad meter, or common meter, which they say underlies all poetry in English. So in a sense it's hard to escape that sound in short poems, the four-stress line / three-stress line. It must be in the very pulse of the language, like the two-stress hemistich of *Beowulf*, which one of my graduate students has found in Whitman.

Music has always been important to me. My mother sang to me often when I was little, and I used to make up long compositions in my head when I was a child, before I studied piano. It was as though everything I saw or thought had a musical correlative. But that fantasy stopped once I learned to read music. Later I wanted, more than anything, to be a composer

But hymns may be just as important to me because of their words and imagery. They were certainly one of the art forms I was exposed to most as a child, along with readings from the Bible and the fine rhetoric of pulpit and prayer. I'm still haunted by the phrases of those lyrics: "There's a land that is fairer than day," "The land beyond the blue," "The river . . . that flows from the throne of God," "Beautiful, beautiful Zion," "By Jordan's stormy banks I'll stand."

SB: You've worked in areas virtually untouched by your contemporaries: anagrams, the complex French chant royal, and a stanza form William Harmon calls the "morganelle." Would you discuss how you began to work with these, and any experiments in progress or planned?

RM: As I said earlier, I began working with traditional forms in 1974, after *Red Owl* was published. I'd tried some experiments, wedding the rich imagistic phrase with a more talky poem, and I'd not been happy with the results. Also, I was very busy teaching then, and almost quit writing for a while. But late in that year I suddenly began several projects at once. One was a series of poems on the ancient Near East, Sumer, and Akkad, which was never finished. Another was the long poem never finished but published in fragments as *Trunk & Thicket*. The original idea was to write a long poem incorporating every verse form, from prose poem to free verse to blank verse to couplets right on through to triolets and rhyme royal. I saw the poem as a river gathering itself from many different-colored tributaries and passing through narrow gorges, over falls and shoals, through lakes and locks, and then unraveling itself through the delta and dispersing into the ocean. But I also tried to invent several new rhyme forms, including the one Harmon calls the "morganelle." I wanted to get a new cultural and historical richness and density in my work. At the same time, I wanted to recover some of the incantatory power of "prophesying" as I'd heard it as a child. Suddenly I was able to confront and use that part of myself that had been rejected so long before. The result was "Mockingbird" and a pile of other poems I've never published but still plan to work on.

SB: To what extent is language a correlative of place in your poems? Does, then, a poem about a mountain carry with it the sense of stability, roughness, isolation that we associate with a mountain?

RM: This seems to be the area of poetics where contemporary literary theory has completely failed us. We seem to be living through a new age of nominalism in criticism. It's as though we have leapt back to the thirteenth century somehow. Theorists want to remind us that no word, no phrase, no sentence, has more than an arbitrary relationship with any fact, object, experience. In fact the only thing "real" about language is the structure and texture of language itself. But of course it is against the background of this very arbitrariness, this clutter, that any artist of language begins work. The fact that words are not written on gold in heaven in no way lessens their impact when put in the right order by a great poet. Poetry creates the *impression* of authority and plausibility; it delights and seems to be true to our experience.

As for a poem being like a mountain, nature is our only language for experience. If a poem is not to be big and grand and rough like a mountain, it would have to be big and rough as a bear, or wide as a river, or rough as the ocean in a gale, or long as the Milky Way. All description is metaphor, seeing one thing and saying another. I wanted to write a poem big as the Cicero Mountain because that was the landform most familiar to me. I had grown up looking across the river valley at its woolly mammoth dome and long sloping shoulders, at the sparkling diamond eye where seepage froze on the cliff face in January. But image or fact in itself is never enough either. It is the equation of language with mountain (strange that it's named after old Cicero Ward, who was named after the orator). So mountain equals poem, grand, rough, isolate. The dirt and rocks and hollows of the mountains have not been changed in the least, and yet they have.

SB: What is your routine for writing? Do you set aside a certain amount of time each day?

RM: Poetry is so unpredictable you never know when you can start something, or if you do start it whether it will work out. Sometimes I've gone back through half-finished manuscripts and found one or two I could complete, often years after the first draft. At other times I've waited weeks for a new idea to come along. Poetry simply can't be written without enthusiasm for an image, a character, a tone of voice, that triggers a sense of possibility. Sometimes I don't have the confidence to write, and sometimes I wonder how I could have written what I have, much less something better, something different. You can't plan to write poetry, because the best things happen by surprise, while actually writing, while planning one kind of thing and finding that you've done another.

Hard as you may work on a poem, it's still a gift. A poem can't be worried into being, though it can certainly be revised and polished up. At the moment of writing, when things are coming together, you don't care much whether it's a great poem, or even a really good poem, as long as you can make it do what you have in mind, uncovering more and more possibilities. At the most intense times of composition you don't even care about "poetry" as long as you can make this one thing powerful in its own way. Literature is far from a working poet's mind.

SB: I haven't said much about your fiction, but I know you've written some short stories lately. What proportion of your writing time do you spend on that and how do you determine whether an idea is better suited to poetry or prose?

RM: Yes, I started writing stories again this summer for the first time in many years. I wrote a lot of fiction in college and started a couple of novels then, and actually published three or four stories, including one in the *Carolina Quarterly* way back. I've always been interested in fiction, and in fact have been working on a novel set in the sixties on a university campus in North Carolina (not any campus I was ever actually on, but a campus with elements of NC State maybe). It seemed like a very interesting setting for a novel.

I've always hated the overspecialization in American writing. Most people do either poetry or fiction, even specialize in a particular kind of poem or story or novel. I like to feel I have the freedom and ability to do both. I've also written some critical essays and reviews over the years. To some degree they all overlap. Certainly writing the poems has made me a better critic of poetry, and also a better prose stylist, a more accurate observer. But I had the experience when young of starting a story and becoming so interested in an image or a metaphor or rhythm I turned it into a poem. Gradually, I wrote fewer and fewer stories and more and more poems. I was interested in compactness, and what I called "nonjournalistic" language. I hoped to find a new way of looking at the world around me. It seemed at the time that Faulkner and others had done the "southern fiction" idea to death. But there was almost no southern poetry. I wanted to work against the clichés of southern writing, and do something spare and precise, free of classical allusion and archaic diction. I found models in translations from Chinese poetry, and from the Greek anthology, and perhaps in laconic mountain speech.

Recently I have begun to take ideas that could become poems—but have not—and expand them into stories. That's the great difference between stories and poems, besides the line unit; the story is much more detailed. In poems most details are left to implication.

SB: How do you know when a poem is finished?
RM: As someone else has said, they're never really finished, but abandoned at some stage. But you do know when you can do no more with them. A line or image locks into place and you're willing to turn aside and work on something else in more need of revision.

SB: How do you explain the lack of critical attention you've received?
RM: I'm probably not the best person to answer that: I don't think there's been a lot of criticism of anybody of my generation. I've had a few very fine articles written on me. Harmon's is the longest, but there've been shorter

ones from time to time. But I really think that my whole generation of poets has been neglected. The generation of poets born in the 1920s was so successful and so dominant that it has never been replaced, so that if anybody thinks of having a festival or writing an article, they think of somebody in the generation of Ashbery and Robert Bly and Gary Snyder, not of my generation. It's really just now that people in their late thirties and early forties are being taken all that seriously. That's a very complicated thing—the differences in generations. I think it has something to do with the fact that the older poets were the people who were in World War II and became writers after the war. It was a generation of great confidence and aggressiveness: they'd won the war. They believed in themselves and they took over. They were very critical of people older than them. I'm thinking about Ginsberg and Bly and Robert Creeley. Very critical of the New Critics—Allen Tate and people like that.

My generation, the Vietnam War generation, lost the war—lost the antiwar movement even—and have always been very confused about what they were up to and terribly polite to the older generation of poets. You never see an attack written by somebody my age on the generation of Ashbery and James Merrill. They always want to agree with them—very polite. And I think that's cost them tremendously. They haven't cleared any space for themselves. There are a few people who've had a little bit of critical attention, but very few. And this is not true of the older generation: by the time they were forty they'd been anthologized and written about.

Another reason for this is that my generation does not specialize in criticism, so that even the outstanding poets very rarely write articles on poetry. They are people who believe in the art of writing but not developing critical approaches. The good side is I think my generation is just now beginning to come into its own. I think you'll see a change. It has taken a long time for us to really get going as writers. And I think that's true of other fields, not just poetry. But poetry, because it's the essential art, reflects it most dramatically.

SB: You've been labeled a "place poet," a poet of "landscape"; William Harmon has called your poems "Pelagian georgics." Are you comfortable with these labels or do you feel they're too limiting? How would you categorize your poetry?

RM: I think all these terms apply in one way or another to what I've done. But you won't find many poets happy to categorize themselves. I think of myself as, hopefully, a poet, period. Certainly Harmon's phrase is the most unexpected, and the most resonant. He picked out the line in "Mockingbird" where I talk about the statute of limitations running out on original sin. That was said in fun, but I meant it too. I think that for me just becoming a writer, becoming a poet, necessitated a kind of distance from the fundamentalist Baptist doctrine that I grew up with. It seemed so negative; it just cut off all possibility of creativity and growth. And I think this is true not only of me but of many American poets, going all the way back to Emerson and Thoreau and Whitman—coming out from under Calvinism and discovering something that worked better for them. The strange thing is that people like me repeat the process in the twentieth century. This has a lot to do with the place I come from and the world I grew up in. But even though I don't know where I stand theologically, I think Harmon is right that spiritually and emotionally I am a Pelagian. I have to believe in possibility, that there's not some great sin to be expiated but that there's a world there we can accept and appreciate, however doomed it may seem at times.

Why not try to work with what we have, what is here. As I say elsewhere, we are paradise's fools, surrounded by an Eden we can't even see. But the landscape I'm interested in is as much the landscape of language as the literal terrain. It has to work both ways to be interesting poetry. We live and speak in a landscape of symbols and references and cultural images and conditioning, as well as a world of trees and windy fields. Poems seem to explore the ways in which these things collide and contradict each other. If I felt older poetry adequately represented the world I've seen and imagined, there would be no need to write more. So you work partly out of a sense of failure, both your own and other poets'. If literature had said it all already I would just shut up and read and rake the yard. At the same time, you know the odds are against you, even as you're driven to put more words on paper, to put your money where your mouth is, and all the nerve you have, and then some. What a rebellious act it is for an American to even think of writing poetry. I'm still nervous about telling strangers I write. It's so much easier to call yourself a teacher. That sounds okay; it doesn't embarrass anybody.

SB: What kinds of things can we expect to see from you after *At the Edge of the Orchard Country*?
RM: That really I can't say. I have lots of ideas for poems, and forms I want to try, and half-finished poems I want to work again. And there's the stories, and the novel, and another book of poems that may be called *Detours*, but

is a long way from completion. But I may never write another poem. It's just possible I've already had my say, and nothing new will surprise me into trying again. I hope not. For nothing else has pleased me quite as much. And it's possible that the best ideas and measures, ever, could be just waiting in the blue marrow of this pen.

Imagination, Memory, and Region: A Conversation

William Harmon / 1990

From *Iron Mountain Review* 6 (Spring 1990): 11–16. Reprinted by permission.

William Harmon: I've been conversing with Robert Morgan for going on twenty years now, but not out loud or necessarily in public, as far as I know, so let me just invite you all to join the two of us in a conversation that began years ago and will continue for many years more, I hope. Recently, the things that we have been talking about are Buicks, including Karl Shapiro's poem, "Buick," and the perfidy and fecklessness of all publishers, among other topics. I brought almost all of Bob's book along. I've got a copy of *Zirconia Poems*, the first book, which is out of stock, also the great volume *Trunk & Thicket*, which is also no longer for sale. Most of the others seem to be available. Let me invite you to take part in the conversation actively, please.

Yesterday, a couple of people were asking how it is that a writer who is from this place and writes of this place doesn't really live in this place. There was a kind of question there about what you write about and where you truly dwell. . . . I don't think I could live away from North Carolina. I've tried it for fourteen years in various places, but it didn't work. I had to come back. How do you do it? How do you stay away?

Robert Morgan: Cornell offered me a job in 1971. I was unemployed except when I could pick up house painting jobs at two dollars an hour in Henderson County. Cornell paid a little more and the work was steadier. But I went up north for one year—they gave me a job for one academic year and I expected to be back in Henderson County at the end of that year. Somebody else went on leave the next year at Cornell and they invited me to stay for 1972–1973. In the spring of 1973 the department chairman called me into his office, and I thought he was going to say, "There's nothing left for you"; instead he said, "Would you like to be a professor here?" And in a perhaps weak moment I said, yes, I would stay on. I think it never really occurred to me that I was a southern writer and an Appalachian writer until I left the region. To tell you the truth, when I was writing the early poems, the poems in *Red Owl*, I kind of thought of myself in the company of Baudelaire in Paris and Pasternak in Moscow and Gary Snyder in Berkeley. I had not thought that much about the region. It was only after I had left it that I got increasingly interested in the history and geography and geology of the southern mountains. And I'm not sure I would have ever written as much about the place if I had stayed down here. I can't know that, but because I was away from it I was awfully nostalgic and began to think more and more about it. I still do; particularly in the wintertime up north I just ache to be back in the South and see that sunshine on the south slopes and this time of year to see the trees budding out. I miss the speech, the accent. This is not to say I don't like it in upstate New York. I do like it at Cornell.

WH: I believe you said to me once that this title, *At the Edge of the Orchard Country*, is true of Henderson County, but it's also true of where you live in New York.
RM: Tompkins County, New York.

WH: It's also orchard country, though it may not be that daily.
RM: It turns out that upstate New York, which is where I live, is part of Appalachia—a northern extension, and during the War-on-Poverty years, it was considered part of Appalachia. If you get away from Ithaca and away from Cornell, some of the hollows look very much like western North Carolina, even down to the old cars sitting out in front of the houses, and bathtubs with flowers in them. There are so many examples of writers who have written about a place they're living away from. The best example is Joyce, who left Dublin when he was twenty-two, I believe, and never lived there again. He moved to Paris and then Trieste and to Zurich and Paris again. Everything he wrote is about Ireland, about Dublin. They say you can reconstruct a map of Dublin circa 1904 from *Ulysses*. A lot of American writers of course went to Paris in the twenties—Gertrude Stein lived in Paris all her life after she left medical school at Johns Hopkins, and most of her writing is about America in one way or another, even about the American language. Pound lived away from America most of his life and was obsessed with American vernacular and, as you know, American history and economics, and he knew a lot more about the Revolutionary period and Federalist period than most of us.

WH: I read a thing once about Hilda Doolittle, known as H.D., who lived most of her adult life in Europe after growing up in Pennsylvania; and then somebody speculated that, if your language is the stuff of daily life for you, then it's not a very good aesthetic medium. The aesthetic medium needs to be a little bit removed from the commerce and so forth, but if you were away from home, exiled in some way, and the language that you had to use for daily life was French, say, or German—even British English—then this frees up your native dialect to be an aesthetic medium and also do the same kind of aestheticizing to your native landscape and people, and so forth. So it may be that one way at least is to leave home, and it then permits your home materials to become aesthetic more easily; but some writers have stayed right where they were born and done all right. They have had to be creative.

RM: There are not many writers who have stayed always within their region. Hardy could be used as an example of somebody who stayed in Dorset and wrote about Dorset all his life. Though in fact he started writing, I think, when he was living in London as an architect.

WH: He may be like Faulkner, to and from New Orleans, eventually back home again. I was going to ask you about Hardy because, like Hardy, you have now combined writing prose fiction with poetry. Even like Hardy you began as a fiction writer and the poetry came afterwards, and now you've gone back to fiction. . . . Robert Creeley said that he began as a writer in the forties and regarded himself as a writer of prose fiction—and the poetry only came later. It baffles me that this can be done. I could not write fiction. I've never done it. I began writing a short story one time and I wrote the first clause; I wrote, "It had been in all the papers." Then I went back and said, "It had been in all of the papers." Then I said, "It had been in all the newspapers." Then I said, "It had been in all of the newspapers." See the poet's habit of squeezing every word. Then I saw I never could do it. And I had no voice to speak in and no medium, so I left. It's a pretty good story so far and I'll finish it maybe some decade soon but I've had the wrong habits for it. Two things about Hardy: one is that he achieved something like a level of genius in both fiction and poetry, and that he did them in the wrong order. He did the fiction first. He wrote fourteen novels and maybe fifty stories and then wrote most of the poems after age fifty-eight. He didn't know that he had thirty more years to live, but he really had two consecutive thirty-year careers, the first in fiction, the second in poetry. That is really astonishing. What interests me—is the prose written by somebody who is a poet different from other people's prose? It's an interesting question. I didn't notice in *The Blue Valleys* that your prose, as such, is poetical.

RM: Well, it's a well-known pitfall to poets who write fiction that they try to write fancy poetic prose and I tried to make clean-cut prose. I think writing poetry helps me as a prose writer, with the economy of language.

WH: Are you still working on that novel you said you were writing?

RM: I'm still working on it. I started a novel in 1980 and worked on it for a year and put it aside, and went back to it in the mid-eighties and have gone back to it again recently. I find it very difficult to write. I think short stories and poems are much closer than short stories are to novels. The difficult thing about the novel is it's so big and there are so many characters and you've got to keep so many things going on simultaneously. It's just plain hard work, but most people know that. Poets lack the navigational skills for novel writing.

WH: But you're still working on it, right?

RM: I hope to finish it in the next year or two.

WH: I'll ask people about a number of writers like Kipling and George Meredith who could be both poetry and fiction writers. Fairly often there is a very distinct discrepancy. Is there a doctrine about this? Why is Hardy by himself? Or is he?

RM: No, he's not. D. H. Lawrence is almost equally ambidextrous. Lawrence has such a powerful voice that it comes through in whatever he writes. Melville is certainly a better novelist, but he wrote very, very good poems. And Dylan Thomas. William Carlos Williams's best writing, I think, is in his short stories. There's a tendency in American culture, or perhaps modern culture, to be specialized. You become an electrical engineer, you become a television electrical engineer—you work one part of the television technology. I think it is more interesting for writers to deal in many literary forms. I find it refreshing when I reach an impasse in poetry and can turn back to fiction writing or vice versa. I have gotten ideas from writing poetry that I have used in fiction and vice versa.

WH: Philip Larkin said once that something was either a short short story or a novel. To him, the idea of a long poem was uncongenial. Anybody want to join in?

Q: Have you started any poems that then turned into fiction or vice versa?
RM: Not recently, but back in the sixties, when I switched increasingly to poetry, that happened. I would have an idea and start working on it and get intrigued by association or metaphor and it would turn into a poem. That doesn't happen so much now. I have an idea for a story and I usually pursue it. One of the things you learn to do when you practice writing a lot is to try to finish whatever you start, at least in a draft. It's very helpful to do that—not to give up midway. Often something that seems unpromising midway will turn out to be pretty good. You never know. I used to work with my dad, who is a house painter as well as a farmer, and he would tell me no matter how bad things are going in the morning they will probably get better—just keep going. And he was right. I do get ideas for poems in the process of writing stories. When they come to mind, I jot them down in my notebook and come back to them.

Q: Do you think it is true, and why, if it is true, that people who write about New York City are "writers" and people who write about the Appalachian mountains are "regional writers?"
WH: I once heard John Hollander describe himself as a "New York hick."
RM: There's a tendency of a dominant culture to look upon the other parts of the kingdom or the country as regional perhaps. But it also works the other way. People who are at what is perceived as the center of the culture are often fascinated by people from the outlands. In the British Isles, this is true of Ireland, say. They've admired Irish writers even though they might have treated Ireland shabbily; and the British theater, and to some extent poetry and fiction, have been Irish for a hundred years or so. You can see this in American culture, both in the fascination with the southern fiction of the twentieth century and with Hollywood's obsession with the South and the Civil War. The first great American movie was *The Birth of a Nation*, the most famous movie of all time is *Gone with the Wind*. It's a pattern that's repeated in history many times: the Normans conquer England in the eleventh century and become obsessed with the Celtic past of Britain and create the Arthurian and Grail literature and pass this on to the Continent. Southern writers may seem important because they are from a different place. That "difference" is useful.

WH: We've discussed this before, but I remember as a kid in North Carolina I made two discoveries: I lived in the same place as *Gone with the Wind*, and I lived in the same place as Li'l Abner. I was not the aristocracy of the columned mansion, nor could I identify with the picturesque peasantry of Al Capp or Erskine Caldwell. I was surprised to find out that this was the same region Concord, North Carolina, was in. I couldn't recognize the accent, as you say. This was a shock to me, and I was also surprised to find out that we had lost the war; they had not told me, you know. "The War"—there was only one war back then. There was another war in Europe at the time, but we used to have May 10 as Confederate Memorial Day in North Carolina in my child-hood. We put flowers on the monument and sang "The Bonnie Blue Flag." If anybody mentioned that the South was on the losing side, I wouldn't believe it. I'll tell you a story about my hometown. There used to be a house on Union Street in Concord where Jefferson Davis had spent the night after the war had ended. The old sign said, "Jefferson Davis, President of the Confederacy, flee-ing south after Lee's surrender, spent the night of April 18, 1865, in this house." Then the house was torn down and the sign was taken away, and later a sign reappeared with many more spaces, just as a computer justifies the right margins, and said, "Jefferson Davis, President of the Confederacy, spent the night of April 18, 1865, in a house near here." They had left out that nonsense about fleeing south after Lee's surrender. That "southern-ness" that we find in various movies and cartoons and other media was not immediately some-thing I identified with as a southern child. I grew up in the specific South of a cotton-mill town. Nunnally Johnson is a writer from Savannah, Georgia, and somebody asked him in the thirties if he thought Erskine Caldwell drew an accurate picture of life in that part of Georgia, and Johnson said, "Oh my Lord, those country people are just terrible snobs."

RM: In 1967 or '68, I started writing about things that I had never seen poems about, like hog pens and manure piles. And people would come up to me and say, "You're so lucky you have all this wonderful material to write about." And, at the same time, I felt disadvantaged that I didn't go to Harvard like John Ashbery and I didn't live in Paris or London. It turns out that you can write about anything.

WH: *You* can. I think you have us all beat. You write a poem about an odometer or glove compartment, but I think it's *Sigodlin* that has a poem that is the extreme of writing a poem about something that nobody else would ever think of writing a poem about. It's called "Stretching." It's a won-derful poem. It never occurred to me to write a poem about stretching, even though this is exactly something I go through forty or fifty times a day.

I've written down a couple of other things I wanted to ask you about—your notebook, for instance. That interests me. I don't have one. I can't remember what I write down so it doesn't make any sense to me to say something like "coat hanger." Do I buy a coat hanger or do I write about one, or what? I'm like MacGyver, the unarmed policeman. I exist that way. Maybe I should do something different, but I'm too old to change. What are your notebooks like?

RM: Well, they change. They used to be a lot better than they are now. Back in the sixties and seventies, I kept notebooks and would write out paragraphs about poetics, and history, or quotations I thought were impressive, ideas for poems, or even a few lines of a poem. I don't know what happened, but in the late seventies, my notebooks got thinner and thinner—words, maybe a phrase, an idea, something that I had read in a history book that I thought might make for an interesting poem, odd facts. In 1975 I typed up notes from several notebooks for Danny Marion's special issue of *The Small Farm*. Back then I had real notebooks. But once I started writing more essays and working on fiction, I spent less time on the notebooks.

WH: They used to tell us in school to hand in our notes and outline. Everybody I knew did the outline after they had written the paper. How do you know what you're going to say until you see what you've done? I never could take notes.

RM: All fiction writers keep notebooks to write down ideas for stories, the characters, their relationships, or a plot idea. Even though you don't use most of them, it is something you can go back to if you have an idea.

WH: What's the farthest you ever went in a poem toward chaos?

RM: Oh, passages in *Trunk & Thicket*. I was trying to write incantatory poetry. In 1974 I got very interested in writing a totally different kind of poetry. Among other things, I went back and started reading the Bible for the first time since my teens. And I also read Christopher Smart's great poem *Jubilate Agno*—"Rejoice the Lamb"—which is a wonderful incantatory poem. And for several months I wrote in a style unlike anything I had ever done before, or since. I think I was a little mad. It was a style I plan to return to sometime. You once wrote an essay called "Robert Morgan's Pelagian Georgics" and took the line from *Trunk & Thicket* that said the statute of limitations had run out on original sin as your theme. The heresy that denies original sin was originated by the theologian Pelagius. He was a Briton, and his name back in Britain was Morgan. *Morgan* in Welsh means "of the sea" or "by the sea," and *Pelagius* is Morgan translated into Greek.

Q: I grew up in the mountains of North Carolina. I detect a remarkable loss of local color in language. If this is so, how will it affect our literature?

RM: I think it is why so many people are writing about the area. As you lose something, it becomes more important and it also becomes available for writing. At the end of the Puritan era, people like Hawthorne could write about it. It's very hard to write about something as it's going on—you can't see it while it's around you. I think I, and a lot of other people, are writing about the mountain past because we feel we are very quickly losing it and we want to recapture it. Once I gave a reading in Hendersonville and one of my cousins, I think the only relative of mine who has ever come to a poetry reading, came to me and said: "It's wonderful. You can actually remember how it was. I had forgotten those things." I think that's an important function of writing.

Q: New generations will not have this understanding?

RM: Except in writing perhaps.

Q: What makes "things Appalachian" appeal on the outside, at a national level, like Cormac McCarthy does? Much of the writing is nostalgic and pastoral. Do you consider yourself an Appalachian writer?

RM: They tell me that when I came up for tenure at Cornell one of my colleagues said: "Well, he doesn't write about anything except North Carolina. Why should we give him tenure and keep him here?" And other colleagues obviously disagreed with that. I think you're absolutely right that the kind of writing that tends to be popular in any time and from any area is the kind that answers stereotypes. And Hollywood and pop culture have taught America what to look for in the South and in the mountains. If you conform to those stereotypes it is easier to be popular, because people like things they are accustomed to. They like to go to horror movies because they like to be scared, but scared by something they know is going to be over soon and fulfills certain formulas. I have tried in my writing to avoid stereotypes as far as I understand them and to tell what I knew and to present people by not writing down about them. I think that's apt to be less popular, at least immediately, and it's harder to do. We like to read about things very different from our experience. Somebody sitting in the suburbs and in the university enjoys reading something really exotic and grotesque. The word *novel* means something new and different. I had never thought of the term *Appalachian* really until in the mid-to-late seventies. I originally said "mountain people." *Appalachian* is not a term we used very much. I guess the best answer is that my writing is Appalachian because the setting is there; beyond that I would find it very hard to identify motifs or patterns that make something specifically Appalachian.

WH: The questioner sounds kind of skeptical, even resentful, about what the term *Appalachian* had been turned into.

Q: Most of the notion of *Appalachian* is created from outside. Part of the problem is in trying to define who we are in relation to a national image. I have a problem with writing as nostalgia, without a vision of the future.

RM: But can you think of any great creative writing that envisions the future that way? There's a passage in Shelley's "Defense of Poetry" where he talks about what he calls the moral imagination, and he lists the great writers he thinks have the moral imagination. Then he says there's a lesser kind of poet. Now Shelley was an activist, a political poet, a radical poet. He says there's a lesser kind of poet who tries to address issues directly; he does not recreate his world. Shelley thinks that is a lesser kind of poetry. I think most current political issues can be addressed more effectively in speeches and editorials and by getting out in the picket line than in a poem that might be read by about fifty people—if you're lucky. Language is by its own nature narrative. When you get up and start telling people a story, you say "this happened," not "this is going to happen." And they want to know what happened. I don't think language was invented by people for utilitarian purposes primarily, but as a medium of delight. When you got back from the buffalo hunt, you said, "I saw this big thing, it was really big, and I chased it," and everybody was listening.

WH: Is that more true of the southern or mountain or Appalachian spirit?
RM: No, I think it's in every culture and every people. We are closer to it because we have not been as urbanized and perhaps have not been reading as long. People closer to the oral tradition are usually the better storytellers. New England had all these schools and educated preachers while people in this part of the world had a tradition of Baptist preachers who were not so schooled but were wonderful users of rhetoric, and improvisation. Our tradition is that, and frontier humor—the tall tale, which is a thing that Mark Twain used and other writers like Faulkner. But people in other parts of the country and other cultures have just as much trouble identifying what is really definitive. Nobody in New England can agree on what is really New England; they can't agree on what is really Massachusetts's culture. Eudora Welty said one of the most interesting things I've heard about the mountains. Her mother came from West Virginia and in her book *One Writer's*

Beginnings, she talks about going back to West Virginia with her mother and discovering the peculiar combination of sentiment and fear that the mountain people have.

I once came across a word in Welsh, *hiraeth*. It means an intense longing for home, which Welsh people are supposed to feel—or Celtic people. Most of the people from my part of the mountains are of Welsh ancestry: Thomas, Morgan, Powell. But there's no such thing as pure Appalachian. Let me give you an example. I had a cousin—my father's second cousin—who grew up on Green River where I did, and at the turn of the century he went off to Wake Forest and worked his way through Wake Forest College. He was in the army in World War I. He went to Cornell and then attended Harvard, and he got a doctorate in engineering from the Sorbonne. That's somebody from Green River, you know. So you could say, "No, none of your family had any formal education." But there are always exceptions to any generalizations. It's pretty hard to make a statement and have it apply everywhere. I knew other people who were educated even though they never left the farm.

Something that I have identified in my own writing, after the fact, is a pattern or people trying to escape the mountains. I've discovered that many of the stories that I have written are about people, even back into the nineteenth century, who were trying to escape the walls of the mountains to go to Charleston, or Columbia, or Raleigh, to get away, and almost invariably coming back because some invisible tether pulled them back. I know in my own family, my uncles moved away and then returned, except the one who was killed in World War II. My dad tried to leave the mountains several times to be a trapper in Canada, to go to Minnesota and raise wheat, but he always came back. It's very hard to escape that repulsion and attraction.

Q: Do you write poetry and fiction for an ideal reader?
RM: I think maybe different works are for different people. Insofar as I visualize a reader, I try to write for somebody smarter than I am—somebody who can pick up very quickly what I'm getting at. I try not to write down to people. I think you should write up to people, assume that they're more intelligent and much better read, and make the writing as sophisticated and as true as you can.

WH: Is the audience for a poem restricted?
RM: It's bigger than Donne's audience. Poetry has never needed a big audience. It's the one literary art that can thrive almost in solitude. Some of our greatest poets, both in England and in America, have written for tiny

audiences, often seemingly for no audience at all. Dickinson is probably the greatest American poet. She showed her poems to about a half dozen people; she published nine anonymously in her life. Stevens until he was middle-aged was known to very few people, and many people consider him the greatest American poet of the twentieth century. Hardy was famous for his novels and nobody much liked his poems. You can't imagine novels being written for a tiny audience or for no audience. Short stories were developed in magazines and were a child of journalism. The novel developed in the eighteenth century for the middle-class reader—the newly literate middle-class reader. Poetry is primeval. You can't find a language or culture that doesn't have it. It just seems to be the essence of language. Emerson said, "Every word is a fossil poem."

But I don't think you need a big audience. You don't need prizes. You don't need popularity as a writer. In fact, it may be more satisfying to write almost in private. I think the luckiest poets perhaps are those who have a devoted small audience. For a long time, I did not give readings because I thought my poems did not sound like they were for a big audience. I thought they had been written in solitude and they should be read in solitude. It was only after I went off to Cornell and started to write longer, more conversational, narrative poems, that I began to feel comfortable reading them before audiences.

WH: We have a quarter of a billion people in this country, and the successful book of poetry may sell no more than couple of thousand copies.
RM: There's a wonderful audience for poetry. I have had such great experiences at different places, giving readings and meeting people. There are readers. They like poetry. Sometimes we wish that poetry sold like Judith Krantz. Then you could live on the royalties.

Q: You once talked about the need to get out from under Calvinism, yet yesterday in a class meeting you said there was no such thing as secular poetry. Would you comment on that?
RM: I don't think there's any real doubt that it's relevant that I grew up in a fundamentalist church and heard the language of the Bible and the language of preachers; and perhaps more important was being among people who thought of things in spiritual terms—moral and spiritual terms. I can't imagine poetry without some sense of worlds beyond the merely physical; perhaps poetry is the unifier, seeing at once the spiritual and the physical. As Emerson said in the last paragraph of his essay "The Poet," "The ideal shall be real to

thee." The great poets like Milton, Dante, and Virgil talk about the interaction of the divine world and the world of time. A poet like Walt Whitman begins great American poetry with some sort of revelation—we don't know the nature of it, but it seems to have been some kind of radical visitation.

One of the great surprises to me in going back through my notebooks to edit my selected poems was to discover that almost all of my better poems were written in one draft. I've been teaching for twenty years and telling students how important revisions, hard work, and patience are. But most of the poems I consider my best poems came all at once and were written virtually intact in the first draft. There really is such a thing as inspiration. You never know when you can write a poem and you never know if you can do it again. Roethke said that after he wrote a good poem, he got down on his knees and prayed that could do it again. One of the pleasures of writing fiction is that it's given to you every day to get up and work for a few hours. With poetry, it either comes or it doesn't. A poem is a gift.

Q: You discovered the influence of your father and grandfather. I wonder about the influence of women on your work.

RM: I think that most male poets are very much influenced by their mothers and most women poets are very much influenced by their fathers. Dickinson would be the type of that; she was very close to her father and she had his gift of language, colorful rhetoric, intellectual authority. I have actually written more about women than most people seem to realize. There are a lot of poems about my grandmother Levi, one about my great-grandmother Capps called "White Autumn," and "Halley's Comet" about my grandmother Morgan. Much of my fiction is about women and spoken by women. I've often found it easier to write a story if I put it in the mouth of a woman character. In some cases, very old women looking back on their lives. I've recently written a novella about a woman in her seventies who has just had a leg amputated and she's sitting in a rest home remembering her life. Once I hear the voice, I can just go with it. I sort of sit and listen and write it down. But I can't explain why I've written more about women in prose than in poetry. In some cases, I don't want to know too much about what I'm doing. As long as it's working, I go with it.

WH: Let me conclude by speaking for everybody here and telling you how much we love and appreciate and praise what you have done. We hope you continue for a long time.

RM: It has been a great honor.

A Conversation with Robert Morgan

Donald Anderson / 1992

From *Xavier Review* 12 (1992): 17–38. Reprinted by permission.

Robert Morgan has published nine books of poetry: *Zirconia Poems*, 1969; *Red* Owl, 1972; *Land Diving*, 1976; *Trunk & Thicket*, 1978; *Groundwork*, 1979; *Bronze Age*, 1981; *At the Edge of the Orchard Country*, 1987; *Sigodlin*, 1990; and *Green River: New and Selected Poems*, 1991. Morgan's first book of stories, *The Blue Valleys*, was published in 1989; the second, *The Mountains Won't Remember Us*, was published in 1992. Forthcoming in 1993 are a book of essays and interviews and a trio of novellas.

Donald Anderson: Your professional reputation has been as a poet—you've had nine books of poetry published—but three years ago, a book of stories appeared, followed this year by a second book of stories, and you have a book of novellas coming out next fall.
Robert Morgan: I started out as a fiction writer, not as a poet. When I began writing, in my teens and then in college, most of the things I wrote were short stories. One of the things that really started me writing was the response of Guy Owen to a story I brought into class. I was a math major at the time. Owen came into class and said, "When I read this story I wept." None of my math teachers had ever said anything like that.

DA: Who is Guy Owen?
RM: He published a number of novels set in eastern North Carolina—he was also a poet and editor of a magazine called *Southern Poetry Review*—but that was so exciting, to get that kind of response from a teacher. The story, "Sunday Afternoon," I then rewrote a number of times and finally got published in the late sixties. So, in fact, I began as a fiction writer and really discovered poetry in, oh, the mid-sixties in the time of the poetry of the beatniks and people like Robert Bly who were very popular then. I

went to poetry readings and got more and more interested in poetry. But I kept writing stories throughout the late sixties. I wrote the last story of that early period in January of 1970, then put the story aside and didn't come back to it until 1984.

DA: What brought you back?
RM: I wanted to start telling stories again. I realized there are certain kinds of things you can do better in prose than in verse. You can talk about people's lives in ways in prose that you can't as easily in verse. You can do it, but . . .

DA: You've done it. In much of your poetry, you tell stories.
RM: I think almost all my poems, other than the early imagist poems, are narrative, but the big difference between the two media is one of detail. In poetry you have to imply almost everything. You don't have space to get in all the facts. Short stories are also an implicit medium, but you get in more of the details.

DA: Are you writing poetry now?
RM: I still write poetry, but not as much as fiction. I don't ever want to stop working on poetry.

DA: What makes a story a story for you? How do you know you have a story when you're finished?
RM: I think a story is about something happening to people that changes them. I hate to use words like "epiphany" or "revelation"—that seems too big, too grand. But a story is about some event in a person's life or several people's lives that really alters them in some way. It's the same as a novel with the difference that you leave out everything except the incident of change. A story is usually the focusing on that one event, and you don't have time to build up to it; you just jump into the middle of it.

DA: Two of your recent stories have been selected for *New Stories from the South*. I'm wondering if you make a distinction between an "American" story and a "southern" story?
RM: I don't think there is anymore. There are obvious features of southern stories—that the story's set in the South or that it's a story written by someone born in the South or who lives in the South—but one of the astonishing things about anthologies, like *New Stories from the South*, is that there is such range—from, in my case, historical fiction, to very contemporary stories about the

suburbs and marriages that could have been written about any part of the country or by writers from any part of the country. It's always been a vexed question in American writing about what "regional" means—that is, what is truly New England about, say, Hawthorne? He's setting his stories in New England and he writes about the history of New England, but beyond that, is there something in his style that's New England? We all know what these regional labels mean, sort of, but when you look at them closely, they tend to disintegrate.

DA: If your stories are not set in North Carolina, then your characters are trying to get back to North Carolina, so the stories seem to me almost all set there. How long have you been away?

RM: I came to Ithaca—to Cornell—in 1971. I go back a lot, and I lived in North Carolina for six months in 1979 when I was on a sabbatical, but I have really been away for twenty-one years.

DA: What is it about mountains that makes you write about *those* mountains—the Blue Ridge Mountains—and not, say, the Adirondacks, a closer range?

RM: I think it's because I feel it's material that was given to me—I didn't choose it. When I started out as a writer of poetry, I certainly didn't think of myself as a southern writer or an Appalachian writer, but gradually, as I kept writing, I discovered I had this material, which was stories told me by members of my family, or just the history of the area, the geology and geography of the area. I would like sometime to write about upstate New York and the Alleghenies—the northern part of Appalachia—but I haven't had time yet. I'm still exploring the southern mountains, and, recently, I've been going farther back into the past—going back instead of forward, and writing about even the eighteenth century and the period of the American Revolution and thinking about how people talked in 1780 and 1810. In fact, I've pushed it back so far, I've got to the Indians and the first explorers and the people who were more Scotsmen and Welsh than they were American.

DA: Your people were Welsh.

RM: The Morgans were Welsh people. I grew up in an area in western North Carolina that was at one time called the Morgan District because there were so many Welsh people.

DA: What originally drew them? Did they come in a group, like Pilgrims?

RM: They came in the eighteenth century—no, not like Pilgrims—they were just looking for free land I think. There was a depression in South Wales, in the valleys of South Wales. The coal mines were closing. It became the thing to leave Wales and to go to Philadelphia—they almost all came to Philadelphia—and then fan out south, down along the Appalachian Mountains. The newest free land was in the foothills of the Blue Ridge Mountains at that time. About three years ago, I went to South Wales and the hills there looked so much like the southern mountains that I could see why people coming from Wales felt at home in the North Carolina ridges. And, as I say, I think they were looking for free land. And here was this great tract of wilderness to be divided up.

DA: Your characters care about land. In fact, it seems to me a principal "presence" in your stories is this attraction to *land*, in particular, *family* land. Getting and holding land is a serious endeavor for your characters.
RM: I think it derives partly from this tradition of people who didn't have anything back in the British Isles, who had never owned land, who had worked on the land as serfs, as coal miners, as common laborers. They get to North America and suddenly they can either get free land or very cheap land, and they were obsessed by that. They would do anything to claim it, if it meant running Indians out or clearing these great forests. I knew people who seemed to me still of the frontier. My grandfather Levi, who was born in the nineteenth century, would look at a grove of trees and say, "Boy, if I was a young man, I'd like to cut those down."

DA: One of your characters says just that.
RM: Well, that's taken from my grandfather. It was because when he was growing up, the mountains were covered with forests—the hard work that people had to do was clearing them. You showed your character by getting out there and clearing land.

DA: One of the images I carry from the stories is this business of selling trees and shrubbery as a way of making a living—the replanting to keep selling more and more shrubs and trees to homeowners in the suburbs of the larger cities. But the image I mean—the image that haunts—is that of the land being given away forever in the root balls of these shrubs and trees.
RM: This is literally true—if you grow shrubbery on an acre long enough, you sell off the topsoil. But shrubbery has been very important for small farmers in western North Carolina in the past thirty years.

DA: As a cash crop?

RM: As a cash crop, because of the location. The climate is very good for raising many kinds of evergreens—northern evergreens that don't grow particularly well farther down in the South. Shrubbery is something you can grow on small acreage. It's labor intensive and you don't need huge tracts to raise a lot of pine trees and dogwood trees.

DA: But eventually this endeavor is dead-ended.

RM: It destroys your soil in the long run. You keep selling off the topsoil.

DA: And if we're to believe the vision of economics of your characters, then they turn such mined places into trailer parks.

RM: The area of North Carolina I grew up in has changed radically during my lifetime. It was still pretty isolated in the forties and early fifties, when I was growing up. It became a resort area. I think this may be one reason I like to write about that area's past—I'm writing about a world that's gone. Memory is very important for writers—the recovery of past events—and all fiction writers know this. What I would like to be able to do is write about the past and about places like the southern mountains with the sophistication of the best fiction writers. I want to write stories set in the southern mountains or among people clearing the forests or people fighting the Indians, and not to sacrifice sophistication and subtlety for "local color." Just because a story is set in a place associated with local color writing doesn't mean it has to be any less serious fiction.

DA: What influenced you as a writer the most?

RM: I read books at a very young age. I grew up in a family that told stories, and I really think that's one of the most important influences. I grew up in a pre-television world where people actually sat by the fire in the wintertime, or sat on the porch in the summertime, and told stories—ghost stories, stories about the Civil War, stories about the nineteenth century, stories about panthers, stories about strange people who'd come through, and, in particular, family stories. It's hard to find a good writer who doesn't have some connection with an oral tradition. Then when I was about thirteen, the bookmobile started coming out from the Henderson County Library. It parked in front of Green River Church the first Monday afternoon of every month. I remember going there and grabbing all the books I could. The kind of books I got were Jack London, *White Fang*, I was very interested in things about the Arctic and the North. I read all the novels of James

Oliver Curwood. I got interested in Dickens and read *Oliver Twist* and *David Copperfield*. I got a copy of *War and Peace* when I was fourteen, and it was so exciting, I read it twice. Last spring, I actually met the lady who drove that bookmobile. She remembered me coming there and getting all those books. My first encounter with poetry came from memorizing poems in school. I went to a school so old-fashioned that we actually memorized lots of things. "Daffodils" by Wordsworth. Lots of Sidney Lanier: "The Marshes of Glynn," "Song of the Chattahoochee." Edgar Allan Poe's "The Raven." We memorized the Gettysburg Address, the Declaration of Independence, the Preamble to the Constitution. I remember getting up and reciting hundreds of lines of "Hiawatha." My sister went off to Bob Jones University down in Greenville when I was about fourteen. When she came back at the end of the first year, she brought her freshman anthology of American literature. I remember reading through it and coming on Walt Whitman and Wallace Stevens.

DA: Do you have other brothers or sisters?
RM: I just have one sister. She's about three and a half years older.

DA: You say your stories are based to some degree on family stories. How do your relatives take to your stories, now that they're manufactured for the public?
RM: For a long time, I don't think my relatives read anything I wrote. But some of them do now that I'm publishing fiction. So far, none has seemed to be offended, except my mother who disapproves of the use of profanity in my stories. Oddly enough, my relatives seem more disappointed if I don't include them in stories than if I do. There's an old joke about Thomas Wolfe, who, after he published *Look Homeward, Angel*, couldn't go back to Asheville because everybody who was portrayed in the book was angry with him. Ten years later he couldn't go back because everybody he didn't portray was angry with him.

DA: It's probably true that we value people by writing about them, that art values humans by describing them.
RM: I rarely take something from real life and just transcribe into fiction. I create characters based on people, then change them around and make up stories. My stories are almost entirely made-up, though there will be incidents taken from history or from real life. I have a novella I've just finished which is almost two hundred pages long. It's loosely based on a story I've long heard about a man who built a highway by surveying the route with his

sow. He figured the pig could find the shortest way over the mountains. That was the only fact I had, but out of that I spun a two hundred-page novella.

DA: How did the sow do?
RM: She found the perfect route!

DA: Who among your peers writing short fiction today do you admire?
RM: I feel very lucky to be writing fiction at this time because the standards are so high, whether it's southern fiction in particular or American fiction in general. I feel fortunate to be writing fiction at the same time as someone like Fred Chappell, or like Lee Smith who is also writing about the mountains, or Bobbie Ann Mason who is writing stories set in Kentucky, or Mary Hood writing stories mostly set in rural Georgia. The list could go on. There are dozens and dozens of writers, good writers.

DA: You're naming southern writers.
RM: I feel a great affinity for these southern writers. It's just a fact, the South is blessed with many good fiction writers.

DA: Has being away from the South been an advantage? Is this—Ithaca, New York; Freeville, New York—your Paris?
RM: It's been an advantage in that I have a perspective on things that I wouldn't have had if I'd stayed in North Carolina. It's a disadvantage that I'm simply not as closely in touch with southern culture now as if I were there. I suspect this is one thing that encourages me to write more about the southern past than about the present. It's no disadvantage being in upstate New York if you're writing about the southern mountains in 1860 or 1772. In fact, it may be an advantage to try to visualize what the wilderness looked like 175 years ago, to try to recreate that landscape without having to see every day what's been done to it since then.

DA: I feel in your stories that kind of longing and sadness, especially in the more contemporary stories.
RM: I've always felt very close to the past. My family likes to talk about the past. I had a father who knew an awful lot about the history of America and of the South and of the area where I was raised. From the time I was a kid, I was very much aware of the Indian past in the mountains, and I would look for arrowheads. I was always asking about the Indians. My dad had been a hunter and a trapper when he was young. I have an uncle who still is a

trapper, even though he's eighty-six years old. I suppose I feel a connection to the frontier past that most people do not. Where I was raised there was lots of talk of deer and bear and panthers and people went out on trap lines in wintertime.

DA: War gets mentioned in nearly every one of your stories. What's that about?

RM: I've always been interested in stories of war. I think it's because war is so definitive in history. The great changes in history often derive from battles. It's almost a cliché, but what happened, say, at the Battle of Cowpens—what happened in forty-five minutes in upper South Carolina—changed the history of North America. That has always fascinated me: to know how people behave in war, to try to figure out the significance of war to civilization. I'm very interested in issues of courage and bravery, and also the science of war—war tactics, strategy, particularly in modern warfare and the air force, and especially the World War II air force. I can't really explain it beyond that. Growing up, I heard stories about the Revolution and the Civil War. This is probably true of most southerners, but I grew up hearing stories about my great-grandfathers in the Civil War and other people, about the outlaws who operated in the mountains during the Civil War, the stories my great-grandfather Pace told about fighting at Fredericksburg and Petersburg, about being a prisoner of war.

DA: Your great-grandfather was alive when you were a child?

RM: No—he died in 1918, but my dad had known him, and it was almost as though he were still alive. I heard all of his stories, and stories about other ancestors. My great-greatgrandfather Levi fought in the Texas War of Independence in 1835–36. I heard many stories about him, stories about his going off to war.

DA: You're named for an uncle who lost his life in a war.

RM: He died in World War II, in a B-17 crash. I heard lots of stories about him. I never knew him, but I was always being compared to him. I would see somebody at church and she would say, "Oh, you look just like your Uncle Robert." Or, "You talk just like your Uncle Robert." I discovered later that many of these women had been his girlfriends. I always felt I could never measure up to him, being told how tall he was, how great an athlete he was, what a good Christian he was, what a good swimmer. I knew his fiancée a little bit. I want to write a full-length book about him and World War II.

DA: The novella in your most recent book seems to me to be based on your Uncle Robert.

RM: It is based loosely on his story, though I got so much interested in writing about the fiancée that I just created this female character. She carried the story away, which often happens when I write. The character starts talking and it's so exciting that you just follow it—you let the character take charge. In fact, it gets so interesting that you can't wait to get up in the morning so you can find out what happens next.

DA: Is that your writing habit, a morning habit?

RM: I typically write in the morning. I keep farmer's hours. I go to bed early and get up early.

DA: In your forthcoming collection of novellas, are the stories set in the past?

RM: In the deep past. One novella is set in the Revolutionary War period in the mountains, one is set at the beginning of the nineteenth century, and the third is set in the 1840s. They're loosely connected, as the characters are members of the same family. I trace the family through four generations.

DA: When did your people first arrive in North Carolina?

RM: Most of my family were originally South Carolinians. They settled in the mountains and foothills of upper South Carolina, and then came into North Carolina early in the nineteenth century. Over the past fifteen or twenty years, as I've studied the history of the southern mountains, I have come to recognize that my family, my community, is somewhat different from those of, say, Kentucky and western Virginia and West Virginia. Those folks were mostly Scots-Irish people and spoke a slightly different dialect. The major difference is that my folks were largely poor whites from upper South Carolina and Welsh people. I've grown increasingly interested in the history of South Carolina as a result.

DA: Wait. Your characters will put a foot over the border into South Carolina, but they won't keep it there long. They'll look, but they won't stay.

RM: Well, they've certainly acquired an identity as Tarheels.

DA: Another presence I feel in your stories is that of religion. Would you talk to that a bit?

RM: I was raised by people who were fundamentalists. My mother was, and is, a Southern Baptist, extremely devout. My father had been a member of the Baptist church, but he also attended the Pentecostal Holiness services, and his family had also been involved in Pentecostal Holiness groups, prayer groups and revival groups, going back into the nineteenth century—in fact, going all the way back to the Civil War. His grandfather had participated in the Pentecostal Holiness meetings even as a prisoner of war up in Elmira, New York. There was a lot of controversy in the family about the differences between the Baptists and the Pentecostal; as far back as I can trace it, my great-grandfather's wife had been a hard-shell Baptist and was very much opposed to his attending meetings where people shouted and spoke in tongues and danced, and this prejudice was passed on to the next generation. My great-grandmother's daughter, my grandmother, was involved in Holiness meetings, and my grandfather Morgan just hated her involvement, and they quarreled constantly about this.

DA: That's a problem in one of your stories, for a Civil War–era couple, and the husband is a prisoner of war right here down the road, in Elmira.
RM: That story is based on my great-grandfather and my great-grand-mother, though a lot of it is made up, but I had the outlines of the story. My great-grandmother was a Jones and very dogmatic about being a hard-shell Baptist. These quarrels were passed down even to my generation—people being thrown out of the church because they had attended Pentecostal Holiness services, because they didn't subscribe to doctrine. Both sides of my family at different times were thrown out by the other side in very bitter quarrels about theology. Mountain people tend to be very interested in doctrine—everybody is an amateur theologian. I think I benefited from hearing disputes between my grandfather and my father, and my father and his aunts, and his cousins, often spirited arguments, bitter arguments. These were intellectual arguments: they were quoting scripture, and arguing about this passage meaning one thing and this another—explication, real hermeneutics—a scholarly tradition.

DA: This surfaces in the stories.
RM: In fact, I want to write more about this spiritual tradition of the mountains, which is also a kind of intellectual and theological tradition, far more sophisticated than many people realize. These were not ignorant people. They read the Bible and they had opinions, and they loved to dispute. They were most fascinated by the Book of Revelation, because it is the most difficult book of the Bible and probably the most ambiguous and militant book of the New Testament.

DA: And the most futuristic.

RM: It's full of prophecies told in deep symbols—very hard to interpret—and I grew up in families where everybody had their own interpretations. They could argue in the cornfields or sitting on porches—about when the Second Coming was, what the Tribulation was, who the Anti-Christ was. Such was the subject of discussion year round.

DA: Your characters may be bright and able, or mad or inept, employed or unemployed, educated or uneducated, but the majority of your characters seem to be able to accommodate whatever their life is through *work*—they have jobs and skills, professions and vocations, avocations—they *work*. In most contemporary fiction, not only do the people not seem to work, we often don't know what they do, beyond, that is, being sort of "natural sufferers." I like that in your stories people work.

RM: I've discovered from my writing that I'm very interested in the way people do things, especially in the way they do work. This was not intentional—it just came out in the writing. I'm very interested in the way things get done—the process of labor—both the technical aspects and the psychological aspects, how people sustain themselves through jobs, their attitudes. So, in a lot of stories I've concentrated on how you build roads, how you do masonry, how you do carpentry, how you set traps for animals. Another thing I've discovered from the writing is that apparently I've a lot of interest in property, and how you acquire property or lose it—how you buy and own land, how it may be stolen from you. I have a story called "The Schoolhouse" which is partly about a man owning land, clearing it up and then losing it because he doesn't know anything about titles, the legal aspects of owning land. He just assumes that everyone knows that your land is your land and that you work it. One day a lawyer drives up and says, "You realize this is not your land, and you have to get off." The interactions between the "practical" world and the "legal" world—the world registered in the office of deeds in the courthouse—interest me. Or, put another way, I'm interested in the way in which the abstract—and actually that's the word we use, the "abstract" of the deed—the way the legal abstraction interacts with the physical world. Lots of moral and emotional questions arise in that conflict.

DA: It seems to me in your stories that the land is more important than any structures that can be put up on it, as if land were truly spiritual for these people. The land is something more than just soil, and certainly something more than a place on which you can pour concrete slabs or foundations.

RM: I can remember distinctly as a child coming out of church on Sunday—after a long hot service of preaching and exhortation and the threat of hell—coming out and seeing the world out there—the trees, the wind, the mountains—this world seemed so restful and going about its business, so wonderful in contrast to what people were doing inside the church. That's one of my earliest memories—that feeling—the beauty of the natural world and the way in which it had no particular design upon you as an individual. I think I've always felt that. I've always enjoyed showing how nature doesn't need us, how it goes on, how its processes and cycles transcend the egos of people, the individual. Instead of being frightening to me, this indifference has always seemed comforting.

DA: But it seems to me, especially in your more contemporary stories, that you're very aware that man can inflict damage on this "uncaring" or "enduring" land, and that it bothers you.

RM: It certainly does, both as a writer and as a human being. It's painful to look at a mountain that's been clear cut and is washing away, knowing that those forests, at least for hundreds of years, will never grow back, or to see garbage dumped all over the river valley. I rarely try to make my stories or poems directly political, but this political issue certainly comes up.

DA: In addition to the land, there is in your stories the important presence of water, especially *spring* water.

RM: That's a mountain preoccupation. In the community I grew up in, you always talked about a place partly in terms of the quality of its water—a good place had a good spring, and usually a good spring came out from under a poplar. People who had moved away would come back and say they couldn't live in a "place like that" because the water was no good. After I started writing about springs in both poetry and fiction, somebody pointed out to me that there's a whole tradition of springs as sacred places in the Celtic world—in both Wales and in Ireland, and well worship and fountain worship are very important in both those cultures. There is something, I guess, in my genes that I was not even aware of. One of the glories of the mountains is fine spring water. I grew up on a place that had one of the best springs in the valley. Everybody bragged on it. They'd come and have a drink and say, "Boy, is that good water!" The first house that my great-great-grandfather built in the valley was right near this spring. The spring is still there, but it's not used anymore.

DA: Is there still Morgan land in North Carolina?

RM: We still own part of the original square mile that my great-great-grandfather Pace bought. My grandfather Morgan married into the family and got some of the land. Grandfather Pace bought that square mile in 1840. It's been divided up through the generations and my parents probably have a bit less than seventy acres of it. I will inherit about half of that. The boundaries of the original piece were always pointed out to me.

DA: I hate to ask this. I hope there are no trailer parks on the original square mile.

RM: Oh, there's some trailers. I have cousins who have started trailer parks on it.

DA: That's always such a terrible moment in your stories, when a spring is muddied because the ground has been razed, carved up for trailer lots.

RM: I have a story in my most recent collection, a story called "The Bullnoser," where a character is burying industrial chemicals on the property. Now I just made this up. One of my cousins said, "How did you know?," and then she named another cousin who had been burying waste from the G.E. plant on his property, and I said, "I didn't know." So life is a page of fiction.

DA: I wanted to ask about Freeville, this town where you live. Is Freeville so named in connection with the Civil War?

RM: It's my understanding that there are a number of houses in the area that have cellars—hideaways where escaped slaves were hidden until the locals could get them to Canada. This was back in the days of the Fugitive Slave Law, and slaves could still be caught even north of the Mason-Dixon Line. Freeville, New York, was right on the Underground Railroad. Everything is connected, you discover. You move eight hundred miles north to upstate New York, and you're on the other end of the Underground Railroad.

DA: And close to where your great-grandfather was in prison.

RM: Very close to Elmira. The first time I ever heard of upstate New York was in stories about great-grandpa Pace spending the terrible winter of 1864–65 up in Elmira, New York, where "he like to froze to death." The Civil War is particularly interesting to me because I come from an area where people fought on both sides—I have ancestors who served in both armies— so it really is an ambiguous, very complicated thing. But events that are complex and elusive are always more interesting than those that are simple and clear-cut. My great-great-grandfather Jones fought on the Union side and died at Cumberland Gap. And three other great-grandfathers fought on the Confederate side. I was always hearing stories about this, and about the problems after the Civil War when people came back. The problems didn't have so much to do with who had fought on the Northern and who on the Southern side, but with who had taken advantage of people while the menfolk were away—the outlaws who had come and robbed and raped and burned houses.

DA: A couple of your stories focus on just this—the effects of war, the aftermath.
RM: It was a very troubled era, little or no law and order. But, you know, recently I've become more interested in the American Revolution than in the Civil War. I believe that American writers have neglected the Revolution. The Civil War is such a powerful event that it has drawn the attention of filmmakers and fiction writers much more than the Revolution.

DA: When I think of the Revolution, I think of northern states rather than of southern states. I don't think of the South.
RM: The majority of battles were fought in the South, and the decisive battles were fought in the South. The only decisive battle fought in the North—and won by the Americans—was the Battle of Saratoga. General Gates claimed credit for that battle, but it was actually won by Daniel Morgan and his Virginia riflemen. Washington knew this, and so did other military people, but Gates was such a good PR man, he got credit. The Battle of Saratoga was actually won by Benedict Arnold and Daniel Morgan, both of whom were very good fighters.

DA: It's my ignorance, but when I think of the Revolution, I think of Concord and the Boston Tea Party and Valley Forge, but I don't go much farther south than that.
RM: Battles in the Revolution were often a matter of one hundred men confronting one hundred men, or even fewer, skirmishes, very small battles. This is one reason we're more interested in the Civil War, with its big battles. The Revolution was a stalemate and a war of attrition, and a war where the British won most of the battles for a long time. But the Americans would vanish into the woods again, like the Viet Cong in Vietnam, so the Americans really couldn't claim a victory until Kings Mountain in October 1780. That battle interests me because it's very important in history, because it happened in

the South, and because it was fought by mountain people. And because of the tactics. The British Army—which, by the way, was not mostly British, but Loyalists fighting under British officers—were experts at fighting in rank and file with bayonets. No army in the world could stand up to them. If they could meet an enemy on the field, they always won. Americans did not win until they used their own tactics, and that happened at Kings Mountain. The mountain militia men who showed up there were sharpshooters, expert riflemen, and they had rifles that could hit targets at great distances. The British had only muskets. The British would direct barrages of fire essentially to intimidate, then rush with their bayonets. But the American mountain fighters would hide behind trees and pick off the officers at a distance. When Tarleton, the lieutenant colonel who lost at Cowpens, was pursuing General Morgan to wipe him out—he'd been ordered, once and for all, to destroy the South Carolina and North Carolina militias, and the regular Maryland force under Morgan—he precipitated the battle because he heard that there was a group of Green River militia on the way to join the other Americans. Now why was this British officer so frightened of a company of the Green River militia? Because of Kings Mountain. Ferguson, who was the other best field officer in the British Army, had been killed at Kings Mountain, just before Cowpens. These two battles, both fought in South Carolina, were the battles that turned the tide of the Revolution.

DA: One of your collections of poems is called Green River. Is that near where you were raised?
RM: I grew up on Green River, but the Green River militia was not from the part of Green River where I lived. They were from farther down where the Green River runs into the Broad River, but it's the same stream.

DA: Is General Morgan a relative?
RM: As far as I know, he was not, but I have relatives who fought at both Kings Mountain and at Cowpens. Great-great-great-grandfather Capps, William Capps, was a veteran of Cowpens. And, in fact, just what Tarleton had feared would happen at Cowpens, happened. The mountain sharpshooters picked off the officers, which so surprised the Tory Army that they went to pieces.

DA: Well, instead of the Green Mountain boys, we're going to have to start thinking of the Green River boys. I wonder if my sense of the Revolutionary War being fought farther north is unusual.

RM: Typically, in American high schools, the history of the Revolution in the South is not taught as much as that of the North. When children learn, they learn about Lexington, Concord, Saratoga, Brandywine, Valley Forge, the crossing of the Delaware, the battles of Princeton and Trenton. Those were mostly, except for Saratoga, very indecisive skirmishes—or they were won by the British. The tide of the Revolution was turned absolutely decisively at Cowpens. The cream of Cornwallis's army was routed and captured at Cowpens. There was then a series of battles, some won by the British, some by the Americans. Then there was a Pyrrhic victory at Guilford Court House, in the spring of 1781, that so badly damaged Cornwallis's army he never recovered.

DA: Is there anything you want to talk about that I haven't asked for?
RM: One of the important things that's happened to me in the past three or four years is learning to let my characters tell their own stories. For years and years I wrote fiction almost entirely in the third person. When I started letting these people tell their own stories—in their own words—the narratives came alive in a new way.

DA: In *The Mountains Won't Remember Us*, I think all the stories are in first person.
RM: But that's recent. I wrote lots of stories in the sixties, and through the eighties that were in third person. Actually, in some cases, I've taken a story that was in the third person and put it in the first person only to see that it suddenly lights up. I had not wanted to write very much in dialect. I had so much trouble learning English in the first place. I had a teacher in the sixth grade who really taught me grammar, who taught me English almost as a second language. I had not wanted to go back to the mountain dialect. My poems are certainly not in dialect. But it was an important thing to realize I could recover that language, and let people talk in their own words. It's a more difficult thing than it appears, because, of course, you can't transcribe the way people talk—you just want to give a flavor of the way they speak, and you want to make it accessible, clear to any reader. At the same time, you want to make the voice seem plausible and authentic, so you're always doing this balancing act—keeping the inflections, the special things of the dialect, and at the same time trying to make it clear so it's the story that's coming through and readers are not saying, "Oh, these people talk funny."

DA: You're a teacher of writing. Can writing be taught?

RM: It's fun to teach, especially creative writing courses, but you have to understand that what you're teaching is not writing. What you can teach is a certain care with language, a sensitivity with language, which may help writers when they go back to their typewriters or word processors. You don't really teach anybody to write. You teach them, maybe, to be critics of their writing, or to have greater confidence in their abilities. The teachers that had the most influence on me were the people who taught me to believe in what I could do. If you approach it from that angle, I think you can actually do some good. Beyond that, what you teach in seminars and workshops is how to talk about writing. It is not an easy thing to be articulate about writing, to be able to say what you feel about a story or poem, to be clear about your response. I think that a writing teacher, at best, is a kind of coach, that what a teacher can do for a writer is in some ways what a coach does for runners or basketball players. You encourage them, give them pointers. And writers teach themselves by doing it and doing it and doing it. One of the most surprising things about teaching for many years, as I have now done, is to see that the people you feel are the most talented, are not always those who go ahead and become writers. It's often the people who don't seem quite as gifted, who have the persistence, the doggedness, and the need to write, who go on to develop their talent.

DA: So will is almost as important as talent.

RM: Yes, persistence.

DA: You've suggested that living in a pre-television age was an advantage for you. What about today's young people? Are they at a disadvantage living in a visual age as they do, if they want to be writers?

RM: I don't think any age is really more advantageous than another. The materials of any writer are whatever experience he or she has had. The particular advantage I've had is that I've had one foot in one kind of world, as it were, and the other in another. I've emerged from a world—a virtually nineteenth-century world of small farms, subsistence farming, literally a one-horse farm, water from a spring, light from a kerosene lamp—to a world of electronics, and that gives me a double perspective which is an advantage to a writer. It's often been pointed out that somebody who's an outsider in a society has an advantage as a critic—has an angle of seeing—that people who are immersed in that culture don't have. On the other hand, I think there are things about contemporary society I simply don't and can't know because I didn't grow up in it. I have felt a great difference from students who have grown up almost entirely in the world of television and media and rock-and-roll and who have no connection with another world, and particularly no connection with the religious experience. Their world is totally secular. These students have trouble understanding poetry in particular. Poetry seems related to the language of the church and liturgy. In some cases I have felt great affinity for students who were raised as Orthodox Jews, who seem to have a background similar to mine in religion and ritual and the language of mystery. Religious training gives us a sense of language having connections with the world of spirituality and morality that is very hard to acquire anywhere else.

DA: Young writers are going to be reading this interview. If you had one bit of advice for the student writer, what would it be?

RM: I always say to young writers that there's no one thing you need to know in *particular*. You just have to know *everything in general*. To say that a writer needs to have studied Latin to write poetry or fiction, or to have grown up in a certain kind of environment, or to have had certain kinds of parents is ridiculous. One of the things that attracted me to writing early on was the way in which writers can travel so light. They don't need the studio, they don't need marble, they don't need canvas; all they need is whatever energy and ambition and enthusiasm they can find, and a pencil and piece of paper. Everything is relevant. If you go to the army, then you know things about being in the army that you can use. Or coming out of the army, if you go off to a university, then you can use what you learn there. If you don't go to the university, you can use whatever you learn selling shoes or working at carpentry.

An Interview with Robert Morgan

David L. Elliott / 1993

From *Chattahoochee Review* 13, no. 2 (1993): 78–97. Reprinted by permission.

David Elliot: The first thing I want to ask you about is your most recent book, *Green River: New and Selected Poems*, which is now just a few months old. How did you approach the task of going through all your former volumes and making selections? What sort of principles did you use in putting together this volume?

Robert Morgan: I found it difficult to select down to only eighty-some pages. The publisher told me the book had to be ninety-three pages or less, so I had to go back through seven books and select the text that was less than ninety-three pages. The first thing I did was go through my notebooks and try to figure out the chronology of poems, partly just out of curiosity to find out when the poems were originally written or the first draft was written. I did a lot of that kind of background work to get some sense of which poems followed which. I have several friends who have read my poems over the years, like Michael McFee and William Matthews, and I asked them for suggestions of poems they thought should be included.

But beyond that, I took what I thought were the best poems and my favorite poems and put them all together to see how many pages I had, and then I took out some until I got some eighty-seven pages. I wanted kind of a sampler of my work, something that would represent the whole range of it. For that reason I left out several poems that I would have included, because they seemed like others that were already chosen. I wanted a book that would give the reader an idea of what I have done, the kinds of poems I've written, from the very short poems at the beginning, the experiments in narrative and rhyme forms in the seventies, the science poems of the early eighties, right up to the present.

DE: I remember your saying at the reading in Scranton last October something about how you were surprised at the number of poems you

chose that, when you looked at the manuscripts, were virtual first draft/
last draft poems.

RM: That really surprised me because I had been telling students for years
about how much revision it takes to write poetry. I had the impression that I
have worked over my best poems many times, but I discovered that roughly
90 percent of the poems that I wanted to include had been written virtually
intact on the first draft, and I did only minor revisions after that. Of course
there's the other 10 percent that were very heavily rewritten often over a
period of five to fifteen years. But apparently there really is such a thing as
inspiration. When the juice is flowing you go with it. (*Laughing.*)

DE: "First thought, best thought." Isn't that what Allen Ginsberg says?
RM: It took me by surprise. I felt as though I might have been not practicing
my preaching.

DE: Has it changed either your preaching or your practice since you discovered this?
RM: I'm a little more careful in telling students that I work through many
drafts of my own poems. In fact, I have mentioned this to classes. Another
thing I discovered looking at the notebooks was that the poems are usually
written in clusters. I sort of knew this before, but I hadn't thought about
it much. I realized that over the past twenty-five years I have had periods
when I would write very little. I was always writing something but not very
much, through several weeks, a month. Then I would start writing again
and usually do two or three poems that didn't quite work out, before I got
to one of the better poems, and then I would write three or four or sometimes more, then go through another dry spell. It seemed to be cyclic, but
I couldn't find any principle to it. It wasn't seasonal. It didn't seem to have
anything to do with whether I was teaching or not. So I have no idea what
the real chemistry behind this is. Maybe that's better. The surprise of writing and the sense of discovery and unpredictability are probably important
to a poet. You don't know when you can do your best writing, so you keep
trying and you stay hopeful.

DE: The title of this book and many of the poems in it mention place names
which are from the Carolinas. It seems as if most of the poems have that
geographical location. Without reading the little blurb on the back of the
book, people would hardly know that you've lived in Upstate New York for
twenty years. How do you feel about that? Is there some hesitancy to deal

with the area that you're now living in? I know that there are some poems that could conceivably be set in Upstate New York, but when they specify an area it rarely seems to be here. I think there's one poem where I saw the word "upstate" and thought that must be a New York poem.

RM: Well, it surprises *me* to some extent. I feel as though the Blue Ridge Mountains of North Carolina, the Southern Highlands, were just given to me, almost, as a subject and a location. I was born there and grew up there. It seems that very little writing has been done about that area. It's fresh and unused by American writers, and it's an opportunity. It just happened that I grew up there and knew it. I had no plan to write about the southern mountains, about my family. When I was young I thought of myself as a poet who could write about anything. When I thought of other poets I thought of Baudelaire in Paris and Pasternak in Moscow. I didn't even think of myself as a southern poet. But as I continued writing poetry and trying out subjects and voices, I discovered that I had this material which I could use and which was really exciting. It was something that had been given to me which other poets didn't have. Very few other poets had written about that area at that time. I can remember the excitement of realizing that I could write poems about hog killings or farming, just the most ordinary things. (*Laughing.*) I remember being asked by my father at one point back in the late sixties, "Do you think you can make poems out of just anything?" That was part of the fun—to realize that, yes, you could write about almost anything, things that ordinarily are thought of as not worth looking at twice, but that they often are the *best* subject for a poem.

I also got more interested in the mountains after I left them and came to Upstate New York. It was as though I could see them more clearly, and I began to write poems about my family and stories that had been told to me by my grandfather, sort of folk stories. I began to read about the history of the southern mountains once I got to Cornell, to really study it. But I have written about other things, poems about science and technology and gadgets, and even a few poems about Upstate New York, which is also part of Appalachia. But in both fiction and poetry I feel as though I have been given material which I couldn't resist writing about.

DE: A similar phenomenon, it seems to me, is that when you write poems about family, again they are memories of your family in North Carolina. Your family here in Ithaca doesn't seem to appear in your poetry very much. Would you give the same sort of answer to that, or do you feel, as some people do, that family poems about one's own wife and children have been overdone?

RM: I think that poems based on memory are often much more success-ful than poems based on recent experiences. Whoever said the muses are the daughters of memory knew what they were talking about. One of the functions of poetry is to remember and to make alive things in the past. I don't know if this is true of other writers or not, but for me one of the most crucial things in writing poems or stories is finding the right subject mat-ter. If you get the right subject, the right character, the right incident, the right metaphor, you're inspired to write, you really want to follow through; and I have, for better or worse, followed the ideas that seem to come to me. I wanted to write about some things that maybe not a whole lot of people knew anything about. I've tried to look at people from inside as opposed to outside, to somehow get behind the stereotypes of southern highlanders, poor people. To tell events in the nineteenth century from the point of view of people who have not had much of a voice in fiction and poetry. I find that really exciting—to be able to get into the mind and to find the voice of the character, and let them tell the story, to really tell it from their point of view.

DE: At this point in your career, what percentage of your time and energy do you put into writing fiction as opposed to poetry.

RM: I began as a fiction writer in my teens and really edged into poetry in my early twenties, got increasingly interested in poetry and started learning about poetry. I wrote less and less fiction in the late sixties and eventually abandoned fiction about 1970. For a decade I didn't write any fiction. After I came to Cornell, for almost a decade, I concentrated on poetry and critical prose. I did a lot of essays back then. But in the early eighties I got interested in fiction again and started writing it alternately with poetry. One of the things I discovered, to my pleasure, in the mid-eighties was that I could work on both—just go back and forth. I didn't stand on any ceremony. I'd write a poem and go back and write a story. In recent years, late eighties, I have been writing more fiction and less poetry. I still write both and I want to continue to write both. I feel they are cut from the same cloth, with similar subjects. Short stories are in fact very similar to poems, especially free verse poems. I guess I'm increasingly interested in lives in both poetry and fiction.

DE: Has the increased attention to fiction changed your poetry in any significant way?

RM: Not that I've noticed. If I have an idea about a character that needs to be treated in detail, I obviously go to fiction and not poetry, because poetry is so much more compressed as a medium. It depends on implication. It's a very implicit medium. Prose can include the details, can go more deeply into something. For a while, writing fiction made me more interested in formal poetry. Writing narrative prose made me feel the appeal of forms in poetry more.

DE: You have talked elsewhere about the rather significant changes that began to occur in your poetry after *Red Owl*. Having put this book together, in which you can see different phases and styles in your poetic career, do you feel that your poetry is on the verge of any other major change of that sort, or do you feel pretty comfortable with the ways that you've been writing in recent years?

RM: No, I'd like to try some new things. I don't know exactly what they're going to be. That's the fun of it. One of the things I want to do is go back to working on a long poem I started on in the early seventies and never finished. It's a very long poem. I think I have more than a hundred pages of it. There are many things I want to try in poetry and I haven't.

DE: The few new poems in the section at the beginning of this book seem almost like a cross-section because there is quite a range of different styles there. So as I was looking at them I was wondering if you felt there was any one certain direction that you were tending to go in more than the others—perhaps the greater philosophical density of something like "Middle Sea." Or, because of the sonnet in that section, I wondered if you were going in an even more formalistic direction.

RM: There may be a direction I'm edging in, but part of the excitement of writing is you never know quite what you're going to do until you do it. I don't have any sense of picking out this direction or that. I would like to continue to experiment with all kinds of poems. I'm very interested in formal issues in poetry and trying new forms and perhaps even different voices and styles. But as I said before, I think the thing that really triggers poems for me is subject matter. If I have a subject that excites me enough I will start working on it and usually stay with it until I get the poem written. I'm more a content-oriented poet than a form-oriented one. I really am interested in stories, landscapes, nature, science, that sort of thing—particularly metaphoric connections between different levels of experience. Often poems start with a metaphoric idea, some very unexpected connection.

DE: I'm interested in the relationship between the great number of nature poems and what you call the science poems, to which I would add what

I think of as technology poems. I know that you started out in math and moved away from that into writing. What is the appeal in terms of subject matter of science and technology, and how do those poems relate to what you have been saying about the appeal of memory, family, geographical location, and so on?

RM: I've always been interested in objects and the poetics of objects. I can't explain it, but I love to write about the perception of things. Somebody has compared my poetry to German *Dingegedichte*, which means "thing poetry." It's a tradition in German poetry. I've always loved imaginative perception of the world and objects, and I've felt that they are important—to rediscover things that seem very ordinary, to see them in new ways. We're surrounded by machines all the time in the modern world. It seems that we have a kinship with them. One of the things that poetry can do is find out about those kinships and express them in seemingly new ways. One reviewer said my poetry was very democratic; it was willing to consider not only other people but things and stones and trees. I never thought there was any real split between people, landscapes, and process in nature. I love the tradition of poetry that somebody like Whitman belongs to, who is willing to say, "I'm the poet of the body, I'm the poet of the soul." The spirit and the physical world seem to be the same thing; they are located in each other, and poetry reminds us of that connection. It's one of the things the poetic imagination keeps rediscovering.

DE: Whitman is certainly the American poet of getting it all in.

RM: You find very few truly gnostic poets. There are a few, but most poets perceive this world as an image of other worlds and are not just trying to escape it. Poe would be an exception. But poets like Dickinson, Emerson, Whitman are very much interested in experience of this world, at least as analogy or metaphor of experience of the spirit.

DE: Two of the more recent poems in *Green River*, "Vietnam War Memorial" and "We Are the Dream of Jefferson," with its line about the "painful dissonance of the present," both border on being political, which your poetry does not usually do directly. How do you feel about political poetry, and are those poems about as close as you would want to go to what many people think of as political poetry?

RM: I would prefer the word "historical." I'm very interested in history, and politics is certainly part of history. One of the things I want to write about more in poetry than I have is history. I believe American poets have ignored history for some reason. The way we understand who we are is to know something about the past—political, cultural, spiritual, artistic. But in recent years I have tried to write more about the study, the experience of history and incorporate the historical sense and vision in poetry. I've done it implicitly from the very beginning, but that's harder to see. I've always been very interested in the presence, the haunt of the Indians, who were here before us, and the way in which political history and cultural history inform the present. I've treated history more explicitly and in greater depth in fiction than in poetry. It seems those poems you mentioned, "Vietnam War Memorial" and the Jefferson poem, deal much more directly with the reality of history, and it *is* political.

But for some reasons not clear to me, American poets have always had a lot of trouble dealing directly with political issues. In a sense there's no need for poets who deal directly with current issues because so few people read poetry. (*Laughing.*) If you want to have an impact, a political impact, you need to give speeches and walk a picket line and write editorials to reach people. But I don't think poets should forget political implication, and I think it's good that occasionally poets, like myself, who write about nature and things that seem apolitical are challenged by the political. That doesn't bother me, but I'm much more interested in the historical sense and seeing things in the perspective of long periods of time, and the political is certainly a part of that. A poet like Wendell Berry, who is very much involved in ecological and agricultural issues, certainly has his greatest impact as an essayist and lecturer and not as a poet, though his poems and prose are very much related.

DE: I was just going to mention him. Do you feel kinship with the type of things that he does, as another southern writer working in both poetry and prose?
RM: I certainly do. I admire Wendell Berry. I probably have a less positive sense of the small family farm than he does because I grew up on one that was very poor and went through the struggle with my parents when I was a child and saw how difficult it was to survive. I understand he came back to the farm as a grown-up and has had a very different experience with it. No, I feel very close to his vision of American agriculture and to a poet like Gary Snyder's vision of the wilderness and the feel of the wilderness. Those two are very different things, though people tend to equate them. Primary interest in agriculture is very different from an interest in wilderness.

DE: Snyder is another poet who has an interest in gadgets and tools.

RM: In the technique and the way things are done. I share that. It's one of the ways to enjoy the world, to do things well and to really care about the craft of making things, doing anything, whether it's farming or cutting logs or repairing tools. If we lose touch with that, then we certainly have lost an important part of culture.

DE: A word that comes to mind when I read much of your poetry is "definition," both in terms of details—something having definition, having much sensual detail—and also in the sense of defining something. In many of those thing poems of yours, like "Rearview Mirror" or "Odometer" and also in a poem like "Cedar," you are in a sense creating definitions by listing associations and metaphorical implications. As I was reading some of those poems, I was reminded of one of my favorite poems from hundreds of years ago—Herbert's "Prayer," a sonnet defining prayer. Do you feel much kinship with the Metaphysical Poets in any way?

RM: Well, I like them, but I don't know if I feel a special kinship with them. I do with some of the Romantic poets, and epigrammatists like Robert Herrick I feel very close to. But I believe that definition, as well as redefinition, is one of the things that poetry does. When I was a very young poet, I had the idea that every poet creates his or her own dictionary. To some extent they redefine words and find for them the truer definition. Poetry invents and renews language, and as Emerson says, "All words are fossil poetry." Language comes from poetry and not the other way around. It's the poetic delight in naming and renaming for which language exists, and a poet is rediscovering, to some extent reinventing, language, finding the true name or true definition of something. This is always present in poetry, poetry of all ages. If you are satisfied with the current definition, you wouldn't write poems, perhaps. But I've been told that I write poems that are not unlike Anglo-Saxon riddle poems, gnomic poems that describe or define almost as a teasing game.

DE: The last words of Herbert's poem are "something understood," which is a marvelous way of ending it. The kinds of definition poems you write seem to be striving for that.

RM: The awesome thing about Herbert to me is the simplicity of his poems—the cleanness on the surface and the depth in the poem. They are poems that seem so direct and yet you can't exhaust them. There's a lot of

wisdom and experience in them. I prefer a poem that has a spare, even aus-
tere, surface, with most of the richness inside it.

DE: You mentioned the Romantic poets. Which are the ones, of the British
Romantics, you feel the most affinity for?

RM: Certainly Keats, and Wordsworth. Some of Coleridge's poems. But
I was thinking more of the American Romantics—Emerson, Whitman,
and Dickinson (if she's a Romantic). I think of all of those as coming
out of the Romantic movement, of American poetry of the nineteenth
century as really being inspired by the British Romantics and particularly by Wordsworth and Coleridge. It's as though the two strands of
American poetry come right out of the two sides of Coleridge's brain:
the Wordsworthian affirmative side, and the symbolist, gnostic side.
(*Laughing.*) When I first started reading poetry, the poems that interested
me were things like Pound's translations of Chinese. They seemed like the
most wonderful things I'd ever seen—the simplicity, the poise of those
poems and the depth and subtlety underneath that very quiet surface. The
first poet that ever really attracted me, I believe, was Whitman. I remember reading Whitman in my sister's college textbook she had brought
home from Bob Jones University, and I was taken that somebody could
make gestures like Whitman did in "Song of Myself." I'd never seen something like that. I remember thinking, "Wow!"

DE: I wish I had been introduced to "Song of Myself" at an earlier age,
but my first introduction to Whitman in high school was "O Captain! My
Captain!" and some other shorter poems that I don't particularly care for. It
wasn't until I got to college that I was really introduced to "Song of Myself."

RM: I was introduced to poetry in a way that was much better than I
understood at the time. We had to memorize poems in the sixth, seventh,
eighth, and ninth grades and get up and recite them, and I really learned
some poems then that I carry with me ever since, things like Bryant's
"Thanatopsis," "O Captain! My Captain!," Sidney Lanier's "Marshes of
Glynn," Poe's "Annabel Lee," "The Raven," "Daffodils," by Wordsworth. I went
to a school that was so poor and so old-fashioned that it concentrated on
things like diagraming sentences and memorizing poetry.

DE: You mentioned Pound's *Cathay*, and in *The Generation of 2000* you
mentioned that you have written a few haiku early on in your career. Could
you say more about your interest in Oriental poetry?

RM: My first writing teacher was Guy Owen, the novelist and editor, and he had us write haiku. He introduced us to Oriental poetry in translation, and come to think of it, that's where I first encountered *Cathay*, in his class. A wonderful teacher. But it wasn't haiku that impressed me most; I think it was the slightly longer poems, more Chinese poems than Japanese poems by people like Li Po and Tu Fu and an earlier poet, T'ao Yuan-ming, from the fifth century who is sometimes called the Chinese Robert Frost.

DE: What relationship do you feel to what has been called in recent years the Neo-Formalist movement? There is an anthology edited by Robert Richman, with people in it like Brad Leithauser and Dana Gioia, which tries to make a case for formal poetry as being the way of the future. Similar sorts of pronouncements elsewhere elicited articles from Ira Sadoff and Marvin Bell in *APR* talking about their feelings concerning what they perceived as the limitations of the Neo-Formalists. How do you feel about that movement?

RM: I think it's inevitable that poets rediscover traditional form after a long period of experiment in open form and free verse. The forms and devices of traditional poetry are so powerful and provide such muscle to poetry in this language that it would be inconceivable that poets wouldn't go back to them at some point and use them. So that makes sense to me. What you discover, of course, when you experiment with poems, is that form itself is not enough. You still have to have the idea, the content, the voice, the passion, the obsession when using forms that you have with any other poetry. But I don't think the key to good poetry is in having form or not; it's in other things. It's really in the human spirit. It's in having passions about ideas or peoples or things. But some of my favorite poetry in the twentieth century is the formalist poetry of Yvor Winters, who I think is a model for the New Formalism, both in his theories of poetry and in his own work. He is a very great poet, and all of his poetry written after he's about twenty-eight, I think, is in very traditional forms—almost entirely iambic trimeter or tetrameter. I think young poets would do well to go back to poets like Winters for a model, or to Robert Frost who's always a formal poet. But Frost is not a great poet because he is a formalist; he's a great poet because he has a great vision of the world, a great understanding.

But I believe that probably in the next few decades poets will go increasingly back to traditional forms that have been so useful in English over the last one thousand years. There's a reason they discovered those forms and used them: they work. They carry a lot of force. On the other hand, it's deadly in American poetry if you sound too much like a British poet or sound too literary. This is why I mention Winters. Winters understood that poetry in rhyme and meter had to talk naturally and plainly, and it had to have content. The trick is to do both at once, to have a voice, to speak naturally, to speak dramatically, to tell a story in the poem and not be dominated by the form. It takes years of practice to learn that. The poet who has learned it can, like Philip Larkin, say "form is nothing, content is everything," because he's such a master of form that you don't notice it when you read his poems. But I believe it's natural to English to write on a four-stress line, something like common meter, and for most poetry it's natural for it to rhyme. Rhyme is a device that really works in English. For more elevated poetry you don't need either. That's why Whitman works so well. He's writing in a very elevated voice, often using incantatory techniques, using the psalms as models, the Gospels and Ecclesiastes. But yes, I'm very interested, if not so much in the poets you mentioned, in the idea about going back to form.

DE: In the workshop in Scranton I believe you said, "Arbitrary lines will be the way of the future."

RM: Arbitrary lines, arbitrary forms. You have given up an important dimension of poetry if you don't have an arbitrary form through which the natural voice of poem can play. As you write in sentences and rely on cadence for rhythm, you approach prose. The power of poetry is often in the way in which the cadence, the natural flow of language, is played against a form that is arbitrary, say a sonnet, a tetrameter line. Frost called that the breaking of the English sentence over the end of an iambic line. It's just one of the powerful effects of poetry. You can have it both ways in traditional forms. You can have the arbitrary unit of the tetrameter line, or the pentameter line, plus the natural music and cadence of the sentences. Free verse poetry loses that, the ground base, as it were, of a meter. Rhyme is somewhat different. Rhyme gives you yet another escapement mechanism, to use John Frederick Nims's term—counting off time. The poetry is in measures of several kinds. It has the measure of the natural cadence; it has the measure of line, the visual line, as opposed to the sound unit of the line; it can have the measure of rhyme and the measure of the stanza, with all these simultaneously going on. And that creates quite a polyphony, as it were. A lot of modernistic art is impoverished because it gives up so much of the resources of the media. In abstract painting you've given up the power of representation, not to mention narrative or allegory. In free verse poetry you gain something, but you also lose quite a bit too.

DE: Free verse has been dominant for quite a while now and probably is still dominant in most writing workshop programs, judging from the work that seems to be coming out of them. But some people say that if you want to write free verse, you really should know how to write more traditional metrical verse. Can that formula be reversed? Is there anything that mastering free verse gives you in writing more formal verse that you would not have if you had not tried to master free verse?

RM: Somebody who has learned to write very good free verse has already learned about the compression of language, which is essential to poetry; about the freshness of diction, which is essential to poetry; about the variation in cadence, which is essential to poetry; and they would probably have an advantage in that they could bring all of that to their work in formal poetry. On the other hand, we are creatures of habit and if for twenty years we've been writing one way, it's sometimes hard to stop and go back and write in another. The danger is that if people are concentrating solely on the traditional forms, they may lose the sense of compression of language, freshness of diction, and quickness of thought, which are essential to poetry. You've got to have it all. Part of the beauty of poetry is that is draws on all the faculties—memory, imagination, the sense of surprise, drama, narrative—all at the same time. It can't be just one of these things. If you have the compression and naturalness of free verse, plus this other game of form, you obviously have a richer medium.

DE: To my ear it rarely seems that your poetry is as close to iambic as somebody like Frost, at least not as the norm. For example, in some of the new poems at the beginning of *Green River*, including those that have rhyme schemes, there may be an average of eight syllables per line—in a sense a tetrameter line—but they don't sound as iambic as Frost.

RM: If they are iambic, they are what Frost calls loose iambic. (*Laughing.*)

DE: When you are writing poems like "Middle Sea" or "High Wallow," how consciously do you work in relationship to the iambic line?

RM: Not very much at all, for many of those you mentioned. My interest in the eighties was in combining forms, in writing, say, what was essentially a free verse or at best a syllabic line, and combining that with rhyme, so that it sounded as free as free verse in some ways, but it would have a pattern of rhyme. On the other hand, sometimes I wrote very metrical poems that were unrhymed and often had different line lengths. I got interested in ways of combining different kinds of poetry in new combinations and not going all the way toward doing everything traditional at once. I believe that kind of thing actually works pretty well for modem American poets. It's one way of trying new things, and keeping some of the old.

DE: That's what seems to me to make your more formal poetry more interesting than much of what goes under the name of Neo-Formalism.

RM: It's deadly if a poem sounds like a literary experiment. No matter what form it is in, it has to sound like it's spoken by somebody who really has something to say, concentrating on the emotions, the perceptions, the subject matter, and not just an exercise. If it sounds like form is dominating you, and the whole purpose of the poem is to write that form, then we have lost much of what we go to poetry for, which is experience. The music of poetry comes from the idea, the content, as much as it does from the actual stressed and unstressed syllables. You can write wooden language that is in iambic pentameter. That's verse as opposed to poetry. If you've lost the content and the passion and the vision, and gained a form, then in a sense you've lost everything.

DE: In some of those poems I was mentioning it seems as if the ghost of tetrameter is hovering over it, but you may have three, four, five, even six stresses, at least to my way of hearing it. What sort of affinity do you feel for a prosodist like Hopkins and his sprung rhythm?

RM: I feel great affinity for the *poet* Hopkins, if not for the prosodist. (*Laughing.*) I think the affinity I feel for Hopkins, besides just his vision of the natural world and his sense of awe and the presence of God in nature, is the way in which he rediscovered the heavy Anglo-Saxon line. The fact that he calls it sprung rhythm is in many ways irrelevant. What he discovered was a heavy alliterative sound that is always in great English poetry from the time of *Beowulf* to Robinson Jeffers and Whitman. A lot of times critics, prosodists, seem to be looking in the wrong direction, for something different in Hopkins. They're looking for sprung rhythm because he described his poetry that way. In Jeffers they're looking for a Greek line, because his father taught him Greek when he was young. And in Whitman they're looking for something else. But in fact, if you know Anglo-Saxon poetry, you can see that these great poets keep rediscovering this heavy broken line that has been in English from the very beginning—the heavy accent, alliteration.

I love his poetry but I get lost in his prosodic theory. I admire his prose, particularly his letters and his journals. I really love the vision and passion and voice of his poems. In fact, one of the delights is to keep discovering sonnets that you passed over earlier. He has a very small collected works. But some of the poems are very difficult to get into. I'm still discovering Hopkins. He's one of those poets like Dickinson that you just can't exhaust. You think you know Hopkins but you read another one of his poems that you had completely forgotten or never really read before, and Wow! You see what he's getting at.

DE: When I was thinking about the relationship of some of your poetry to the iambic line, the title of your book *Sigodlin*, came to mind. I'm wondering if in a sense what you are saying about people who are mere versifiers is that their poetry is anti-sigodlin and that a dose of sigodlinism is healthy for poetry.

RM: I love the word "sigodlin" because of the sound and because it seems so strange, even though I discovered that the source isn't so strange. It was apparently a contraction of "side goggling." (*Laughing.*) But yes, there is a crookedness and a slantness to experience, and being too geometrical and too perfect goes against that. It's the crookedness of experience often that is most significant. But what's the quote that Emerson likes, "God writes straight in crooked lines"? (*Laughing.*) But it is also interesting how you can contrast the crystalline lattice of verse's perfection to the roughness and skewedness of experience. Some of the important tension of poetry is between these two things, and it is not unlike the tension in poetry between the narrative voice and the lyric stasis of the poem, the stasis usually coming from the metaphoric depth—that sort of timeless experience with the connection in the metaphor—and that being in tension, in some sort of balance with the *saying*, the motion of the poem, the narrative of the poem. It is important to have both. Every poem talks, has a voice. But almost all lyric poems have that spark of metaphoric connection, which is not in motion.

DE: Given the shift in your poetry toward being more formal, what do you think of as the greatest achievements in free verse in American poetry, or do you not return to many of the freer poets with pleasure anymore?

RM: Well, the greatest achievement in free verse is certainly Whitman. He is the great monument in American poetry, along with Dickinson and Emerson.

DE: I was thinking more of the twentieth century.

RM: There are very few masterpieces in the twentieth century in free verse. I believe the poems we go back to are poems that are variations of traditional forms: Stevens's great blank verse, the blank verse of Eliot—the play between traditional forms, like sestinas, and blank verse in the *Quartets*. Jeffers might be my model of a great free verse poet. Roethke stretches out into some free verse toward the end of his career, echoing Eliot in the *Quartets*, echoing Whitman. But the great revelation of American free verse is still Walt Whitman, I think, and the way in which he broke out of the traditional line through the discovery of Italian music and the free-flowing line of bel canto opera, and how he felt free to use all these rhetorical gestures he had heard in the Bible. But poetry is not only in verse; some of the great American poetry is in prose: the prose of Emerson, the prose of Thoreau, the prose of Faulkner, the prose of James Agee. There are many ways to write poetry, and verse is only one of them. But I guess I would pick Jeffers and possibly D. H. Lawrence as great examples of free verse poetry, though I believe that what Jeffers was doing at his very best was recovering, as I said, the old Anglo-Saxon line, sprung rhythm, if you will. (*Laughing.*)

DE: Did the Pound/Williams strain of American poetry ever appeal to you?
RM: Not Williams very much. Williams appeals to me as a man and as a critic, and I feel I should admire him, but none of his poems ever reached me the way some other poets have. Pound very early appealed to me as a theorist of literature and language. But both of those always seem to be relatively minor poets compared to T. S. Eliot and Stevens. I probably like Williams's short stories better than his poems, and the single text of William Carlos Williams that I admire most is his essay on Poe in *In the American Grain*. I have read essays by Williams that are so good that they made me proud to have tried to be a writer.

DE: You wrote once, "My understanding of tradition is that our language and our age are writing us in ways we can't always see." A number of people over the years have commented on the impoverishment of the language, the effect of mass media and television in particular. Do you feel at all pessimistic about the future of language or poetry? Are there ways in which the language of our age may have a negative effect on poetry of the future?
RM: I grew up without television for the most part, and I've always felt a little bit out of sync with my contemporaries for that reason. It's impossible, of course, to know what the effects of the electronic media are quite yet. But I believe that writing seems to be going better in the parts of the country that were only more recently affected by television. Some of the most exciting writing is coming from the South, from rural Maine, or from Montana—the outlands. (*Laughing.*) It could be that those places still have a closer

relationship to storytelling and an oral tradition. But it is clear that we have had probably more excitement in fiction writing in the past twenty years than in poetry. These things seem to come and go. In the fifties and sixties the excitement was with poetry. I believe to some extent that the revival of poetry in this country was inspired by Dylan Thomas's reading tours. He got people interested in poetry and poets. The most exciting writers of the past two decades have been fiction writers. I'm not sure why that's so. Poetry and fiction seem to trade places somehow in American culture. In the nineteenth century after the explosion of poetry writing—Whitman and people like that—the best writers in the *late* nineteenth century were people like Twain and James who wrote great fiction. Why this happens I really don't know.

DE: Do you feel, from the point of view of somebody in a university literature department, that the great interest in critical theory over the last twenty years has had a positive effect in terms of the readership for new poetry and prose?

RM: The world of literary theory seems not to have affected creative writing in one way or another, but it has affected the critical community; and indirectly I think that has affected writing, because all the attention given to literary theory has taken attention away from fiction and poetry and writing about fiction and poetry, so what the poets especially lack is a critical audience. Poets are there, the poets read poetry and they sometimes even write critical articles; but what's missing are the critics we used to have who serve as interpreters and intermediaries with the audience. The academic critical community affects the journalistic critical community a great deal. What American poets lack now is not only academic critics who might have turned attention to them, but the *New York Times* and the *New York Review of Books* and that kind of critical notice that is essential if you want to reach a bigger audience. There's a wonderful audience out there for poetry if you can reach it. On the rare occasions when I'm invited to read to a public library or at a community center, I find it. There are some good listeners to poetry, people who like poetry. But for the most part you may have no way of reaching them except through poetry readings.

I don't think academic critics have ever been the ones who made readers read poetry or fiction. But I think that reviewers in big magazines and newspapers do. When the *Los Angeles Times* and the *New York Times* quit reviewing poetry and talking about it, that hurt the audience of poetry a great deal. But it is connected with the academic critical community because, to some extent, those critics take their signals from academic critical writing.

On the other hand, poets are lucky perhaps that they don't need large audiences. Poetry is the only literary art that seems to thrive with just a few readers. (*Laughing.*) In fact, I believe that the most necessary audience for a poet is to have one or two very good readers. We spend our lives looking for those one or two true readers, the readers who really understand not only what we're doing but what we might do.

DE: What was Whitman's comment about "great audiences"?
RM: Whitman was very optimistic. (*Laughing.*)

The Art of Far and Near:
An Interview with Robert Morgan

Robert West / 1997

From *Carolina Quarterly* 49, no. 3 (1997): 46–68. Reprinted by permission.

Robert Morgan's relationship with the *Carolina Quarterly* stretches back to his days as an undergraduate at UNC-Chapel Hill, when he served as the magazine's fiction editor. In 1964 *CQ* published his story "A Fading Light," reprinted in our Summer 1993 Forty-Fifth Anniversary issue (45.3). Morgan turned to writing mainly poetry, and in 1969 his first book, *Zirconia Poems*, appeared. Since then Morgan has won a reputation as one of the country's finest poets, and the *Carolina Quarterly* is proud to have featured many of his poems over the past quarter-century.

In recent years Morgan has returned to fiction. He has published two story collections, *The Blue Valleys* (1989) and *The Mountains Won't Remember Us* (1992), followed by two novels, *The Hinterlands* (1994) and *The Truest Pleasure* (1995). Although part of our interview was conducted in writing, most of it took place immediately after Morgan's recent visit to Michael McFee's UNC-Chapel Hill class on North Carolina writers.

Robert West: You're in your early fifties. Philip Levine has remarked that turning fifty brings with it a significant loss of energy, including energy for writing. On the other hand, poets such as Yeats and Wallace Stevens did what many consider their best work after middle age. How do you see getting older affecting your own work?

Robert Morgan: Miraculously some poets do sustain their work and even grow better in their fifties and sixties and seventies. I think of Hardy and Edwin Muir, as well as Yeats and Stevens. But they are the exceptions. The rule is that poets do tend to lose their verve in their late forties and early fifties. But let's be grateful for the exceptions.

On the other hand such late blooming is even rarer among fiction writers. A graduate student once asked me to name a great novel written after the author was sixty. I said, "Why sure." But in fact I came up only with *Billy Budd*, which is perhaps more a novella than a novel.

Now that people are living longer, and keeping their health longer, all this may change. The sustained concentration for writing novels and poems may be possible into the seventies and even eighties in the future. I hope so. I would like to think I am just getting started.

RW: Are there particular ways you see yourself changing as a writer? What kind of changes do you see in your writing up to this point?

RM: Well, I can see when I look back at my early poems that I was interested in elemental things then: I wanted to write poems about simple objects, I wanted to write poems about metals, poems about insects. I think that was the way I had to start out. The ideal poem for me when I was twenty-five would have been a poem that really evoked a sense of, say, evaporation, the elemental process. As I've gotten older I still admire that sort of poetry, but I've gotten increasingly interested in putting things in context—historical, human—telling stories in poems, writing longer poems. I've gotten increasingly involved in the way in which voice and idiom can be used in traditional forms, so you're playing at least two games at once, doing something formal, plus the narrative voice, the meditative voice.

I don't know what my poems in the future will be like. I have a sense that I want to go back to writing poetry full time, when I complete the cycle of stories I've been working on. And I don't know how writing so much fiction will affect the poetry, but I suspect it will make it more voice-dominant, voice-centered, and perhaps more dramatic in the sense that a character is speaking rather than the poet or some anonymous narrator. But I certainly do want to continue developing as a poet, and part of the excitement is you don't know how it's going to go. I have a sense in my own case that poetry has been something given to me at times, and I was often very surprised at the direction it would take, or at the subjects that would come to me. I believe that you change as a poet when you get new subjects; it isn't just a formal thing. Maybe there's a way in which I don't want to know what kind of poems I'll be writing in the future. That will be part of the fun, just to see. But I do plan to write more poems, and probably to write poems more than fiction.

I started this cycle of stories and novels about ten to fifteen years ago, and the idea has been I would finish this one story and get back to poetry.

But every story leads to another one, and as long as I'm excited by them and the fiction keeps me going. . . . I really write as a way of keeping myself going. You build your life around writing, and it's what gets you through. So, it's partly just curiosity to see what you can do. I think that it's more likely that in my sixties and seventies I will be writing poetry rather than fiction.

RW: Your remarks on the poems getting longer brings to mind Michael McFee's essay in *Iron Mountain Review*. He points out a progression from *Zirconia Poems* through *Red Owl* and *Land Diving* toward a longer form: something that's in a sense more relaxed, more drawn-out. Do you think it's typical for the young poet to look for an extremely compressed utterance?
RM: I'm not sure that it's typical. It was necessary for me because of the way I approached poetry. I did not have a very literary background when I got interested in poetry. I came to poetry writing from the sciences and mathematics, and also through an interest in Japanese and Chinese poetry in translation. When I first started writing poems I wanted a poem that was so concise it was almost disembodied. I got that idea partly from these translations of Taoist poems and Zen poems—poems spoken as though they were in a timeless medium, not located in the idiom of the present. Philosophical poems, poems of religious, meditative depth. That partly explains that tone you're talking about. I did not have the idea they would be spoken in American slang or anything like that. But in the late sixties and early seventies I did get interested in voices, and in narration and embodying the voice, making the poem sound like a real person talking. I would have said, if you'd asked me that question in 1967, that I wanted to achieve a sense of impersonality and timelessness.

RW: Did you find Pound and Eliot helpful as American intermediaries between that Japanese and Chinese inspiration and what you wanted to do?
RM: Both of them, extremely. Originally Pound. Pound's translation of Chinese poetry in *Cathay* was maybe the most important thing I read. Eliot a little bit later. Partly through the way I saw in the *Quartets* Eliot could arrange sentences—beautiful sentences—into lines—perfect lines of poetry. For me that was just a breakthrough discovery. So both those poets were very important to me. Probably Pound a little bit more early on. Pound's sense of getting to the essence of poetry. Pound knows how to talk to young poets. He tells them what they want to know about sound, about cadence, about line. My elementalism probably came partly from reading Pound, particularly what I consider his greatest book and one of

the great books of modern poetry, *Cathay*, just a pamphlet really, published about 1915.

RW: There seems to be another progression in your poetry, toward an acceptance of the sufficiency of words to carry meaning. In the early poetry there's a sort of Symbolist tendency to stretch and strain the language; it's bursting with the desire to convey the quiddity of things. For instance in an early poem, "Beginning" from *Zirconia Poems*, you end with "the pines / roaring their blackness at the fields." And even in a somewhat later poem, "Paradise's Fool," from *Land Diving*, there too there's a sense that the language is straining to carry the meaning. But later that sense dissipates.

RM: Yes, I was struggling to find language that would carry the experience of the world, of things. How new this process was to me. I wasn't coming to poetry from a literary angle, the way other writers do, knowing a lot of English poetry. But with this other thing in mind, which was finding a way to make language convey a sense of the world. The pine trees, the wind—it's this elemental thing I was talking about. And conveying as much the haecceity as the quiddity, to use Hopkins's polarities: *quiddity* being the whatness of something, to know it as type, and *haecceity* the specificity, the individual thing.

But what you are talking about is something real. It's the dramatization implicit in the language of the struggle to find words adequate to experience. That's exactly where I was. It was less a literary thing than a linguistic, philosophical preoccupation. Discovering how far you can go with language to create immediate, elementary experience. It has been described by another critic as a drama of someone who feels in a very eerie, unsettled world. Strange. Scary. And that experience dominates the first two books. Then in the later books I am much more at home in the use of language to describe things. I had never thought of that until a critic, I think it was Mary Williams, up at Emory and Henry, pointed that out.

Another way of putting it came from one of my colleagues at Cornell, who said that in my early poems I could have been writing as an Anglo-Saxon poet: in the kenning and the riddle-making, in the sense of being in a haunted world. But I believe that all poetry does that to some extent. Through poetry, especially through that kind of poetry, we recover a sense of animism. That's the Stone Age aspect, when you get back into a world that's spirited, where things are spirits, alive and connected, what philosophers call holistic animism. You have to really dive deep back into yourself and get rid of so much modern analytical categorization to achieve that perception. But it's one of the great things poetry does.

RW: Another poet from the North Carolina mountains, Fred Chappell, has written about his fascination with French Symbolism, which your early approach to language does put me in mind of. Why do you think poets like you and Chappell, growing up in rural western North Carolina, would share such a grappling with language with someone like Stéphane Mallarmé? Or Arthur Rimbaud, whom Chappell talks about in his "Rimbaud Fire Letter"?

RM: It may be that there's a connection across time because of the isolation of western North Carolina. If you are writing poetry as a young native of the mountains of North Carolina, you necessarily have very little sense of connection with a contemporary scene or an American tradition, and therefore may be able to identify with what is most original and greatest in modern poetry, which is probably French poetry.

The great watershed of modern poetry is French, more than English. When I was in my mid-twenties the poets I was reading most were Baudelaire and Nerval and Rimbaud. My sense was that what they were doing cut down to the bedrock—in perception, the use of language—more than anything I knew in English. If you wanted to go to the source that's where you went.

I felt connected a little bit later with New England writing, because culturally and theologically I had gone through experiences similar to what Emerson and Thoreau went through 150 years before in New England. There was a real fundamentalist culture in western North Carolina, very much like what they knew around 1825 or 1830, and perhaps the very isolation of my background enabled me to feel a rapport with what those French writers were doing in the 1850s. When I read Baudelaire and Rimbaud and Nerval, I saw that was the source, that was where it happened, that was the gold standard. And I still think that.

RW: If, as you've remarked, the worst poetry of our time is that which connects directly with literary theory, how would you describe the best poetry of our time?

RM: The best poetry of any time does several things at once. The language feels fresh, feels spoken with passion and discovery. There is concision, and precision, a formal assurance and tightness. But voice and idiom are equally important, the sense of personality, of the gesture being made.

The kinds of contemporary poems that have meant most to me have been those such as Philip Larkin's "Church Going" or "Wedding Wind" where all these come together, where the voice is contemporary, the idiom and form perfect, the lines unforgettable, said with ease. Larkin has a tough honesty and sense of humor that I find irresistible.

Among the American contemporaries I read with most enjoyment are several North Carolinians. I think the best poetry being written these days is being written by southerners, white and black, men and women.

RW: Jonathan Williams recently told the *North Carolina Literary Review* that the whole idea of southern writing is outdated, that in an age of easy air travel, when he can get from North Carolina to Connecticut in two hours, the whole concept is just blown out of the water. What do you think makes a southern writer southern? Why do you think southern writers today make such good poets?

RM: Because they still have subject matter. They believe that poetry's about something. Not just about language, but about stories, about history, about characters, about nature. And that makes an enormous difference. The Language Poets are writing only about language itself. That seems to me a kind of dead end. Southern poets are still writing narrative poems, poems in form, dramatic poems—they're doing something vastly more interesting.

One of the great discoveries in the past year for me was the poetry of Donald Davidson. One of my graduate students at Cornell was doing a tutorial on southern writing with me, and we kept reading things and getting together and talking about them and I made several discoveries. Both he and I were astonished at how good the poems of Donald Davidson were. Davidson was one of the Fugitives but he did not become one of the New Critics, therefore he didn't become one of the Modernists, therefore he was forgotten when Tate and Ransom and Robert Penn Warren went on to fame. But Davidson's poems are primarily descriptive and narrative. And they're all about the South and about the history of the South. And they're done in voices, some of them, country voices, black voices. He's vastly underrated. It's unfortunate he's been forgotten.

In some ways I think that illustrates the difference I'm talking about. A lot of southern poets of our time have kept that sort of quality. And I don't know if it's regional or not, it's just the way it's turned out. Maybe the example of southern fiction writing has been so powerful, that southern poets have sort of keyed themselves to that. Our most famous writers are Faulkner and Eudora Welty and Flannery O'Connor. It would make sense that the poetry would reflect some of those same values, some of the same techniques.

RW: Are you yourself wary of the label "southern writer"?

RM: Oh, I don't care—some people want to call me an "Appalachian writer"—even though I know some people use regional labels to belittle.

But as we enter the period of the new tribalism, etc., I think it's inevitable. And if people associate me with a region, that's fine with me.

Poetry is so located in the particular idiom that regionalism makes sense. Some writers are associated with Concord, Massachusetts, at a certain time, or London, England, at a certain time, or Dublin, Ireland, or with North Carolina. It's interesting that so many writers have come from North Carolina. Just today somebody in class asked me why I thought that was so. And my answer was that I think it's the example of Thomas Wolfe and Paul Green and other people. If you have some famous writers from an area, that gives young people the idea that they can be writers, aspire to it. Why are there so many writers in Mississippi? William Faulkner. When I was a student at NC State, every weekend the Raleigh paper would feature another North Carolina writer. It was clearly a way to get some attention, to be a writer.

RW: And you yourself have won the North Carolina Award for Literature. So there's that sort of official attention.

RM: Yes, the governor recognizes writers from North Carolina.

RW: You're often asked about the relationship between your poetry and your fiction. Since many of your poems are short narratives, sometimes people ask how you decide whether a story should be developed in prose or in poetry. My question is a variation on that: given that you've written both long fiction and a few long nonnarrative poems, why not write long narrative poems?

RM: I began as a short story writer in the early 1960s, before I became involved with poetry at UNC-Chapel Hill. So in a sense returning to prose fiction was a return to my first love. Your question is a good one, and one I've pondered over the years.

First, I like the aspect of prose fiction that Philip Larkin calls "the spread" of the novel. With prose you can incorporate more details, develop scenes, sustain the tension in a special way. Prose has its own speed. In the best fiction the language itself can become almost invisible. Fiction is about intimacy with characters, with events, with places. Poetry almost by definition calls attention to its language and form.

The decision to write in prose instead of poetry is made more by the readers than by writers. Almost no one is interested in reading narrative in verse. If we are looking for a powerful gripping story we go to Dashiell Hammett, not Robinson Jeffers. Jeffers's narratives seem clumsy and overwritten in comparison.

If a story can be handled best by compression and implicitness, rather than by detail and step by step dramatization, I usually try it in verse. "The Gift of Tongues" works better as a poem than it might have in prose. I have both a poem and a story called "Death Crown," written fifteen years apart.

RW: Do you think that long narrative poetry is an obsolete genre? Would you go so far as to call it archaic?

RM: I think so. I mean, we have a lot of long narrative poems written in the twentieth century, but they're not very well known, and they're not read by very many people. When people read a narrative, they want to concentrate on the character, on the action, and not on the Spenserian stanza, or whatever stanza Browning used in *The Ring and the Book*. It still interests people, but it is a dead art to some extent. It's a little bit like reading poetry in Latin: there are people who do it, it's still great poetry, but it's not something that engages a lot of people.

When you have an idea for a story, for characters, you want that story and those characters to reach a lot of people, as many people as you can. And you want to put it in a medium that will be read. And I think you normally think of prose as a way of doing that. It fits our time, fits the culture, and so does film. I considered going to film school; I actually got the applications to UCLA and Southern California. When I was here at Chapel Hill I took a course in film and was very interested in filmmaking as well as film writing. But my wonderful teacher here, Jessie Rehder, said to me, "Bob, your talent is for language, and film is about images up on a screen. I think you will do better as a writer than as a filmmaker." And she was absolutely right. But I'm still enthralled by film.

RW: Over twenty-five years ago you left western North Carolina to teach at Cornell, and you've been there ever since. It's obvious from *Wild Peavines* that you still draw inspiration from the region you grew up in, but is there ever a moment when you think of yourself as a central New York writer?

RM: I often say that I moved from southern Appalachia to northern Appalachia when I went to Cornell in 1971. The areas are similar in many ways, even in landscape. In fact, because of the rapid development in western North Carolina, central New York looks more like the Blue Ridge area used to. So, in many ways I feel at home up there.

I have actually written a number of poems set in central New York, such as "Yellow," and several as yet unpublished short stories. But the work with the New York setting has not been noticed as much. In the future I want to write a series of stories set in the Finger Lakes region. And I have become more and more interested in central New York history.

But my ties to western North Carolina are so deep I doubt that I will ever escape them. My first sixteen years were spent on one particular piece of ground, and that seems to be the landscape that most nurtures my imagination. Being away from Henderson County has perhaps made me focus on it more intensely than I would had I stayed there. Distance not only gives nostalgia, but perspective, and maybe objectivity.

In some everyday ways I've become very much a resident of central New York. And I have taught students from the New York City area so long I have found a special affinity and rapport with them. It surprises me sometimes that there are students from anywhere else.

RW: John Ashbery, who used to support himself by writing art criticism and now teaches creative writing, has remarked that outside pressures can be good for a poet. On the other hand, A. R. Ammons and Thom Gunn, who also teach creative writing, have admitted in recent interviews that their own poetry work has to wait until the school term is over. How do your teaching and writing lives interact?

RM: Well, the real answer to that is I don't know; I haven't analyzed it that closely. But I do think that teaching writing over the years intrudes on your own writing in important ways, not least in taking away some of the excitement of poetry. When you're writing poems, when it's going well, there's a sense of soaringness, there's a real glory to writing, a sense of discovery, things are opening up, you're hearing voices. And when you're working as a teacher you lose some of that. In the workshop there's a concentration on technicalities necessarily, you're dealing with young writers who are really not very good at this point. You're spending a lot of time trying to be objective, and analytical, supportive, and you lose some of that excitement which is so essential for writing poetry.

I have been able to write while I was teaching. But I think over the years it saps some of the enthusiasm that's necessary for writing poetry. And furthermore, I don't think poetry is something that can be taught. We can encourage young writers and coach them, but what you can't teach them is the very essence of poetry, which is that thrill of discovery, of insight, of seeing something new, of hearing the cadence of poetry. It is simply unteachable. I don't think that the creative writing industry has helped American poetry.

RW: The creative writing class does still seem an odd thing to many people.
RM: Some people swear by writing courses, and it's certainly enjoyable to teach them. Of the ways you could make a living teaching is probably one of the better ways. But whether it really helps American poetry I kind of have my doubts. I don't think American poetry has gotten any better in the past thirty-five years, as poetry has moved more and more into creative writing programs. Oddly enough, creative writing programs seem to have been good for fiction, or at least not to have hurt fiction, and I would have not predicted that.

RW: As a creative writing teacher, you must find yourself counseling a number of students who want to write about their families. What sorts of dos and don'ts do you offer them?
RM: First I tell students that writing cannot be taught. I tell them I am more a coach than a teacher, and that they will have to teach themselves to write by endless practice, by persistence.

Young writers take off when they find their subjects. There is no such thing as teaching writing as a skill without a subject. The writer's material might be family, or philosophical ideas, or love, or emotional trauma. Since almost everyone has a family and stories about family, that is often a place to start.

I encourage students to pursue an idea far enough so they can see what the clichés and stereotypes are. Only then do they begin to hit pay dirt. A lot of my students are Asian American, and it has been thrilling to watch them break through the stereotypes into something alive and surprising.

I tell students they will know they are getting somewhere when an idea, a scene, is so painful they can just barely bring themselves to write about it. A writer has to touch quick, and draw blood.

RW: I'd like to ask a few questions about *Wild Peavines*. "Attakullakulla Goes to London," like your earlier poem "Ninety-Six Line," portrays colonial Britain's dealings with the Cherokees. It's one of the few narrative poems in the book. How did you come to write it? Was there really an Attakullakulla?
RM: The most famous chief of the Cherokees in the eighteenth century was Attakullakulla, or "The Little Carpenter." He was a clever, evasive, witty man, famous both for his wisdom and his resourcefulness in negotiations with the British. In the 1970s I spent some time studying the history of the Cherokees, and I always wanted to write about him. I have been told by

a friend of mine who is Choctaw that my sense of history is "Cherokee-centric" because I know more about them than any other tribe.

Since I used to find arrowheads in the dirt while hoeing corn, I have been fascinated by the haunting presence of the Cherokees in western North Carolina. They are a shadow population in most counties, part of the community across time. I have a story called "The Tracks of Chief DeSoto" about their first contact with the whites in the 1540s.

RW: "Mowing" and "Working in the Rain" are both about your father. Is there something about his combination of hard work and solitude that you find particularly inspirational as a poet?

RM: As I say in an essay in the *Southern Review* called "Work and Poetry: The Father Tongue," I seem to keep returning to my father in poems because his personality was so extreme, so driven. He did everything to excess. There was nothing restrained or ordinary about him. That kind of personality lends itself to treatment in both fiction and poetry. He was an unforgettable presence, large in size and gesture, a tireless talker and storyteller, opinionated, intense, obsessed with the Bible and its prophecies, with history, with reading. He was unable to work with other people, and had to work in solitude. For someone with no formal education, he was remarkably well-informed, with a flair for dramatic language.

RW: Why issue the poems of *Wild Peavines* as a chapbook?

RM: Two reasons. I didn't have enough poems for a new book: I went several years without writing poems, or writing very many poems. And I thought that would be a way of keeping my hand in, to publish a chapbook. And my friend Jonathan Greene, who runs Gnomon Press, is such a great book designer that I wanted him to do something else of mine. He did *Groundwork* years and years ago, and it just occurred to me one day to put together nineteen poems.

RW: Why not just wait until there's a full book of poems?

RM: Well, I love chapbooks. They're in some ways the ideal form in which to publish poems and read poems. You can sit down and read nineteen poems in a way you can't sit down and read fifty poems, sixty to seventy pages of poems. I've always regretted that the chapbook can't be put in bookstores. It's sold only by mail; they're bought by collectors. But you reach in some ways the most desirable audience, the best audience for your poetry in a chapbook. I like the look of them, the feel of them.

RW: The first book publication of "Earache" was in your chapbook *Bronze Age*, but it didn't appear in a full-length book until *Green River.* You chose not to include it in either of the two intervening books. Why that sort of delay? I could just as well ask why, although "Chant Royal" was published in *Poetry* in 1978, that poem didn't appear in 1979's *Groundwork.* This goes to the idea of how you conceive of a book.

RM: That's a tough question. It's one of the toughest questions. What is a book of poetry? Some people will tell you that a book of poetry is a unit, has integrity just like a novel does, or a book of essays, a critical book. Other people will say a book of poetry is merely a collection of poems.

And we know there are examples of both these extremes. There are books for which critics make the claim that they're integrated in a highly organized way. People claim that *Les Fleurs du mal* by Baudelaire is. We know that he in fact organized it according to poems to his mistresses, poems written for this woman, and to that woman.

It's a problem I have pondered and worried about over all these years. I would say that the most important thing about a book of poetry is that it be a book of good poems, whether they're thematically linked or sequenced in some carefully orchestrated way or not. The best books of our times have included the three mature volumes of Philip Larkin. They're very short books of poems, and very carefully arranged.

RW: Coming back to you in particular, "Mowing" may be the most recent example of this. When was "Mowing" originally published?
RM: It was published in 1981, in *Poetry.*

RW: And yet it wasn't included in 1987's *At the Edge of the Orchard Country,* in 1990's *Sigodlin.*
RM: I didn't want to publish it in a book as long as my father was alive. I thought it might embarrass him. He didn't read poetry magazines, but he looked at my books of poems when they came out. That's one of the few examples of where I've held a poem back because of the content. Neither of my parents has been very sensitive about my writing, but since that poem is about his obsession, his particular obsession with mowing, I decided not to publish it in a book in his lifetime.

RW: Occasionally you drop a highly unusual word into a poem, something striking that calls attention to itself. A couple of examples are "nous" in "Lightning Bug" and "frampold" in "Chant Royal." You've done this again in *Wild Peavines*: the final poem, "Chicken Scratches," contains the word "incunabula." Is this a deliberate technique?

RM: It fascinates me to bring worlds together that way, to bring a word from one frame of reference into another. The risk is that it will just seem imposed, that it won't add anything to the poem, so you have to be careful. But I love the idea of suddenly pulling in a whole new set of connotations just by diction, by word choice. You're using twentieth-century language and suddenly you use a Shakespearean word like "frampold," or a scholarly word like "incunabula" in talking about chicken scratches in the backyard.

I love to create interesting textures with language. You can do it as long as it doesn't seem completely imposed, and it seems like a discovery. You get to the end of the poem—"the incunabula of morning"—which is a way of not only using the unexpected word, but of comparing the time span of the day to centuries, since "incunabula" takes you back to things printed in the fifteenth century. I love to do that, to compare different time frames and different scales, and if you can do it with one word that way, then it's even more effective. As Bill Harmon says in his essay on versification, poetry can evoke the time of the poetry and the time of the period of the subject, at the same time. And sometimes, by a very careful choice of words you can evoke an era, completely throw the poem into a different time scale.

One of the most powerful devices of poetry is the use of distortions. Time and scale. So, you can go from talking about the way a minute passes to the way a century passes, or a lifetime. You go from talking about something close up to evoking something very distant: a grain of sand here, the moon there, a planet out there. Alchemy is called the art of far and near, and I think poetry is alchemy in that way. It's delightful to distort size, to see something that's tiny as though it were vast, to see something vast as though it were tiny. Stevens talks about "The Planet on the Table." One of the most powerful devices is to distort time, to go from human time to atomic time, geologic time. And sometimes you can actually accomplish that, with one unexpected word choice.

RW: *Wild Peavines* contains one pantoum, "Oxbow Lakes." It's a very difficult form, yet you've published several. What draws you to it?

RM: I like the pantoum perhaps because it is at once so simple and so complex. The simplicity is that every line is merely repeated. The difficulty is that the interlocking quatrains must carry a narrative or argument, make sense with all the repetition. It's a folk form in Malaya, where they have "pantoum parties" where the participants sit in a circle making up interlocking quatrains. The pantoums that have worked best for me are those where reflection, repetition, echo, are part of the subject.

RW: There's a movement afoot that calls itself New Formalism. Although you've written poems in many traditional forms, when I see the New Formalists enumerated your name is not among them. How do you relate to this would-be renaissance of formalistic poetry?

RM: I really don't know the answer to that, since I came to formalism on my own; I'm not a part of any school. But I am certainly interested in the recovery of the resources of English poetry that were lost in the sixties and seventies American free verse movement. It's as though poets tossed out many of the devices that really make poetry work. I'm glad to see them coming back.

Mere formalism doesn't get you very far in poetry. A poem in form still has to have voice, gesture, a sense of discovery, a metaphoric connection, as any poetry does. And what really works in any poem is bringing all these things together. It's the syncretic effect that is so powerful: the image, the sound, the voice, the gesture, form, cadence. You've really got to have most of those things at once to have good poetry. The fact that something is in a rhymed form or in blank verse will not make it good poetry.

What actually makes poetry poetry is of course impossible to define—and we like it that way. We recognize it when we hear it, when we see it, but we can't define it. But we know it. When somebody says, "Shall I compare thee to a summer's day?" we know they're starting to talk poetry. And my test for poetry is related to that: it's in its memorability. We remember things both for the way they sound and what they say, and it's impossible to separate these two things. If a poem is not memorable, if you don't want to repeat it, if you don't want to say it out loud, then there's probably something wrong. One of the problems of free verse is that much of the free verse poetry is not memorable.

RW: You grew up not far at all from a sort of headquarters for the deconstruction of metric. At Black Mountain College, Charles Olson led an attack on traditional approaches to poetry, to meter. Do you have any response to Olson's program for *Open Field* and what it did to American poetry?

RM: Well, the Black Mountain poet I like most is Creeley, the early Creeley. Those early poems by Creeley seem very lyrical and very traditional, very rhyming and with a lot of voice and character in them.

But the poetics of Black Mountain I never quite understood. I'm not sure I ever understood what projective verse was or composition by field.

In many ways I suspect it was just an extension of modernism, which I think is one of the myths of academia—that there was such a thing as modernism and postmodernism.

The idea of avant-garde art is a very suspicious thing to me, particularly avant-garde poetry: the idea that poetry is new, and it keeps being new the way Chevrolets every year are new. It's the newness in conjunction with old-ness that makes it interesting. And part of what we love about poetry is the fact that it seems ancient, that it has an authority of ancient language and ancient form, and that it's timeless, that it reaches back. So, I feel personally that avant-garde poetry is almost a contradiction in terms. Though we have the sense of the originality of a new poet, of a great poet, it's that sense of originality doing very old things that is most interesting.

After all, we have all these other forms that are very contemporary and modern. The young people have MTV and rock and roll music. Why would they go to read poetry? What is it that poetry can give them that they don't get anywhere else? And it's partly the authority, this other thing that is very hard to name. Poetry belongs to the Stone Age, to a preliter-ate culture. It's an oral/aural thing. It awakens in us kinds of perception that go back to those times, to preliterate times, certainly to premedia times, preprint times. And if poetry loses that, then in a sense it's lost what makes it poetry.

That's a roundabout answer to your question. But if you get too far from a metrical tradition in poetry you have lost an essence of poetry in English, I suspect. Someone like Hopkins stretched it about as far as it could be stretched, or Whitman, and that stretching worked because it was stretching away from a very well understood common norm. Something like sprung rhythm doesn't mean anything to people who don't have a firm sense of iambic pentameter and traditional metrics.

RW: I remember somewhere you say you don't like talking about poetry, that you don't like interviews. But you seem very adept at it.
RM: I learned to impersonate the kind of person that talks about poetry. It comes from teaching, I think. One of the biggest changes that ever occurred in my life was going from the isolation of western North Carolina, from being unemployed and working part time as a house painter in Henderson County, to Cornell, where everybody was a literary person. Graduate stu-dents, professors, everybody was talking about writing, and it really changed my poetry. That was one of the watersheds you were talking about earlier.

RW: With the *Carolina Quarterly* nearing its fiftieth anniversary, I wonder if you would share whatever thoughts you may have about the role little magazines play for poets today.

RM: the *Carolina Quarterly* was an important part of my literary education. Working with the magazine, and being published in the magazine, encouraged me in my early fiction writing, and later with my poetry writing. Little magazines and small presses are crucial for young poets and short story writers. They are where the action is, and always have been. And they will be even more important in the future, in the world of blockbuster publishing. Young writers find their first audience in little magazines, and experimental writers find their only audience there.

I'm very pleased that the *Quarterly* has lasted fifty years, and hope it stays around another fifty. It is one of the glories of UNC-Chapel Hill, and the state of North Carolina.

Getting the Voices Right:
A Conversation with Robert Morgan
about *The Gardener's Son*

Peter Josyph / 2000

From *Adventures in Reading Cormac McCarthy* (Lanham, MD: Scarecrow Press, 2010), 143–58.[1] Reprinted by permission.

For a film called *Acting McCarthy: The Making of Richard Pearce's The Gardener's Son*, I asked novelist and poet Robert Morgan to speak with me, on camera, about *The Gardener's Son*. Based on the murder of James Gregg by Robert McEvoy in the mill town of Graniteville, South Carolina, in 1876, the picture was coproduced by Richard Pearce and Michael Hausman on a budget of $200,000, which was provided by Public Television station KCET's Visions series. Fashioned from an original screenplay by Cormac McCarthy, shot in color by cinematographer Fred Murphy on 16mm film, using locations chiefly in North Carolina, *The Gardener's Son* was director Richard Pearce's first full-length feature. The film, which aired on January 6, 1977, was favorably reviewed by John O'Connor in the *New York Times*, who called it "a haunting production" and praised its "almost poetic vividness"; by Alan Kreigsman in the *Washington Post*, who said that it "abounds in privileged moments," and features performances that "lend the drama an almost Aeschylean depth"; and by Tom Allen in the *Village Voice*, who called it "the most provocative American movie of 1976" and rated its ironies "on a par with *The Battle of Algiers*." As I have suggested, it was superbly well cast and is some of the best work by all of its participants.[2] McCarthy himself appears briefly (and silently) as a tophatted investor who is shown around the mill by James Gregg, who is beautifully played by Kevin Conway. The film has never enjoyed a theatrical release.

My conversation with Bob Morgan took place in a small room at the Gramercy Park Hotel in Manhattan on February 12, 2000, when Morgan was in New York to meet with the publishers of his novel *Gap Creek*, which had recently been chosen for the Oprah Book Club. Speaking about Algonquin, which published the book in hardcover, Morgan said: "Before this, the most copies they had sold of a book was 150,000. The day Oprah made the announcement, "they had orders for 650,000 copies overnight."

Peter Josyph: You are one of the few people I know who saw *The Gardener's Son* when it aired in 1977.

Robert Morgan: Purely by accident. I turned on the television to PBS. This film was already in progress. It grabbed my attention because of the voices, the accents. I realized: "My goodness, here's something from National Public Television where they really have the accents right and the dialect is right on the money." I remember the foreman in the cotton mill who says to the kid: "If I'm not mistaken you'll find a broom in there." My goodness—who has done this! So, I kept watching, glued to the show.

I've never forgotten, after over twenty-two years, Ned Beatty coming to the door of that old tavern. He's told the mother is dead, and he says: "I didn't know that. C'mon in, honey, and get ye a drink. I'm mighty sorry t'hear that." That was so perfect. I was enthralled. Watched the whole thing. Very sad, very dark story. Credits came on, said it was directed by Richard Pearce, script by Cormac McCarthy. I, of course, knew about McCarthy, but I had never read him.

It was a very important thing for me to see that film because it showed me what you could do with the voices of that region. The cotton mills of upper South Carolina mostly employed poor whites from the mountains. Many of my family members had worked in those cotton mills. My mother worked in a cotton mill when I was young. She supported us. So, I was quite taken to see the anger in the character of the boy. It was a breath of fresh air to see that kind of realism. Particularly in terms of the voices, and the way in which these cotton mill workers were at such a disadvantage, but were, in a way, happy to be working there, to be making wages. They had come down from the mountains, having sold and abandoned their farms.

I did not start writing fiction immediately after that, but within the next four years I did, and I believe that's one of the things that inspired me to start telling stories about Appalachia, about the mountains where I had grown up.

PJ: Prior to that, had you not thought of using your native land as material?
RM: I had published several short stories and they were all set in the area, but then I published only poetry for about fifteen years. The important thing for me in going back to fiction was learning to use voices. I had not done that in my earlier stories very much. It was a process of learning to let my characters tell their own stories, reveal themselves in the way they talk. The genius of Cormac McCarthy is partly in his ability to get the voices right. In all of his fiction and in the screenplay he has an amazing ear. That was a kind of revelation to me, to see that's where so much of the life of the characters was, in the voices. This is certainly true in all of his books, especially in the Appalachian novels.

PJ: Brad Dourif told me that he enjoyed watching McCarthy's delight in local speech patterns during the filming around Glencoe, North Carolina. "I guess there's something about the way characters use language," Brad told me. "You know, Dickens always defined his characters so well with language. And I'm just remembering what a kick it was. We were out looking at locations, and this old guy was showing us around and he'd say: 'Well, y'know, th'other day . . . . went over, got in m'car, so t'speak. . . . turned on the engine, so t'speak . . . ' And I remember McCarthy's *delight* at that. He was describing it to somebody, saying: 'My God—this guy was talking about things that'd really happened, but he'd always say *so to speak* as if it were a metaphor, as if it didn't happen!' There it is. There's the writer. How the way this guy used the language was telling you so much about him. So easy to do, so easy to write—but so clear." Does one have to *cultivate* that kind of an ear?
RM: I think you have to teach yourself to do that. Often the people who have the greatest trouble writing dialogue and dialect accurately are the people who have spoken it themselves. Because they do it, they are not aware of how to write it down. It can be an advantage to come in from the outside and consciously study it, listen to it. It probably begins for any writer, including Cormac McCarthy, with an ability to listen. My experience is that writers are often better listeners than talkers. Other people may talk better about fiction than writers, but almost all the good writers I know listen and watch people.

They say Faulkner used to sit on the square in Oxford and listen to people tell stories. People often ask me: "How can you write so accurately about women. You're a man." My answer is, "I have known a lot of women and I listen to them talk." I used to listen to them as they strung beans or peeled peaches. I am sure McCarthy worked that way. I have heard that he used to hang around a country store in Tennessee and talk to trappers, construction workers.

But *it is a made thing*, that's the answer to your question. It doesn't come naturally. Nothing about writing is natural. But if you work *really hard* at storytelling, at language, you can make it seem *perfectly* natural, as though it happened spontaneously. The best art does seem to be virtually spontaneous. I tell my students that you do not take a story from real life and transcribe it to the page, you *create* a sense of reality, one detail, one sentence, one image at a time.

PJ: In a lot of fiction that tries to capture a region, or a class or a category of person, the writer assumes that once he gets the language the way that he heard it, that's the prize, that's literature. But it has to attain a level of poetry, doesn't it? Often that's missing. It isn't missing in your books. It isn't missing in *The Gardener's Son*. McCarthy is a poet, is he not?

RM: He certainly is. His writing, his dialogue, is so compact. If you look at a page of *The Gardener's Son*, or *Child of God*, it's amazing to see the poetic energy there, the way he's caught the flavor of speech but compressed it. If you transcribed a conversation among the people like that and printed it, it wouldn't be very interesting. McCarthy's writing is art. It is a made thing. He has caught those tropes, those expressions, and put them into a very compact form.

I believe a lot of people writing about poor people, people in Appalachia, may approach it with an agenda instead of trying to get inside the characters and let them tell their own story. I believe that if you write from someone's point of view, let's say Lester Ballard in *Child of God*, it can only be done if you really try to see the world as he sees it. This is the great thing that McCarthy learned, perhaps, from writers like Dostoyevsky. That you take characters who may be repellent to a lot of people, and who would be considered criminals or insane, but as a writer you try to get inside those characters and tell their story from their point of view, and that makes it live. It's very different from having an agenda, where you are going to show the world what poverty is like, or what the criminally insane are like. It's like the difference between fiction and nonfiction, perhaps. The fiction writer is not writing an argument. You want to show real people.

PJ: Were there elements of place that rang true to you in the film?

RM: The scene that I remember most vividly is the tavern scene. That was just astonishingly real to me. You have a tavern that was really just a shack, a barn, with these men sitting around passing a jug of moonshine and slicing off a bit of potato as chaser. Also, the house where the mother is lying in state was particularly well done. I think the script mentions black cloths hung over the mirrors. That was a particularly good detail. But beyond the detail, the tone of the piece, the realism, the hardness of it impressed me. This was not romanticization of cotton mill life, and it was not an essay. Here was a filmmaker, a writer, and actors who were willing to look at poor people as they were.

PJ: James Cagney used to have an expression, "dropping the goodies," for some actorial touch that, even if he were playing the bad guy, would charm the audience, warm them up to him. Most of the performances in this film don't attempt that. Certainly, Dourif's doesn't. Were your sympathies with the kid? He *is* a murderer.

RM: I certainly sympathized with him. Because you know that had he had a good lawyer, and if he had had money, he might have been convicted but he probably would not have been hanged. The story is about moral ambiguity to a great extent. You don't know, finally, why he is so angry. It may have been almost an accident. In modern times it would have been judged differently—he was unbalanced, he was angry, it happened spur-of-the-moment, it was not premeditated, it would have been Murder Two instead of Murder One—so you have to be sympathetic to a character like that.

One of the great things about the story is that it's not a story of moral judgment. You do feel Gregg, the mill owner, taking advantage of the people. He's propositioning his women employees. I know that happened all the time. I've been told stories about that. McEvoy certainly knows that the owner does that, so that even if Gregg didn't proposition his sister, McEvoy knows he *might* have. It was considered more or less a right to the cotton mill owner.

I guess my greatest sympathy is for the sister, the female characters. I really wish more of the script had been kept in the movie. Some of the greatest writing McCarthy has ever done, probably, is in the later scene where the sister is in the hospital in Columbia, that monologue where she keeps circling back to the horse called Captain, who they sold and who she sees in the streets of Graniteville later. *That* was a very telling detail, that the horse was important. The loss of that horse symbolized the loss of their farm and their identity as rural people. They had moved to the cotton mill and they had lost their house. The loyalty of the horse, the fact that the horse recognizes them years later on the streets of Bingle, that's a wonderful detail.

I think McCarthy thought his way very deeply into that story.

PJ: It's also poignant that the horse is named Captain. It's a boss's name—"Cap'n"—plus Gregg is "Captain Gregg"—but here it means something different.

RM: Yes, it's her memory of the farm, which is probably viewed as a kind of Eden lost. It certainly was not when they were living there. But living in a cotton mill town with all the problems they've had—the father's alcoholism, the son's murder conviction, the mother's death—she certainly looks back to that mountain farm as a much better place and time, and the horse is symbolic of that.

Horses are so close to the people in rural life. You work with a horse. That's why it fascinates me so much. I worked with horses when I was young. The horse has a *name*, it's not just a *horse*. It's Captain.

PJ: In Graniteville I spoke to a girl who was working in a convenience store just outside of town. She said: "What d'you want to go *there* for?" I told her we were doing some research. She said: "Well I *live* there. You don't want to go *there*." I told her that we needed a place to stay. She said: "There's *nowhere* you can stay in Graniteville." She just didn't want me to go there. Being there of your own volition was crazy to her. I had to be warned off, chased away. I saw her point. It's still a small town . . . still a company town to a degree that the cops pulled up and came over, a pair of them, and tried to prevent my pointing a video camera at the mill—which I did anyway and I can tell you, those smokestacks are *smoking* . . . there are "cardboard" company houses, uniform, depressing, all in a row . . . and the stench is, at times, overwhelming. In the cemetery on the outskirts of town, where James Gregg is buried and where you can still hear the mill and you can still smell it, clearly, I thought: "Having been here, I could see why a guy would commit a murder just to get *out*."

RM: They paid *very* low wages before the year of the minimum wage. My mother, on her first job, made nine dollars a week. She was the only person in her family employed. This was 1931, when she graduated from high school. In the nineteenth century they paid even less. The same people who had owned the plantations, after the Civil War, in the Reconstruction period, built cotton mills. They had lost the slave labor and they replaced it with the poor whites of the Piedmont and the mountains. They could pay them almost nothing, because these are people who were not used to a cash economy. They had practiced subsistence farming. They were attracted to the cotton mills because, hey, they were making wages, they could live in town and buy things. But it was a pretty bad system.

Yes, I could see where somebody would be so angry. But the brilliance of the film is partly that it's never explained. McCarthy is a writer who doesn't *explain* his characters. They do what they do and you can interpret that however you want. I think that's part of the fascination of his stories. They're not stories of moral judgment, they're about people.

PJ: It would be nice to have the film reshown. Nan Martin (Mrs. Gregg) said to me: "I have always been puzzled by *The Garderner's Son*. Did they think so little of it that they just put it off in a dusty warehouse? This is Americana. This is *pure* Americana. It is *almost* a documentary. We shot it in a town where the mill was still there, where the looms were still set up. I was wearing a bustle that came from somebody's attic, I had a parasol from the 1880s. And you think this wouldn't intrigue people? You think there's much more interest in Jane Austen? No!" Kevin Conway (James Gregg) said: "Just the fact that it's an early work by someone who evolved into one of the great American writers—that's important in and of itself, right? There aren't that many Cormac McCarthys writing in American where you can just say well, we're not going to show it. The beauty of the film—the only reason to *do* film—is that it's going to be around for a while. You can preserve special moments in our cultural history. There's no point in preserving them if you're not going to show them."

How would you answer someone who says: "Why bother with this one? It's an old film, it's about a very small region of the country, it's the nineteenth century, it's not *like* that anymore, it's a murder by an unknown guy no one cared about then and no one cares about now. It's important to you, Bob Morgan, because it influenced you, but does it have a lick of importance beyond that?"

RM: My first answer is the artistic quality of it. Works of art are important not only because of the subject, but because of the way they are made. It is so brilliantly written, directed, and acted, that it should be brought back. But it's also about a very important issue and a very important time in history. I believe that fiction and film are the main ways people know about history, and to know who you are you have to know something about history. I think there would be a real audience for this movie, because we are, now, looking more into our roots than we have in the recent past. If you want to know something about this country, you have to know what happened in the nineteenth century and the early twentieth century.

Often the best stories are set way off in places nobody's ever been, about incidents they've never heard of, and this is a particularly interesting story because it's about one of the great transition periods in American history. Most viewers of film and television know more about the Civil War than they know about the period just after it, when the upper South, the Piedmont South, was in a *terrible* period of poverty. I've heard stories in my family about this period. There just wasn't *anything*. There was no way to make a living. The land had been devastated. That was one reason these people went down to work in the cotton mill towns and were enticed to work for wages, because everybody was having such a hard time. So I would say it's important for people to know about this period and these kinds of people.

What makes a story accessible to a general audience is the artistry. We like stories that are real, that are detailed, that are local. Oddly enough, what would make a story set in an exotic place accessible is the specificity. Paradoxically, it's that local color, that local detail, that makes it accessible to any audience. Instead of *stripping that away* to make it accessible, you do exactly the opposite: you get the dialect right, you get the details rights, and that makes it understandable to somebody in Russia or Japan, or to somebody a hundred years later.

PJ: You gave a talk in which you referred to something that you, certainly, achieve in your own work. You said that it's in the detail that a story achieves a cosmic element. You said: "The greatest writers evoke a sense of the poise and scale of eternity in their work."[3] That's a fascinating phrase, *the poise and scale of eternity.*

RM: I believe that's one of the things that makes a writer a poet. To bring into play a very local story, in the foreground you have a very angry character, you have a very angry young man, McEvoy, in South Carolina, who inadvertently—or with a plan, we're not sure—commits a murder. It's an engaging story, partly because the detail is so specific to the time and place, so it seems real, we get involved in it. But *the effect* of a story such as that, one that is really well done, is that it seems universal, it seems to fit the way we view humanity, history.

It's a tragedy. Cormac McCarthy is a tragic writer. When you pull back from a story like that, you feel that it fits into the larger world and into the larger human condition. It isn't *just* a local story. Viewed from a distance, it seems even more tragic, these individuals caught up in the great processes of history, economics. And it's that combination of double vision that's one of the marks of a great writer. They see the *local* in this story, but you also feel it connects to the larger patterns of nature and history.

In some ways, McCarthy is a great naturalistic writer. You can feel the forces of nature as well as of the personalities of the characters. You see this in a novel such as *Child of God*. You see it particularly in *Suttree.* The story's all about the city, but at the end, as Suttree is leaving the city, you expand to the countryside and then to a mythic sense of nature and destiny.

PJ: Where would you rank McCarthy among American writers, particularly those of the twentieth century?

RM: My sense is that some of the writers of the last half of the twentieth century and the beginning of the twenty-first are as good as the great writers of the earlier twentieth century. In the future, writers like Cormac McCarthy, Tim O'Brien, Louise Erdrich, Lee Smith, Doris Betts, Reynolds Price, Alice Walker, will be seen as great writers the way Faulkner, Hemingway, and Fitzgerald are. Academia has canonized certain modernist writers, talked and talked about them so long that we think of them as deities, and nobody can ever be that great. I suspect that that is just a myth created by academia, as I suspect modernism is a myth created by academia.

In the longer context, you can see that Cormac McCarthy links up with Melville and Dostoyevsky and it has very little to do with modernism, it has to do with these great tragic stories, with the drama and the power of them. Perhaps some of the great modernists are not as good as the great contemporary novelists. It would be hard to find a writer about war better than Tim O'Brien, for instance, even considering Tolstoy and Stendhal and the writers about World War II. Of course we don't know how these people will be ranked because we don't know what the tastes of the future will be, but I suspect McCarthy will be thought of as one of the great American writers a hundred years from now.

PJ: I used to say to academics: "I don't acknowledge postmodernism because I don't acknowledge modernism. There are things in Laurence Sterne that are every bit as postmodern as Pynchon!"

RM: (*Laughs*) Absolutely. All the elements of fiction seem to have been present at the beginning, in the eighteenth century. Nothing has happened that's entirely different from what Sterne, Richardson, Fielding, and Defoe did at the very beginning. The great dramas, the historical epics, the ironies, the experimental tongue-in-cheek writing in Sterne, the comedy of Fielding—it was all there at the very beginning.

PJ: Can you think of other films about the South that have struck you with comparable force to *The Gardener's Son*?

RM: So many films about the South have been romanticized. One of the most realistic films that I have seen recently is *Sling Blade*, by Billy Bob Thornton. That seemed to hit that note of the real. The voices have that sense of discovery. A character says: "Are you going to carry me over?" Meaning, am I going to ride with you. Hollywood *can* get the South right, but it rarely does. In television and film they usually rely on stereotypes. The first major American movie was about the Civil War, and the most famous movie of all time is about the Civil War, so around the world that's the audience's view of the South. What you get in *The Gardener's Son* is the smaller picture. You get down to the finer details, and it has a realism and a toughness that's very special. I would like to see more films like that.

PJ: To get such fine performances, it does seem to help, doesn't it, to have good writing? In talking about McCarthy, Anne O'Sullivan (Martha) told me: "You wanted to rise to the occasion because it had so much texture and depth, and you wanted to be as good as you could be to do it."
RM: It's a lot easier to be a really good actor if you have really good lines to say and a really good character. I'll never forget that when he was given a lifetime achievement award, Cary Grant thanked the writers, and he named half a dozen.

PJ: Billy Bob Thornton directed *All the Pretty Horses.*
RM: He has a wonderful sense of characterization through voice, both as an actor and as a writer. I noticed this in *The Apostle.* He's the man who tries to run the preacher off. That just seemed *absolutely* right. That anger—he got that anger right, and the fear of religion, of the spirit—and the way he changes on camera. *That* was an awfully good movie, also. But both as a writer and as an actor, Thornton has such a feeling for the complexity of characters who are poor, or are not well-educated. He doesn't think of them as simple. He sees their complexity.

PJ: *Sling Blade* has something in common with *The Gardener's Son* in that there are no easy answers there, either. Even in the way that it is lit, you get the sense that parts of Karl will remain dark to the viewer and, perhaps, to anyone who knows him.
RM: Well, the good writer and the good actor will find the character often through the paradoxes, the contradictions that will make him or her most real. Nobody is either all good or all bad. The challenge is to include those

contradictions and yet, at the same time, to give the character an overall unity, and I think Thornton is one of the best at doing that.

PJ: In my own work, I have allies who support me by what they do. I look at them and say: "Someone else is aiming at the same sort of thing." I couldn't get by without the touchstone of knowing they've done it, or are doing it. Is there any sense in which McCarthy has been an ally to you?

RM: Yes, he is one of the writers who showed me the possibilities of working within the region, with characters who are at the fringe of society, as it were. I believe it was easier to get back to fiction writing after discovering his work, encountering the power of language, the way in which he will look at the world in its contradictions and pain. He is one of several writers I rely on for a sense of encouragement and of possibility.

My first writing teacher was the novelist Guy Owen, who planted seeds I'm sure he never realized, talking about dialect, learning the terms local people used, that sort of thing. Owen was a great influence on me. Not at the time. Later. And certainly Cormac McCarthy. Lee Smith, another writer about Appalachia. Fred Chappell was one of my teachers. I've learned a lot from Fred. He's been very encouraging over the years. A short story that has meant a lot to me over the years is Alice Walker's "Everyday Use," which is about a family of farm women in Georgia. The older woman brags how she can kill a hog all by herself. (*Laughs*) She can run the place all by herself. That has a wonderful realism and toughness to it.

It is easier to write knowing that there are writers like Cormac McCarthy who are successful, that great writing is not something of the past, but also of the present.

PJ: What will you do when they come to you and say: "It's not enough that *Gap Creek* is a novel—we're going to film it—will you do the screenplay?"

RM: I would like to have a shot at it. Screenwriting is very different from writing fiction. I believe literary people don't realize how hard it is to adapt something for film. It seems easy, perhaps, because it's not about writing but about visualization and drama. I think it would be a great challenge. I would like to try it. I love movies. I had never seen a movie in a theatre until I went off to college. I grew up in the country and my parents wouldn't let us go see movies, but when I moved off to college I just went wild going to see movies and loved them. I believe that film has had a lot of impact on fiction writing. We have learned a lot from film, particularly about pacing and compression. So I would be thrilled if someone made a film of one of my books, and yes, I would enjoy at least trying to write a script.

PJ: I won't ask whether you'd feel a loss of power being stripped of your prose. As a poet you work very sparsely, don't you?

RM: I believe film and poetry do have a lot in common, and film and the short story. But I'm in awe of film and its power. It's different from language. Often the hardest novels to adapt are the best written, the novels that live in their language, in the narration, in the descriptions. That's very hard to adapt. It may be easier to adapt novels that are not that great. The way you tell a story in film is different. I tell my students that film is, oddly enough, a medium of *reaction*. To know what something means, the camera turns to the face of the actor, and we know, by extension, if it's moving or mysterious. Since you don't have that actor or the camera in fiction writing, you have to show what happens and the reader responds to that. Paradoxically, film is more the medium of reaction, and fiction the medium of action. You can tell the reader *what happens* and you don't have to explain what it means.

PJ: Your face is very congenial to the camera. Have you done any acting?

RM: No. I sort of wish I had. I believe fiction writing is very similar to acting. The great pleasure of writing fiction is that you don't have to be yourself. You can get into your characters. You can forget your own troubles for a while and think of the troubles of your character, Julie, or Jimmy, or Hank. I feel there's something very close to acting in writing. I often wish I had tried acting, but I never did.

PJ: When they film *Gap Creek* they'll probably find a part for you.

RM: (*Laughs*) I can be the old guy!

PJ: James Dickey tells the story of playing the sheriff in *Deliverance*: "Well, they just had a costume that fit me . . ." But when you look at *the size* of Dickey . . . (*Laughter*)

When we make our own dramatic films, we might have to put you to work.

RM: Okay. That's a deal.

Notes

1. This interview was originally published in *Southern Quarterly* 40.1 (2001): 121–31, and later revised for inclusion in Peter Josyph's *Adventures in Reading Cormac McCarthy* (Lanham, MD: Scarecrow Press, 2010), 143–58.

2. In *The Gardener's Son*, Kevin Conway plays James Gregg, who is shot in the office of his mill by Robert McEvoy, played by Brad Dourif. Robert's father, Patrick, a gardener at the mill, is played by Jerry Hardin; his mother is played by Penny Allen; his sister, Martha, from whom Gregg tries to buy sexual favors, is played by Anne O'Sullivan. Nan Martin plays James Gregg's mother, and Ned Beatty plays Pinky, a good ole boy with whom Robert takes a drink in a doggery when he returns to Graniteville to see that his mother is *not* buried there. Paul Benjamin plays the attorney hired to defend Robert, who is hanged at the end of the film.

3. The full sentence is: "It has been said that the greatest writers evoke a sense of the poise and scale of eternity in their work, no matter how cluttered or twisted or violent the scene in the foreground." See Robert Morgan, "Cormac McCarthy: The Novel Raised from the Dead," in *Sacred Violence: Cormac McCarthy's Appalachian Works, Vol. 1*, 2nd ed., eds. Wade Hall and Rick Wallach (El Paso: Texas Western Press, 2002), 12.

The Poetics of Work: An Interview with Robert Morgan

Patrick Bizzaro and Resa Crane Bizzaro / 2000

Originally published in *North Carolina Literary Review* 10 (2001): 173–90.
Reprinted by permission.

In the fall semester of 2000, Robert Morgan took a sabbatical leave from Cornell University, where he has been a faculty member since 1971. During that semester, he taught at Appalachian State University in Boone, North Carolina, and traveled extensively, reading from his 1999 novel *Gap Creek* (Algonquin), which was by then a selection of Oprah's Book Club. On December 9, 2000, he visited Greenville, North Carolina, sponsored by East Carolina University's Writers' Reading Series, and read from *Gap Creek* and his new collection of poetry, *Topsoil Road*. The following interview was conducted by Patrick Bizzaro and Resa Crane Bizzaro at their home after the December reading.

Patrick Bizzaro: You talked a bit in your reading tonight about the effect that Oprah has had on your career and, generally, on literary careers of people all over the country. Back in 1984, in an interview, Suzanne Booker asked you, "How do you explain the lack of critical attention you've received?" Would you compare that time in your life with this time in your life? Could you talk about the kinds of changes that have happened in your career?

Robert Morgan: Well, the greatest thing that happened as a result of the Oprah Book Club selection is to suddenly have hundreds of thousands of readers as opposed to, at most, tens of thousands before that. I had good readers, loyal readers, before Oprah, but she really gave me a million readers, and we've sold a million copies of the book and some of those books are read by several people—so that's the fabulous thing. I never dreamed that I'd be read by so many people or be a "popular" writer.

When I was talking to Suzanne in 1984, I thought of myself primarily as a poet. I always expected to have a relatively small audience. But I think that I am, perhaps, more of a "popular" writer than I knew, and I realized that maybe, all along, that's what I wanted to be. And since it didn't seem to be an option in the world of poetry, I never thought about it that much. But I realize that I like to write the kind of fiction that a lot of people can read. I want to reach a large audience. I want to write fiction that's accessible to people. I want to write human stories that almost anybody can understand, and, certainly, the Oprah Book Club selection reinforced that sense. But I was beginning to have that before, actually, and I can realize now that all along I wanted to write the kind of fiction that would *really mean* something to a large number of people. My mother has gotten so many phone calls and letters and visits from readers of *Gap Creek* that she has been as astounded as I have.

Resa Crane Bizzaro: Are these complete strangers to her, too?

RM: No, usually they're people she knows or people distantly related to us. But the last time I was home, she said, "You know, that book really *means* something to people." And I realized *that's* what I wanted to do all along: I wanted to write a book that really means something to a lot of readers, a book that would really move them. Any number of people said they'd finished the book in tears—both of my most recent novels [*Gap Creek* and *The Truest Pleasure*]. So, writing fiction in the last fifteen years has changed my ideas about the kind of writer I am and the kind of writer I wanted to be and focused me more on writing for a larger audience—an audience outside of academia. I believe the audience for poetry and short stories is largely in academia. But for novels, the audience is huge and includes literate people from all walks of life.

RCB: How have you personally been affected by all the publicity surrounding *Gap Creek* due to the Oprah show? I know you said you were interviewed by her, and there had been a number of reporters, and others—how has that influenced you?

RM: The publicity has forced me to be a much more public person that I am naturally. I am a very private and shy person, an introvert. But there's no way you can be an introvert if you have to do a lot of radio talk shows and television talk shows and lots of readings. So, I've turned myself much more into a public person to go out and promote the writing and to respond to readers. One of the great surprises of the past year is that I actually enjoy going out and meeting readers. When I was younger, I did not enjoy that; I would not have enjoyed doing *this*. But once I got into my fifties, I discovered that I had spent so much of my life sitting in a room by myself, writing or reading or working alone, that it was actually fun going out and meeting people—like this afternoon. People were enthusiastic about *Gap Creek* if they'd read it or enthusiastic about reading it even if they haven't. And if you have time to talk to them and ask them where they're from, that's actually fun. But I did not feel that way fifteen years ago. I think simply being in the public eye probably made me feel a little bit less self-conscious about it. If you do something day after day after day, you tend to get used to it. There have been days this fall when I've done six radio interviews plus a television spot in one day.

RCB: You said at the reading earlier that one of your poetry publishers called you after Oprah picked up *Gap Creek* and said they wanted to reissue one of your books of poetry. Have you noticed a significant increase in the number of books that have been reprinted or brought back for another edition based upon the number of people who've read *Gap Creek* and want to read more, or do you have any sense of that?
RM: Well, two of the early books of short stories have been reprinted by Scribner—post-Oprah. But the new book of poetry, *Topsoil Road*, went into a second printing before it came out. And that's never happened to me before. I think that's certainly the effect of having a best seller. There's a little bit of a spillover effect, but—in general—the worlds are very separate, poetry and fiction. When I started publishing fiction, I basically discovered a new audience. Some of my poetry readers had read the fiction. But for the most part, they're fiction readers, and there's not as much overlap as you would think. We live in a literary culture where people are typecast as either poets or fiction writers, short story writers or novelists. It's a world of specialization. So, I really had to create a new audience for myself as a fiction writer. I think, initially, I was able to make contact with editors because they knew me as a poet. The editor at Peachtree [Publishers] who first accepted my book of short stories was the wife of poet Leon Stokesbury, and she had read my poetry, so she knew who I was. That was an advantage.

RCB: So there was not any resistance to a poet producing fiction?
RM: There has been resistance to the fiction among the poets. That is, for years, I was publishing stories and my poet friends would say, "Well, Bob is

a pretty good short story writer, but he's *really* a poet." And I felt as though I had to really work against that because my mind was set on novel writing and fiction writing, and it wasn't that I quit writing poetry—I was still writing some poetry—but I had just fallen in love all over again with narrative writing, with fiction. And by the time I had written *The Mountains Won't Remember Us* (1992), I knew that was the best thing I had ever written. But it probably had more poetry in it than the books of poetry I had published. I'd been told by my friend, the late Harold Brodkey, back in the seventies— and I thought this was the weirdest thing anyone had ever said to me—he said, "Bob, you know reading your poetry I can tell what a gifted writer you are, but you have the cadence of a prose writer."

RCB: Did you think about prose poems?

RM: Well, I thought about that, but I also knew that I started out as a prose writer. What I really wanted to do—when I was eighteen and nineteen and I was just beginning to write—was be a novelist, more than anything in the world, and then I got more and more into poetry and the poetry was reinforced by early publication, my fellowships, a job teaching poetry at Cornell University. So, I went with the poetry until I was about thirty-four or thirty-five, when I did start writing fiction again. And I think I have been able to do in prose many of the things I did in poetry.

PB: What kinds of things does poetry allow you to do that prose does not?

RM: The thing you can't do in prose is achieve the effect of metrical poetry and formal poetry. You can do everything else—you can do metaphor, you can do description, you can write musical language, lyrical language—but there *is no equivalent* to what you can do in the metrical patterns or the rhyme patterns. It's that ceremonial—ritual. And as far as I know, there is no way you can duplicate that in prose. What Dylan Thomas does in "Do Not Go Gentle into That Good Night" can't be achieved in any other way. So, as a prose writer, I have become increasingly interested in the formal aspects of poetry.

PB: *Topsoil Road* seems to have more formal poems in it than your earlier volumes.

RM: The new book is almost completely in syllabics or metrics with some rhymed poems, and that reflects the evolution of my ideas about poetry over the past fifteen years.

PB: You have said that in 1974, or thereabouts, you were "very busy teaching and almost quit writing." I wonder if things have turned around almost completely; that is, that now you are very busy writing and, as a result, are less interested in teaching.

RM: Well, I can see that I'm going to have to retire from teaching or go on half time. I'm so busy not only writing but traveling, giving readings and lectures. Also, I'm getting older; I don't have the energy I used to have. I used to be able to get up at 5:00 in the morning, sometimes even 4:00 in the morning, and write. I'd do a full day's work of writing before I ever thought of going to Cornell. And in those years I was writing full-time, and teaching winter sessions—helping to raise three children. I had more energy, but around 1974 when I was really teaching myself to be a professor, a teacher, I had to put aside the writing for a while, and, when I came back to it, it was in a very different way. It was a great break between the early, imagistic poems: the poems became narrative and I experimented with voice. There was a period—it lasted less than a year—when I wrote a kind of incantatory poetry that I have never written since; it was inspired by rereading the New Testament for the first time since I was a child—and reading Christopher Smart's *Jubilate Agno*. I'd never read that before. It had a deep effect on me. So I spent months writing this kind of incantatory poetry and published a bit of it in the poem called "Mockingbird." That was maybe a tenth or even less of what I had actually written. I wrote an enormous amount. Sometime I want to go back to that voice. I still want to do that again.

PB: You said that when you went to Cornell, your writing changed in some ways?

RM: Well, I had lived in such isolation before I went to Cornell. For two years, we had lived in an old farmhouse outside Hendersonville, and I saw no literary people. In fact, I saw very few people. I was working part-time as a housepainter and odd-job man. I did some freelance writing. And the poems I wrote in that period show it: they're mostly descriptive, imagistic, and the voice in them is almost oracular. It sounds like some cosmic voice—not a person talking to other people. After I went to Cornell, I was talking every day to students and to other writers; the poems show that—that I became much more conversational. There was something conversant about the new poems, and they became longer. I got increasingly interested in the use of voice, which led to prose writing.

RCB: At the reading this evening you said that in writing one book [of fiction] you had to wait for the voice of one narrator to "get out of your head" before you could move on to the other book. Is the feeling of voice as strong in poetry as it is in fiction for you?

RM: The voice in my poems is different. It's more formal, it's educated—usually—it's more like my voice, whereas the voice in narrative prose is usually the voice of the character. And writing in the voice of the character is a lot like acting—so that you live with the voice every day for months, even years. You get back into character, as it were, to write the story. It can be hard to get out of that—like an actor who has played a role so long that—that you just naturally fall into it. I've never been able to erase myself in the poetry and become the character the way I can in fiction writing. One of the reasons I love to write fiction is I can escape from my own life into the lives of the characters and think through them and speak through them. Supposedly, actors feel this way, that they don't know how to be themselves but they know how to play the roles they play. And I think a fiction writer is, to some extent, that way. I've felt most alive at times when writing a story, and I work early in the morning, usually, and I look forward to that time of day when I can live with my characters. I immerse myself in their world and forget the year 2000, the problems now, and focus on the problems of a century ago—eighty years ago.

The greatest novelist in English is probably Dickens, and late in his life he discovered what he really wanted to do was go out and give dramatic readings from his novels. And I understand that perfectly. He'd spent all his life writing and writing, and he liked that contact—that eye contact, that electricity—of acting out his novels, scenes from the novels for a live audience. And they say he shortened his life, he did so much reading, both in America and in England. He got so involved in playing the parts, doing the voices; but I understand that, and I think that the inspiration for writing fiction is *very* close to the inspiration for acting. The way you revise fiction is often to act it out, to say it out loud, to *imagine* the way somebody would really say it. Can you say it the way you hear it? Could you imagine how this character would say it? And if you can't, you probably need to revise it. "Will it play?" as they say in Hollywood.

RCB: Do the voices of characters stay with you? Once you leave your work area, do you still hear them during the day? Or is that something that you try to tune out until you're actually able to work?

RM: Mostly, I tune it out. And that surprises me—that I can work very hard for two or three hours, put it aside, and go spend the rest of the day doing something else, and the next day come and put it on. If I have an idea about the story, I'll make a note in my notebook or something. A phrase I want to use, a change in point of view, in attitude, but—for the most part—I don't worry about the story until I go back to it. And that surprised me, that I had that sort of *ease* with fiction writing. I think it has to do with my age. [*He laughs.*] After you reach a certain age, you know you've got to do your work. I've got to do my teaching; I've got to go get my car fixed. And you can only do one thing at a time. If you're going to survive, you've got to pace yourself and, to some extent, compartmentalize. I began writing fiction in a period when I was working as an administrator at Cornell, and I may have had to learn this then. I directed the undergraduate program for this big English Department. I directed the graduate program. I was acting chair of the department.

PB: You draw from your own experiences in both your poetry and your fiction, yet they seem to be portrayed differently. I'm thinking in particular of "The Gift of Tongues," and I find that to be just an absolutely wonderful poem, and it's drawing from something that, no doubt, is part of your personal past. But also in *The Truest Pleasure*, you're drawing on a similar theme. I'm thinking in particular of chapter one. I'd never imagined someone being able to tell the experience of speaking in tongues from the inside out—not only to tell that experience but to tell it from inside the mind of a woman. Do you use your experiences differently in your poetry than in your fiction?
RM: Well, I did attend Pentecostal services as a kid. My dad was a Pentecostal Holiness. I was so scared by the services that I wasn't able to write about it until I was beyond forty years old.

RCB: What does a typical service involve?
RM: Well, there would certainly be singing and praying and shouting, and often people would raise their hands and shout and dance in the aisles. Somebody who got particularly stirred would speak in tongues usually in eye contact with the charismatic leader. It's a semi-hypnotic state. The thing can be faked, but real glossolalia is triggered by eye contact with the authority figure, usually. Sometimes people rolled on the floor. Sometimes people would get so carried away, they would run. I've seen men run and jump up against the wall or run outside—make strange noises—the Pentecostal people called barkers—seem to bark.

PB: How old were you when you observed this?

RM: Oh, between the ages of five and twelve. But once I was able to write the "Gift of Tongues" I realized that I could write about it. When I was planning to write *The Truest Pleasure*, I decided it had to be done from the inside. Typically, in our culture, fiction writers writing about religion, particularly Protestant fundamentalism, do it from the side, ironically, critique it, see it as though from some great height—some critical height—and I knew I didn't want to do that. I wanted to get inside the mind of somebody who was not a hypocrite, somebody who really believes what they're doing and to show what the experience was and why it was important. I've actually gotten letters from Pentecostal Holiness people saying, "I never dreamed that anybody could describe the experience of a service." So that was the main thing, to do it from the inside and not laugh at it and not feel *superior* to the experience—but to get into the personality.

And I think this is exactly where fiction is; this is where great fiction writers do their great work, whether it's Dostoyevsky getting into the mind of a murderer or Tolstoy into the mind of an adulteress. An author who's there to judge the character has already given the game away and should be writing other things—should be writing essays. The point of fiction is to really show characters as full persons and to not be so quick to judge them. Or, as I like to tell students, fiction is rarely about good versus evil; it's about loyalty versus loyalty. You're loyal to this or to that. Loyal to your country or to your idealism, or you're loyal to your lover or your spouse. I mean that's what creates good fiction. It's not bad versus good. It was important to me to come to that point where I realized that you were not there to judge but to get inside the character, and once I understood that and once I had the voice, I could go with it. Voice, to me, is the key to writing fiction. I can hear the person describing an experience; I can go with it and go with it. So it's not an issue of plot. The plot comes, of course, from the trouble the person is in. The best advice I ever got from a teacher was from Bill Hardy at Chapel Hill teaching screenwriting. He said, "Well, you get a story when you get somebody who wants something *real bad*, and it's hard to get." [*He laughs.*] I've never been able to improve on that.

PB: What inspired you to narrate two novels from the point of view of two women?

RM: I decided that Ginny had to tell the story of *The Truest Pleasure* because she's the garrulous one; she's the talker. She loves language, just loves to play with words. I realized that if I tried to tell it from Tom's point of view he wouldn't have much to say. He's a hard worker. He distrusts language. He distrusts people who talk with great facility. I knew it would be a better story if Ginny told it. Perhaps I sympathize with the woman's point of view more, I'm not sure. Women interest me a lot, particularly the women like Julie [of *Gap Creek*] who have to work so hard. Dreiser says in an interview that he became a fiction writer because he could remember his mother's broken-down shoes. You can just *feel* the sympathy. And if you know Dreiser's fiction, you can see that that's essentially what it's about. I think something of that is true for me, particularly in a book like *Gap Creek*. I mean, I wanted to get into this character who doesn't know *anything* but hard work and spends her life working for other people. She's not a saint. She complains. But she always goes ahead and does the work. When the Oprah people interviewed my mother, who's eighty-eight years old and not used to being on camera with lights in her face, she really couldn't think of much to say. As soon as they turned the cameras off, she said exactly what they had been hoping to get from her. They turned the lights off, put the camera back in the van, and she said, "You know, it's a good thing Mama's getting some honor now; she never got any in her lifetime."

PB: Is that part of the message, if there is a message, in these two novels, that, oftentimes, women who work that hard really don't get the attention they deserve?

RM: Well, I think it's the culture that expected that they would do the work. Women in those days had to do so much work both inside and outside the house. The men worked hard: they chopped wood; they plowed the fields; they went hunting; they killed the hogs. But the women would have to get up and start the fire, cook the breakfast, milk the cow, and then go out and work in the fields, often, with the men, and come back and still fix dinner—not to mention all the work of looking after the children. That has been forgotten to some extent. We have so many modern conveniences. Women still work very hard, but they don't have to carry water from the spring if they're going to wash clothes; they don't have to carry wood to start a fire under the pot, carry the clothes and wash them on a washboard.

RCB: In considering how our lives have changed over the years, did you have to do a lot of research for *Gap Creek* and your other fiction?

RM: My whole life was the research. I actually did grow up on a farm where we did that sort of work. In fact, as a kid I was assigned to carry water from the spring for the washing because that was one thing a kid could do, carry a small bucket—not a huge bucket—but I helped kill hogs, kill chickens, hoe the corn. After I moved to Cornell in 1971, to my surprise, I became a student of southern Appalachia—in a way I'd never been when I lived here. While I was turning myself into an Ivy League English professor, I was also going to the library constantly and getting county histories of western North Carolina, East Tennessee, upper South Carolina, regional histories, histories of the Cherokee Indians, histories of the early settlements and explorations, studies of the dialects, the geology of the mountains, the botany of the mountains, economic histories of the mountains, religious history.

PB: Historical accuracy is really important to you; would you talk a little about that? I felt sometimes when I was reading your novels that I was also getting a history lesson. How and why are you interested in this kind of accuracy?

RM: I think I inherited from my dad an interest in history. He just loved to read it and talk about it. I think one of the motivations to write fiction is to make the past come alive—to try to understand it, to get into it, to see it in the kind of intimate detail and complexity with which we see contemporary life. We know who we are by knowing something about the past. I do love to read history. When I have leisure time, I prefer to read history to almost anything else. As a fiction writer you want to establish authority, believability, but you often make little mistakes, no matter how hard you try. I do try to check facts—and *words*. I don't want to have characters using words that would not have been used at a certain time, and probably the hardest research I do when I'm writing a book is to check the vocabulary.

RCB: How do you do that?

RM: The two easiest ways are the *Random House Unabridged Dictionary*, which has the dates of first usage—at least in America—and the *Oxford English Dictionary*, which has a lot more dates. So, if somebody says "tin can" in 1850, you can check and see if that's listed as being used at the time. Somebody can always argue with you; there's no way to prove that you're absolutely right. But it's probably been the hardest thing to check, in some cases, to see if a word or phrase was actually used at a given time. From reading literature of the past and documents of the past, you do get a sense of the speech. One of the most *valuable* things I ever read was the journals of Lewis and Clark because those are written phonetically, and we get a sense of how these Virginia frontiersmen spoke from their spelling. So, it's very useful if you're writing a story set in 1800 that you have this document written phonetically in 1803, 1804, or 1805 by a native of the Blue Ridge Mountains of Virginia, or a native of Kentucky, on the Kentucky frontier. But, mostly, writing fiction, you go for plausibility. You're not a historian, and you can't know for sure about certain things. You mostly try to make the story *believable* to the reader, making it as accurate as you can. And you will slip up somewhere, probably; you can't make it perfect.

RCB: How much of that plausibility do you think involves the reader's willing suspension of disbelief? Or do you think readers even notice?
RM: This is a *very* interesting question, because if you violate the preconceptions of readers too much, they won't believe what you've done. And to this extent, you can't get too far from expectation or stereotype. But you try to make it as original and accurate as you can—and still believable to the general reader. If you're going to write popular fiction, or fiction that a lot of people like, it's a delicate issue—because you certainly don't want to write stereotypes. In fact, I want to do just the opposite. But if you write something that completely violates the readers' expectations, they simply won't believe it—even if it's true. People have the hardest time believing the truth, particularly if it violates the clichés they've heard.

RCB: What was the great appeal for you to the time period in that particular location? The two novels both pretty much hit around post–Civil War, around the turn of the century. What's the great appeal for you there?
RM: It's just on the brink of the industrialization of western North Carolina, and that fascinates me. It's about to disappear. I think that cultures become particularly available for fiction writing just as they're disappearing. Hawthorne can write about Puritan New England just as it's gone. The mountains of North Carolina had been isolated and had stayed pretty much the same for a hundred to 125 years. Also, I'm fascinated with the generation just before my parents' and knew some people in that generation—people who had lived through Reconstruction who could remember the post–Civil War mountains and who spoke the old dialect, which I do not get much into in *Gap Creek*. I decided it would be too hard for readers—the really hard, harsh speech of the older people I knew when I was a kid.

RCB: Did you have family members who encouraged your interest in the time period?
RM: Yes, I had a great-grandmother who could remember the Civil War. When I was a little kid and she was in her nineties, she would talk about

being a little girl in Walterboro, South Carolina, where she had been taken by her mother to be safe during the Civil War because the mountains were overrun with outlaws and deserters. And they were safe—until Sherman got to Savannah and turned north in 1865. She was just a little girl, but she could remember bodies being brought, laid on the porch, and blood dripping down, and dogs coming to lick up the blood. So, I actually knew somebody who could remember the Civil War. It was like a contact with the past, the living past.

Mountain people, particularly my family, were storytellers. They just talked all the time, and I grew up among people who could remember which ancestors fought in the Revolution, where they fought in the Civil War, who was on the Union side, who was on the Confederate side, where people were put in prison by the Union Army. And they had all these tall tales about panthers, snakes, and ghosts. So, in that sense, I think my writing comes out of an oral tradition—as so much writing does—it's getting down an oral tradition of storytelling and living storytelling. The reason I think Irish writing has been so lively in the twentieth century is Ireland still has an oral tradition. One of the sources of great African American writing is the oral tradition in the black community, and the same is true in southern Appalachia.

PB: Your men don't necessarily come across as great guys in your novels. But one thing that I've found about Tom [of *The Truest Pleasure*], that I really admired, was his willingness to go out and work. And he worked so hard that, at the end of the novel, it would have been really hard to unravel what he did—or to maintain what he had done. I wonder if you could talk a little about work and the [role of] work in the novels.
RM: I went off to college to escape the hard work of the mountain farm, the hog killing and wood cutting—so I was surprised, as I began to write more and more poetry and fiction, how often I returned to descriptions of work and to narratives about work. But over the years I got so interested in describing how people do work, how they experience work, what we might call "the poetics of work," that it occurred to me that work is our most definitive activity, that we define ourselves through our work, not through our leisure activities.

It's what we do day after day, what we have to do, that *is* most us. And insofar as we have any wisdom, it's probably in our work—the way we sustain ourselves, the way we get through, is in the work we do and in the satisfaction of a job well done—probably the greatest satisfaction that people have. They don't like to think that; they like to think it's in the time they spend on their boat on the weekend or traveling down to the beach. But in fact, it's their work that gives them a sense of who they are—of their worth—and probably helps them to get through day after day after day.

Over the years, I discovered that I wanted to dramatize for the reader how people do work, particularly the kind of work that's rarely done anymore, such as road building with a plow and a shovel, making molasses, stripping cane, milking a cow by hand, using a cross-cut saw, which I've done a lot of. Most of that I have done myself, so I didn't need to do any research about describing how it's done. And I've used a lot of information I got from my dad and the people of his generation who really did a lot of heavy work. A lot of them were reduced to hewing crossties with an axe to make any money—out of chestnut wood, which is a hard wood, and it would take you a whole day—even if you were good—at hewing a crosstie. And if you did a really good job with it, you could get ninety cents for it from the railroad.

PB: Tom did a good deal of that, didn't he?

RM: Mm hmm. It was the hardest work there was. He could also split rails. He's based on my grandpa Morgan, who died before I was born, but he left things in such ship-shape that even as a kid I could see the rail fences he built, the terraces in the orchard hill, and, of course, all this stuff went to ruin after he was dead because there was nobody around who had that much interest in keeping everything perfect. The gates he had built were still usable through my childhood. All you had to do was bring a little grease and put it in the socket of a rock—he'd fixed a rock for the post-turn—but of course nobody ever did that. So, it groaned. But you could see where he had put grease in it. He was an absolutely tireless worker, and he made that farm into a very profitable thing in a way that his wife's family never had and nobody did afterwards.

RCB: What kind of farm was it?

RM: It was mostly subsistence farming; you raised what you lived on. There were small money crops. As it says in the book [*The Truest Pleasure*], he grew extra sorghum cane, and he'd sell molasses—particularly down at the cotton mill village—he'd take jugs of molasses and peddle them. He was known as such a good maker of molasses that people would come to buy the molasses he made. He would sell a calf from time to time; he would sell vegetables. The only steady source of money throughout the year was butter and eggs. He would take some eggs down to the store. So we're talking about a cash income of a dollar or two a week. You'd live on what you grew and what you preserved and raise hogs and chickens and that sort of thing. But when the Depression came, he had four hundred dollars in the bank, which he lost. Both my grandpas—the other one had three hundred dollars in the bank, and he lost that. And nobody in my family used banks again until the late fifties; you kept your money in a shoebox if you had any. Or the post office—you could actually put money in the post office in those days.

RCB: What did your family do? Did they farm, as well? I know you said you went off to college to escape farm life; so your parents and your grandparents farmed?

RM: My dad kept the farm going. His money crop was pole beans, but he never really made any money. We were supported by a mother who worked in the cotton mill, and she worked in a beauty shop. Then she got a job—and this was the greatest thing that ever happened to her—in the GE plant. She actually worked in the GE plant when I was in college and helped me. I mostly sent myself to college, but she helped me also.

RCB: What did she do in the cotton mill?

RM: She worked in the spinning room; then she went to beauty school and worked as a beautician for a few years. She managed a beauty shop until she became allergic to the chemicals—permanent wave chemicals—and got the job at GE working as an assembler. They were making outdoor lights. She held a screwdriver and put some kind of part in. My dad never made any money; I mean he would make a little bit, and then he'd give it away. He never had any sense of money. He belonged to a pre-industrial society, or something. He'd live by barter or by subsistence agriculture.

PB: Julie and Hank [of *Gap Creek*] are also members of that pre-industrial society. As a result of attitudes during that time period, did you have trouble writing about sexuality, especially about Julie? Readers might get the feeling that her physical relationship with Hank was pretty good and she had passionate moments, but she would also say that there's some things that people don't need to know about married people's lives. With Julie you had at least three sex scenes, where she really lets readers know what was going on. But you've chosen to do it metaphorically. What have been some of the responses by women to your effort—not only the effort that you've talked about before of describing giving birth—but the effort to describe the sexual experience from the woman's point of view?

RM: I have gotten unanimously good response from readers of *Gap Creek*. A number of women have said to me, "You really have given Julie a wonderful sense of color." And, eventually, I realized that they were talking about one of the sex scenes.

PB: Yes, color as metaphor.

RM: Yes, but they really didn't want to say that. But that's clearly what they meant. The way you describe sexual experience metaphorically. That is, if you make it graphic, it will not be as interesting or as evocative.

PB: This is a conscious decision that you've made, that you weren't going to give the graphic details but you were going to describe it indirectly.

RM: Very few graphic details—because I wanted to communicate her experience, the way she felt, and what it meant to her. That was more important than being too literal or graphic. I've been amazed at the response of women readers. The only reader who has disagreed with anything in the book—the only woman reader—was a woman who said when the baby is coming on, that Julie says she has this terrible pain between her legs. And this reader said, "I'm telling you, the pain is so bad that it's all over you."

RCB: You have said that you clearly hear characters' voices. Did you get that same kind of sense in writing the scenes that involved sexual encounters? For Julie or for any of the women who you've written about?

RM: Well, when you're writing a dramatic, particularly emotional scene, the voice changes. If you do it right, the reader doesn't notice. But you will see most fiction writers doing this. The chapter might start out in a very simple voice, but by the time Julie is describing her intense experience—of lovemaking or some emotional experience—the language gets a lot richer. And the idea is that you have the language, the feeling, the thought—language adequate to the experience. It's probably not what she would literally say if you were sitting in a chair opposite her and she was telling you about her experience. You move from the tone of voice and the style that she *would* use if she were telling the story to somebody face to face, to language that reflects the way she really feels. That's the way art operates.

I once pointed out this technique to my students about a story by Lee Smith—the character at the beginning seems relatively inarticulate, but—as the story progresses—there's a scene where she's standing out under the stars and she really gets eloquent, virtually Shakespearean, and it's truly effective. But it would be literally almost impossible. It's the way art works; art works through *expressive distortion*, and when you want that moment of epiphany under the stars, you pull out all the stops. And the reader doesn't notice that. They're experiencing the epiphany. And the language—if it's working right—is almost invisible—in the experience.

PB: Speaking of experience, you're able to successfully portray a variety of events to readers, including the devastation of fire. And fire seems to be a recurring problem in much of your writing. What's the attraction there? We had talked before about the idea of being terrified by the concept of baptism by fire; yet early in *The Truest Pleasure* there's a fire during one of the revival meetings. Fire occurs in *Gap Creek*. Is it just a natural disaster, or is it something more?

RM: I don't think it was anything I have planned in either case. You live in a little wooden house, and you heat the house with a fireplace, and you cook with a wood stove, and you have fires out in the back under a furnace. The fire gets out in *The Truest Pleasure* from the molasses furnace, as I remember. It is pretty common, but the way my stories work—and I was not conscious of this in writing them—but looking back at them I can see the way they work is that I've put the characters in physical danger and facing physical adversity, and the story's about how they deal with it, whether it's a lightning storm, flash flood, pasture fire, house catching fire, hunger. But the story is how they confront physical adversity again and again. And I guess fire is one of the obvious ones, and it's easy to write. I *love* to describe fire.

PB: Oh, you do it very well. I enjoy reading those scenes, in particular in *The Truest Pleasure*, when they were all running around the pasture. I really found myself able to locate them, and maybe I was envisioning it better, but I had a sense of where these people might be in relation to each other—even though they couldn't see each other. And then the scene where Pa's in the middle of the creek throwing water on himself.

RM: Well, I was thinking of the description of the Battle of the Wilderness— when it had been dry, and the fire got out. This was on the field, the old Chancellorsville battlefield, and there were still bodies lying there. Wounded soldiers simply got burned up; they couldn't get out of the fire. A lot of people died of fire—more, perhaps, than died of gunshot wounds. And he had been there, so in a sense he's reliving, as he jumps in the spring, his survival from 1864.

PB: The Civil War was a very powerful influence on a lot of things that he did, including that particular scene.

RM: I grew up in a house where my dad talked a lot about the Civil War because he had known the model of Pa, my great-grandfather, who was a veteran of the 64th North Carolina infantry and the Elmira Prison Camp—one of the soldiers who survived it. He passed on to my dad an enormous amount of information about what it was like to be in the Civil War as well as in that prison camp. So this was all vivid to me from the time I was a kid. All the many other stories about my other great-grandfathers, my great-great-grandfathers—one story after another, after another, after another—what it was like on the battlefield. Pa had been to Fredericksburg and said he didn't know how anybody survived with so much firing for so long. With so much lead in the air, it seemed impossible that anybody could have survived Fredericksburg. What he didn't say was that it was the Confederate Army firing down the hill on Joshua Lawrence Chamberlain and his men trying to come up the hill—and just cutting them down hour after hour after hour. It was one of the heaviest losses of the Civil War. He was there. He was also at Chickamauga. He was in Longstreet's army, another good day for the Confederate Army. And then he was home on leave when Gettysburg happened. He was captured the next summer around Petersburg and taken up to Elmira. But he was a very literate man; this is the side of the family that were readers, very bookish people. And he knew a lot about the Civil War and passed a lot of it on to my dad. He had a first edition of *Webster's Unabridged Dictionary* and history books.

PB: It seems odd that, coming from a family so strongly interested in history and books, you started out interested in math and science when you entered college in the mid-sixties.

RM: I was interested in *everything* as a teenager. I wanted to go to West Point; I wanted to fly B-52s; I wanted to be a composer; I wanted to be a writer—even then—I wanted to be a scientist. I particularly got into mathematics at Emory College at Oxford because I had never been particularly good at math in high school, but I got off to college and started taking calculus and realized I finally had teachers who understood the concepts of mathematics, understood the philosophy of mathematics, and it was *so easy*. And I was the best in the class.

PB: How old were you then?

RM: I was sixteen, and I never graduated from high school. I wanted to get away from home, to more opportunities, more books. I was tired of staying

on the farm, and I heard Emory would admit you—if you had a certain minimum SAT score—without a diploma.

RCB: What did your parents think of that? Of you going off to college before
you'd finished high school? Of going off in general?
RM: They pretty much supported it. My mother, particularly, had told us
from the very beginning that we were going to college. She was the one who
had the ambition, oddly enough, and she thought it was a good idea. They'd
hoped I would do something like go to medical school or study science, and
because I did so well in mathematics—this was the age of the space program
and "beat the Russians"—it occurred to me to study rocket science—aerospace—so I transferred to NC State in aerospace engineering and applied
mathematics and did very well, making straight A's taking differential equations and vector analysis, physics. Then my advisor told me I couldn't take
the more advanced course because I had never made up the deficiency in
solid geometry from high school.

PB: That's when you took the course from Guy Owen?
RM: Guy Owen—and it was the thing to do. I mean I wasn't really a mathematician or a scientist. I was a poet; I was a writer. I could do math, but—I
have never been a great mathematician.

PB: And you were writing poetry at that time?
RM: I was always writing a little of everything. I wrote my poetry and fiction for Guy Owen's class, but he particularly encouraged the fiction writing. I went ahead in that. At Chapel Hill I got involved with poetry.

PB: You made a conscious decision to write poetry?
RM: Well, I thought I was going to write both up until 1970, but the poetry
was getting published; it was getting reprinted. I got fellowships in poetry,
and Fred [Chappell] certainly encouraged the poetry more than the fiction.
And I was a better poet than fiction writer then.

PB: Were you a southern poet then?
RM: No, the poets I was imitating were Ezra Pound and Gary Snyder and
Kenneth Rexroth. The poetry that meant the most to me probably was the
translations of Chinese poetry by Rexroth, Pound, and Arthur Waley. I
started there, and people said that those short poems are kind of like mathematical proofs. From pure mathematics to short, imagist poems.

PB: As I read your poems, the rhythms seem almost to be mathematical, worked out in a particular way. I wonder if this is a conscious thing for you, even in the early poems.

RM: I certainly wasn't conscious that it was mathematical, that it would be like mathematics. But I can remember spending days at Greensboro, and then in Hendersonville, writing and rewriting and rewriting the same little poem—changing the line breaks, changing the word, changing the shape of it a little bit. But my sense of poetry was more visual then. I wanted it to look right, and I wanted it to sound right. And I had time then; I had patience. I could spend the whole day, and this was in the days before computers, and you had to rewrite it and retype it every time if you changed the line. And I didn't even have an electric typewriter. I had one of those old manuals. I would do hundreds of drafts in notebooks and on yellow pads, even before I typed it.

PB: In your estimation, how has your poetry changed over the years?

RM: Well, the poetry has certainly gotten more formal. I'm increasingly interested in rhyme and traditional forms, as well as metrics. But I think also the poetry shows the way in which I have worked more and more with fluent voices. The early poetry is so laconic; it's almost gnomic with its short sentences, and very little sense of voice—conversational voice—in the early poems.

PB: That's why I asked earlier about the impact of science. The poem "Yellow" in particular, seems to be a poem that maybe a scientist would write: "May is the yellow month. At this / latitude the woods are a fog of different / yellow greens . . ." It's almost scientific—see what I'm saying?

RM: It may have been my first poem set in upstate New York—since May is not the yellow month in North Carolina, but it is in upstate New York.

PB: You mentioned typing and retyping your work, but I know you have a laptop with you. Do you compose poetry on your laptop?

RM: No, I compose everything longhand in a spiral notebook and then put it on the computer or on a typewriter.

PB: You also have a history of keeping journals, don't you?

RM: I keep notebooks—I don't call them journals. I write down ideas, words, phrases, seeds of plots, lines of poetry. And I don't write in them nearly as much as I used to; there's simply not enough time to. And I'm also working on novels most of the time, which means I put everything in the novel I'm working on at the time. I have an idea, I put it in there.

PB: Today at the reading you said some people had complained—or maybe it's something that you had noticed—that you tend to write more poetry about your father and men and fiction about women. But I was also impressed with how many women appear in your poetry. Some of them seem to be models for the women who end up in your fiction. This seems to be the case with "White Autumn," for instance, and "Bare Yard."

RM: Yes, the poem "White Autumn" is based on my great-grandmother, the one who could remember the Civil War. And I have a number of poems about Julie [Morgan's maternal grandmother], including "Bare Yard," where we gather the leaves for cow bedding. She kept me when I was a little kid while my mother was working in the cotton mill. But people have pointed out that there are more poems about my dad and men than women, and I can't explain that. And the fiction is a little bit more, maybe a lot more, about the women characters.

RCB: Your female characters tend to observe more details and tend to be able to talk more about their feelings. Do you think that, comparatively, poetry is pretty spare compared to prose? Do you think that the fact that the men in your life have been less inclined to talk about their feelings—do you think there may be some connection between those men in your poetry and women in your prose? I mean, do you think it's a personality trait?

RM: Well, I think the poetry may be closer to the way I am. Much of the time, I'm the listener, the reticent talker, the person who wants to say something quickly, who would love to say the pithy sentence. So, in that sense, the poetry is in my voice and the fiction is in the voice of the characters.

PB: Back in the mid-sixties you said, "Southern poetry is nearly non-existent"; has that situation changed?

RM: Oh yeah. There's so much more poetry in the South and in North Carolina now than there was then.

PB: Why do you think it's changed? Why are there so many more writers in the South, do you think?

RM: Well, there were always writers in the South, but there wasn't very much poetry in the South. It's a very good question. I used to teach nineteenth-century American literature and early twentieth-century poetry a whole lot. One of the things you noticed was how little there was from the South—great writing, great poetry, most of it was from New England in the nineteenth century—and in the twentieth century, for that matter. The poets I taught were Eliot, Stevens, and Frost, all of whom are, essentially, New Englanders. Poetry depends on a kind of moral and intellectual authority. In the South, genius was in storytelling and tall tales and humor. The South always lacked the particular moral authority that people like Emerson had—and Whitman and Dickinson and Thoreau. It's a very different kind of culture.

The Old South was much more feudal and much more like Europe in many ways. The great genius of American literature, and particularly of American poetry, came out of the collision of New England Puritan zeal with the Enlightenment. So that Emerson in 1832 resigns his pulpit, leaves the country for a year, comes back, and sets himself up as a freelance writer and lecturer; his first series of lectures are on natural philosophy, geology, astronomy, botany, and that sort of thing. And his first book is not called Salvation or The Soul, it's called *Nature.*

The South did not have the Puritan zeal. It had more of the Enlightenment— Jefferson, the great man of the Enlightenment. There was nothing in the South in the eighteenth century comparable to Jonathan Edwards; Edwards was one of the great American writers. The intensity of Edwards's writing, the power of it. I think he was the greatest, but he was not atypical. There were people, great preachers and pastors, in New England who really were of that caliber. And that's one of the great sources of American literature.

PB: Who are some of your favorite southern writers now—southern poets?
RM: Well, I have not kept up with poetry very much in recent years. I have given, I would say, 95 percent of my energy to fiction writing, and to reading fiction, and I think that some of the greatest living writers are in the South— even in North Carolina. I jokingly said to a reporter earlier this year, who asked me who I thought were the best living writers, that the greatest living writers all have Irish names and were living in Texas: Cormac McCarthy, Larry McMurtry, and Tim O'Brien. But I think we're living in a renaissance in fiction, and I wish I had more time to read my contemporaries. There are so many very, very good ones.

Interview with Robert Morgan

Sandra Ballard / 2001

Sandra L. Ballard's "Interview with Robert Morgan" first appeared in
Appalachian Journal 29, no. 4 (2002): 494–504. Copyright, *Appalachian
Journal* & Appalachian State University. Used by permission.

Robert Morgan is widely known for his best-selling novel *Gap Creek*
(Chapel Hill: Algonquin, 1999), the first book selected for Oprah Winfrey's
Book Club in 2000. He also continues to write short stories and poetry, with
his most recent collections including *Wild Peavines: New Poems* (Frankfort,
KY: Gnomon Press, 1996), *The Balm of Gilead Tree: New and Selected
Stories* (Gnomon Press, 1999), and *Topsoil Road* (Baton Rouge: Louisiana
State University Press, 2000). His newest novel, *This Rock* (Algonquin,
2001), is a sequel to *The Truest Pleasure* (Algonquin, 1995).

This interview was conducted at the home of Robert Morgan's mother in
the Green River Valley, North Carolina, on November 21, 2001.

Sandra Ballard: Let's start with all this time you're spending on the road.
How is your schedule affecting your writing?
Robert Morgan: I feel like I've been on the road continuously since *Gap
Creek* came out in the fall of 1999. I did book tours for the hardback then,
and I thought it was all over until Oprah chose the book, and I went back
out on the road and did it again in the spring of 2000. Then the paperback
came out from Scribner in fall of 2000, while I was at Appalachian [State
University]. It seemed to me I was away about half of the time I was in residence at ASU. I don't think I could have done that much travel when I was
younger. Somehow, now that I'm in my fifties, I find that I actually enjoy the
tours. I like the readings and the book signings. What I don't enjoy so much
is the travel itself. I'm tired of airports and airplanes and rushing and sitting
down and waiting. The worst thing about traveling by air is that you have

no control. If the plane is late or the flight is cancelled, you're stuck because there's no way to get where you want to go.

One of the good things about the past few years of traveling is that I actually have done more writing. I've discovered that once I have a draft or a novel on my laptop, I can sit in a hotel room and revise it. If you're in a hotel and you have nothing to do until an interview at noon or 1 o'clock, what are you going to do? Watch television or read the Gideon Bible? Or work on your book?

One of the things I've missed most is reading. I can never get caught up on all of the dozens of books I want to read.

SB: What do you want to read?

RM: I want to finish a biography of John Bunyon that I've started. I want to read some of the new novels. There are lots and lots of history books I want to read. I need to do some more research for a novel set in the American Revolution, the campaign in the South in 1780–81. I need to look at Harriette Arnow's *Seedtime on the Cumberland* and a number of other books. I particularly want to find things like diaries and letters. Without those, it's a little hard to connect those events with people rather than distant historical abstractions. I need to know what they were wearing, how they talked, their expectations. So I'm reading for that one project.

SB: Does the book have a title yet?

RM: I have a working title, "The Battle of Thicketty Mountain," which is what local people called the Battle of Cowpens. If you go to Cowpens and look across Thicketty Creek, you'll see this low ridge called Thicketty Mountain. The story takes place there.

SB: You talked once about liking Eudora Welty's comment about going to West Virginia with her mother and sensing a "peculiar combination of sentiment and fear" in her West Virginia relatives. Does that comment apply in any way to your work?

RM: That quote really did strike a note with me. I realized just how accurate it was. Mountain people feel sentiment, deep sentiment, strong feelings of loyalty, kinship—and resentment if they feel they've been slighted. But the key to understanding the culture is realizing how important sentiment is. On the other side is fear, a fear of change, fear of travel, and a very special fear of the unknown, of a different place, a different city, probably springing partly from a sense of inferiority.

The more I thought about it, the more I realized that Appalachian people had sorted themselves out, selected themselves, as did their cousins and relatives all through the nineteenth century and even the twentieth century. Some of them moved on. But who were the people who stayed here in the early nineteenth century when a lot of people were moving on? The people who stayed liked this place. They were people who liked to stay put. I think the most adventuresome ones went West. The ones who stayed were satisfied with their work. They didn't want to leave.

SB: In an interview you gave last year, you said it was easier to write about a time that was past.

RM: I think a culture becomes *available* in a special way once it's waning. We can see it more clearly then. It's hard to know what's happening at the time it's going on. We don't have the perspective that we do when you view it across time. We may misunderstand. But when a culture has waned, say, like Puritan culture by the time of Hawthorne, we can see it very clearly because we have a different connection to it. And I believe that's partly true of Appalachian culture. At this moment in history, there's been an awful lot of culture absorbed into this homogenous American culture, media culture. We see the influence of highways, shopping centers—so fiction, the most distinctive stories, can be written now about times that are gone.

Some people say, "Well, you really ought to be writing about the contemporary world and its problems; you should focus on these times, current problems, political issues." That's valid. But I think it's also fair to say fiction *may* not be the best way to address the here and now. Essays, editorials, and activism may, in fact, be more relevant than a story. Most fiction is set in the past. One of the delights of reading is learning about a time that is different from ours—sometimes extremely different. The time of a story is the past, but we learn that we're not isolated from understanding. We can read a novel set in the nineteenth century and say, "Oh, that's the way it was." We can see the way our ancestors did things versus the new ways. We become a part of that community, what I call the "community, a culture" that's not isolated, but a community that's ongoing. A story can give us a sense of community across time.

SB: Because *Appalachian Journal* has long had an interest in publishing the poets of our region, I wonder how you see the role of poetry in regional studies?

RM: I think that poetry and fiction often reveal the essence of a culture. We read a good novel that presents a place and a time with authority, with details, with intimacy with the characters' lives.

A scholar in Kentucky wrote a book about Jefferson's nephews Lilburn and Isham Lewis, who murdered one of their slaves. It's a good book, published by Princeton University Press. The author quotes several times Robert Penn Warren's poem *Brother to Dragons* which gets into the psychology and personality of the brothers. The scholar relies on Warren's imaginative recreation of the events. I have no doubt that adds a great deal to the scholarly book. The poem is certainly more memorable than just scholarly commentary. The most powerful portraits we have are stories, narratives. Two basic functions of the language are naming and narration. With words we can name things, emotions, experiences. All names are metaphors, seeing one thing in terms of another. The second is narrative, storytelling. I don't think we'll ever get away from our love stories—it's in movies, television, ballads, songs, opera, short stories, history books.

Watching the past—seeing people in trouble, experiencing the stress, the danger, watching people solve problems—seems to delight us, it's been said, often because it allows us to see that other people have problems, often much worse than ours. If we consider our daily problems—finding a parking place, getting a speeding ticket—while we're looking at Hamlet, who's lost everything, somehow our sympathies with Hamlet make us feel better and make us better people, seeing our own problems in a different light.

Appalachian studies is like anything else—it's about Appalachian life, its people, and one of the best ways of understanding and preserving that life is with narratives, and poems.

SB: You've talked about studying Appalachia after you moved away from home. Besides wanting to learn historical facts, did you have any other motivation for that study.

RM: I think the first motivation for my study after I left the region was simply homesickness. I'd moved away for the first time in my life. I'd lived in Atlanta, Raleigh, Chapel Hill, but until I moved to upstate New York in 1971, I'd never really left home. That's when I discovered how little I knew about the place I came from.

There's also the fact that as you become older, you become much more concerned with the world you came from. As you mature, you become more interested in seeking your roots. But I would say the single most important thing that motivated me was wanting to be back in North Carolina. I was in my mid-twenties when I went to the Cornell library and began to read all the county histories, all the regional histories. I read all the classic studies of the western North Carolina highlands. I read the diaries of Michaux and Bartram, again (I had already read that once before). I read histories of the Cherokee Indians. I read about the geology of the mountains, mining in the mountains. I just loved to do it. The books were sheer delight, but I also learned a lot.

I love to write about the past, about work, about how you build a shot tower, how to build a road, how to build a bridge, how to sharpen a mill stone. By then, I understood that good writers had to have a vocabulary adequate to what they want to write about. And one of the ways to learn the words was to study histories of the dialects, also to study histories of building, of mining, to learn the words, the names of things. There were things I didn't know, though I knew a lot of the physical details of farming. I'd plowed with a horse, carried water from a spring.

I was in a museum one time—I won't say which one—that featured a number of farm tools. The guide, the curator, pointed toward something and said that it was a "singletree." I looked at it and said, "No, that's a doubletree. It's for two horses, not for one." It wasn't that the guide didn't know anything, but I knew the difference because I'd used one. For a lot of the physical details I did not need research because I knew them already, but some of my memories were prompted by my reading. For instance, I'd forgotten the word "sigodlin." I was reading an essay on Appalachian speech, saw it, and thought, wow, I haven't used that word in forty years. I ended up writing a poem. Memory and scholarship are both important to me. They enable me, in the process of writing, to feel that all kinds of knowledge are relevant.

SB: I wanted to ask a couple of questions about teaching. What kinds of things do you think that writing classes can teach writers?
RM: Well, you certainly can't teach anybody to write. But one of the things you can teach is a *care* about language. The best way that I've found to teach is by example, to show young writers with your own writing how much you care about using the right word, using the right structure. That goes a long way to show them that you *care* that it's said right, that you *care* about the details. You can help a young writer to build a vocabulary adequate to his or her purposes, to read, to get into the character, to know it matters.

But there's nothing you can do that will really help writers who are not themselves driven. No amount of information you can impart to them will give them the inner drive to write. You can help them to learn about the subject matter. For writers who have that drive, there is, in fact, quite a bit you can do to help. I call it a kind of coaching. You can help writers to see their strengths, to learn to trust their own judgements. Perhaps the greatest thing you can do for talented young writers is to make them feel that when they're good, they can recognize it.

The single thing I remember most vividly about the teaching of Fred Chappell was realizing that he could understand how my poems worked. He could help me see what had happened in my writing. That was very important for me. And I thought "wow."

SB: Would you talk about your affiliation with the Hindman Settlement School's Appalachian Writers Workshop? When did you first go there and how is it different from other writing workshops?

RM: I was a visiting poet and I gave a reading in 1987. That was the first year I was at Hindman.

The special thing about Hindman's Appalachian Writers Workshop is that it's such an open place, unlike, let's say, others where there are all kinds of levels of hierarchy. In some writers' workshops, some of those attending aren't allowed to talk. Some are scholars, some are fellows, junior professors, senior writers. At Hindman, there's a wonderful informality and openness. Virtually anybody can show up, sit in on the classes, talk to the writers. There's an amazing generosity among the participants. A lot of friendships are made. The participants are helpful to each other. But it's also special in that the focus is on Appalachia. People have a place to gather in eastern Kentucky. I don't know of another writers' workshop that's focused to that extent on a region of the country. In fact, the people who come to Hindman are often from all over the country, yet all but a few of them have some connection to Appalachia, a grandma or grandpa, someone from the region.

SB: What advice do you have about MFA (master of fine arts) programs?

RM: When students ask me about MFA programs, I tend to say that they can be very useful to people who have been out of school for a while, for people who have a backlog of writing, a draft of a novel, and are ready to use that time off. They're usually not so successful for students who are just out of college. I recommend that they take off a year or two and write. And they should not expect too much from an MFA program. It's a place to have the opportunity to master your craft a little more, to meet other writers, to get published in magazines.

I also advise students to go where they will receive the most time for writing, without a number of other responsibilities to teach or work. It obviously makes more sense to go to a program with faculty who are writers you admire, who know their craft.

SB: What did you learn from your experience of editing on the staff of the *Carolina Quarterly* at the University of North Carolina?
RM: Working on the *Carolina Quarterly* was very important for me. I got to read the little magazines. I became the fiction editor simply because there was nobody else to do it.

One of the good things was I got to know some of the contemporary writers who were sending in fiction. That's when I first contacted Jim Wayne Miller. He sent us some short stories which we published. I accepted one of his short stories which became part of his novel *Newfound*. The story was the one about the two brothers in school, and the younger brother answers the teacher's question about what they'd had for breakfast—sawmill gravy [*Carolina Quarterly* 15, no. 3 (Summer 1963): 17–34].

I published a story by Ray Carver. I discovered people like him and suddenly had some sense of connection to the active literary world, rather than just taking classes about literature of the past. I began to connect with living writers. I began a correspondence with some of them. I began to see what the living standards were, what the fashions were.

But I discovered that I did not have real talent for editing. I lacked the ability to stay focused and read carefully and critically for long, sustained periods. I discovered I was a lot better teacher and a lot better writer of criticism than I was an editor.

Working with the *Quarterly* really got me into the literary crowd at Chapel Hill. I had a sense of what was going on, not just with the *Carolina Quarterly*, but with all the magazines we exchanged with. There I was in an office with dozens, scores, of literary journals from all over the country that featured the fiction writers of the day.

SB: Are you feeling more at home these days as a fiction writer than as a poet?
RM: Well, for the past twenty-two years, I have gradually written more and more fiction, less poetry. Within the past couple years, I have written hardly any new poetry. But I think that will probably begin to swing back the other way now. I'll write less and less fiction. I don't have it in me to write novel after novel. I have two underway and ideas for one or two

others, but I expect that over the next decade, if I keep writing, I'll probably write more short stories.

SB: Would you talk about your newest novel, *This Rock*?

RM: *This Rock* is a sequel to *The Truest Pleasure*. Ginny Powell from *The Truest Pleasure* narrates about a third of the story. She's raising her two teenaged sons and has lost her eldest daughter to pneumonia. The rest of the book is narrated by her son Muir, a character who is driven by a call, a vocation, a sense of destiny. After failing as a preacher, he tries all kinds of things.

The only "true" episodes in that novel are three things based on my dad's experiences. I don't know if he ever tried to preach; I know he thought about it. But he did want to go to Canada and be a trapper. He loaded up his traps and guns and mackinaw in his Model T and headed off and got as far as Ohio when he ran into some gangsters who scared him so badly that he turned around and came back. And then he did go down the Tar River to trap. He almost drowned in a flood. He had to sell all his traps and gun to buy a train ticket home. He would tell that story sometimes. He also went camping in the Black Balsams and witnessed the Sunburst Lumber Company stripping the balsams. But except for those few things, everything else is fiction.

SB: What about the story of the hanging of the elephant?

RM: Oh, yes, that story is based on a real incident that happened in Erwin, Tennessee. A circus elephant went crazy and killed a bystander and was sentenced to death. That story was told to me by a student at East Tennessee State University. I couldn't forget it and had to put it in something, so I moved it to North Carolina.

SB: In *The Truest Pleasure* and *Gap Creek*, you used female narrators, but I noticed you dedicated this novel to your father and primarily used a male narrator.

RM: Yes, in *This Rock* I wanted to get back to a male narrator. When I started out, the character of Moody wasn't very important. He was a minor character, a minor irritation to Muir. But I got more and more interested in that character, and I made up more and more about him, the activities that he's involved in. He's defensive, irreverent—and I kept thinking, why? Why? Gradually, he became one of the main characters. He almost took over the novel.

SB: Did you have to do much rewriting or revising of *This Rock*?

RM: I kept adding to the characterization of Moody. He became more and more important. From the first draft, before I ever sent it off to Algonquin, he was a very minor character. Basically, he only appeared early in the novel and then just kind of disappeared. But as I kept writing the sequel, I came back to him, adding and taking out. I learned a little bit about novel-writing with that book.

SB: Would you talk about what you learned? And how did you choose the names for the characters Moody and Muir?

RM: I just wanted a short Scottish name, and Ginny was a great admirer of Dwight L. Moody, the evangelist. She subscribes to the *Moody Monthly*. The name Muir is perhaps homage to my favorite Scottish poet, Edwin Muir, and the great naturalist John Muir.

This Rock is my most carefully structured novel. Scenes toward the end mirror earlier scenes. You remember the scene when Muir is sitting and eating the sardines with the old man, the one who's not entirely right. The old man asks him, "You ain't a preacher, are you?" and Muir says, "No, I ain't a preacher." It's the great issue for Muir: how do you find what you should choose to do? There's a lot more of that in *This Rock*. A phrase here or a line there matches one that comes later. In earlier novels I wasn't paying so much attention to organization.

SB: What kinds of responses are you getting from readers about this book?

RM: A number of people have told me they think it's my best book. More male readers like this novel than the last one. They like the vision of faith, the driven character of Muir. They feel the sermon in the last chapter is one of the best things I've ever written.

I had a reviewer in Charlotte who said he thought that the ideas in Preacher Liner's sermon were most frightening because it said you could not hide your sin. You could not hide it behind good deeds, could not hide it behind sitting in church (*laughs*).

SB: The poet Diane Wakoski once commented that her parents had done her a great disservice by not raising her in any particular church because she felt that she'd grown up with nothing to rebel against. Did you ever go through a phase of rebelling against religion?

RM: I certainly did rebel against religion in my teens. I think that rebellion was necessary for me. I had to break away and look at the world in new ways. But having said that, I might add that religious training offers you the power of language and a sense of mystery about the world. Early on at Cornell, I saw that my best students in poetry had some sort of religious training. They'd already learned about the power of language and mystery. So, an entirely secular education leaves you deprived—to have not been taught when you're young that there's a whole spiritual world that you can't see, but that is significant.

When people compare the effectiveness of parochial schools over public schools, they often see that the parochial students seem to learn twice as much, twice as fast. The reason is that they have a context in which they can place events. I have no doubt that people who have had religious training have elements and dimensions to their understanding that are unavailable otherwise. But rebellion against what you are told to believe can also be important.

In the works of writers very different from myself, with very different background from mine, I could recognize those constants, those connections to a spiritual world, morality, ethics.

When I was young, I was exposed to a lot of discussion, about the meanings of passages in the Bible, about theology, and that helped me as a student, as a scholar. When there was a biblical allusion, I knew it. I saw how it fit in.

SB: It seems to me that in *This Rock* you've made a conscious effort to challenge some stereotypes about Appalachia and Appalachian people, with their levels of education, the books they own.

RM: I decided in *This Rock* to work very sharply against stereotypes, more than I had done before. I wanted to stretch people's ideas about Appalachia in ways that *Gap Creek* couldn't.

There's this fellow who knows *Paradise Lost*. He may be a dirt farmer, but he reads Milton, or Latin. He may have little or nothing, no formal education, but he likes to think about art and architecture and philosophy. Muir looks at Looking Glass Mountain and studies the great rock cliff. He thinks about man-made structures but recognizes the mountain is different; this is nature. He's thinking what Goethe thinks—art versus nature. Accidentally, because his grandpa had these books, Muir studies *A Book of Architecture* by James Gibbs and Henry Adams's *Mont Saint-Michel and Chartres*. He can think about these things *and* live in Green River. He has no money, but he is a dreamer, dreaming his vast dreams.

SB: Are characters in *This Rock* modeled on people you know?

RM: Well, there are people in the family who serve as models. My dad is one. The character of Moody is a little like my uncle who was a bootlegger. Ginny is somewhat based on my paternal grandmother.

SB: When an idea presents itself to you to write about, do you immediately know which genre you'll use—poetry or fiction?
RM: Poems usually come quickly. They are based on an image or a metaphor, or even a form such as a pantoum. I usually build a short story out of one crucial scene. But a novel takes me months and years to plan. A novel is made from characters and voices I want to live with for a while.

Everybody has some creativity, some talent. Many kids like to draw, but once they get a little older and start working consciously on it, they discover they are not so good. I used to be good at drawing, but I never got beyond that early stage. But in the case of words, I was able to work my way through to different levels, to learn about overwriting, pacing, different kinds of clichés. I guess that's what talent is, discovering your drive, discovering what you really should have known all along. *This Rock* is the story of a man who is possessed with trying to discover his occupation, his calling. The advice Muir gives himself has to do with finding his gift—I'd never thought of that in connection with my own experiences as a writer until afterwards. A reader pointed it out. The drivenness, more than anything else, is the mark of an artist.

SB: It takes something to learn to trust your intuition as a writer.
RM: In fiction writing, the key for me was voices. I discovered I could be another person if I could hear the voice. It was a way for me to get away from myself. One of the great breakthroughs for me as a writer was learning that I could speak as a woman character, that I could take on another identity with a voice different from my own.

SB: I wonder if you think about your novels in some of the same terms you would if you were writing screenplays?
RM: Good films ask a great deal of a writer, perhaps in ways I don't even understand. In a film, everything is visual. That's one of the ways I often begin to write a scene, by trying to imagine the time, the class of the characters, as a film. But the big difference when you're writing fiction is that you don't have that camera, you don't have those actors, you don't have the action to watch. What you have are characters that you want readers to care about. It's necessary to make them do things and say things, one word at a time. A film can do it all at once.

One great thing about films is that they're so popular. If you want to break the ice at a party, just say, "Hey, has anybody seen . . . ?" Chekhov said somewhere that if you want to break the ice at a party, talk about chocolate. I would say talk about film.

SB: Are there any plans for a movie of *Gap Creek*?
RM: There's been an awful lot of talk. But so far no one has signed a contract.

SB: I heard you say once that a film novel shouldn't necessarily match the book.
RM: Well, film's a very different medium. One of the things that is so deceptive to students about writing fiction is that they expect writing to be somehow equivalent of film, so they want to write pages about how their characters feel. Of course, you don't do that in writing. You tell the readers what happened, for the most part, making them understand how the characters fell from their actions. In film, you have those actors whose faces are registering emotions, fear, curiosity. Oddly enough, film is a medium of reaction. We watch the actors respond to events. In fiction, we tell what happens and the reader responds to that.

SB: So, you'd be interested in screenwriting if the right opportunity presented itself?
RM: Yes, I would love to try my hand at screenwriting. I'm a little too old to get really involved in it. But I wouldn't mind trying to adapt a novel. I think a film would have to be different from the book. It's almost painful sometimes for an author to watch a novel being adapted to a film. Film gives us another way to think about narrative.

SB: Do you read popular fiction? What do you read for fun?
RM: I read two books this summer just for fun. There are so many books I read because I have to read them, but the two books I've read most recently for pleasure were P. D. James's *A Death in Holy Orders*, a novel set in a theology school. It's amazing for a writer who's eighty years old, writing almost at the top of her form, though I never figured out the motivation for the murder (*laughs*). The other book I read was *The Life of Thomas Aquinas* by G. K. Chesterton. A wonderful surprise of a book.

SB: Are there books you read, films you watch, that are guilty pleasures?
RM: Well, *Brideshead Revisited* with Jeremy Irons. I like the scenes in the

Castle Howard. There's nothing in my writing or style like that, nothing with the same aesthetic.

SB: What contemporary writers do you recommend to your students and to your readers?
RM: There are a number of them, many from North Carolina. I always recommend Fred Chappell, and Lee Smith, Doris Betts, Tony Earley, Reynolds Price, among others.

SB: Would you tell us about your current writing plans and projects-in-progress?
RM: I do want to write a sequel to *Gap Creek*. And the one on the Battle of Thicketty Mountain. So, I have two books underway.

SB: How much time will the *Gap Creek* sequel cover, and when will it be set?
RM: Probably about another year, in the late 1900s. But I won't know until I write it. My books often surprise me—and my characters often surprise me (*laughs*). I think if the story doesn't surprise me, it won't surprise anyone else.

The Moral Ambiguity of That Time: A Conversation with Robert Morgan

Resa Crane Bizzaro and Patrick Bizzaro / 2004

From *Appalachian Heritage* 32, no. 3 (2004): 11–17. Reprinted by permission.

In the spring of 2004, Robert Morgan was Duke University's Visiting Blackburn Professor, and he lived in Durham, North Carolina, not far from campus. This interview was conducted at the residence he shared with his wife, Nancy, surrounded by books and art. After a cold winter, azaleas and daffodils were blooming, and the sun shone over the hilly neighborhood, not at all reminiscent of the setting of his most recent novel.

Patrick Bizzaro: In the acknowledgements to *Brave Enemies*, you say "my father Clyde R. Morgan, first told me the story of the Battle of Cowpens when I was a boy." How about your father as a storyteller? What can you tell us, in particular, about the way that he told this story, the story about the battle, and how your tale differs, maybe, from what he told you?

Robert Morgan: Well, one of my great resources as a writer has been the fact that I grew up among storytellers. My grandpa was a great storyteller, had all these stories about panthers and snakes and ghosts and mad dogs. My dad loved history. He loved to read history, though he had very little formal education. He had only gone to the sixth grade. But he loved the local and regional history, American history, family history, and he had hundreds of stories about the Revolution, the Civil War, the local history.

I don't think my dad had studied that battle in the kind of detail that I studied it. But he had read about it in the history books. He read history of the Revolution, and he knew a good bit about the campaign in the South. He knew a lot more than most Americans do about the Revolution and George Washington. One of the things that I got from him was that sense that the Revolution *ended* in the South. It may have begun in New England, it may have begun at Lexington and Concord, but it ended in four great battles in the South: Kings Mountain, Cowpens, Guilford Courthouse, and Yorktown. One of the reasons I wanted to write *Brave Enemies* was to call attention to the Revolution in the South, which is not too well known, as well as to this great battle. This is one of the greatest victories Americans have ever won. Kings Mountain is a very important battle, often called the turning point of the Revolution. And it had great psychological significance because Patrick Ferguson and his militia were defeated. But in military terms, the Battle of Cowpens was much more important because General Daniel Morgan defeated the cream of the British army. It wasn't a militia he was fighting; it was the best the British had. It was the best army in the world, Cornwallis's army. That gave a boost to the American cause. It's almost impossible for us to really estimate it at this point, to prove the American militia, a small American force, could totally defeat the best Cornwallis had, you know? It hastened the end to the Revolution. Cornwallis was crippled by Cowpens. He lost so much of his best army that he never recovered.

PB: Recently, I've read some books, historical fiction, but also historical poetry. In particular I'm thinking of William Heyen's *Crazy Horse* poems, where as a kind of afterword, he acknowledges certain sources. And I think one thing that we don't teach our students is how writers conduct research. And the research is sometimes, in some ways, very different from the kinds of research a literary scholar or an historian would do. Yet, we teach them methods of literary research, in most places, as a required course. Would you mind talking a little bit about the research you did?

RM: I've always loved to read history, particularly American history and regional history. When I moved to Cornell University in 1971, I was living out of the South for the first time in my life. Out of homesickness and nostalgia, I kept going to the Cornell library and checking out county histories and local histories, regional histories, histories of the Cherokee Indians, histories of the southern Appalachian region during the Revolution and the Civil War. I read the early explorers and their journals, and I became a student of southern Appalachia in a way I never had been when I lived there. I have used an awful lot of that information I acquired.

I like to say that much of the physical detail in my writing is based on my own experience of killing hogs and, you know, shucking corn, milking cows, that kind of thing. But I have, in fact, used a *lot* of the things I have learned in my study of the South, the southern Appalachians. I am not that much of a researcher like, let's say, an historian. I like to read what interests me. And often if I don't know something, I write around it. I just use what I *do* know in writing and later go and check the facts again. So, I primarily read for fun. I love to do the research. It's one of my favorite parts of writing the stories, to go back and read the histories of the Revolution and Daniel Boone and the explorers, that kind of thing. And I love the eighteenth century, the age of exploration. The Enlightenment hitting the American wilderness. The eighteenth century was a time when people believed in nature, and they believed in the authority of nature, and even in the benign-ness of nature. They thought it was a good thing. And I think that spirit influenced people like Bartram and Daniel Boone a lot, because they were so curious, so passionate about going out into the world and exploring the mountains and the rivers and the meadows and the wildlife and the Indians.

PB: Do you think we now have a distrust of nature? Has it changed in that particular way, that it's a source of uncertainty? That maybe adventure wouldn't be the same or interpreted the same way now as then?

RM: I think our sense of nature is more complex now that we know so much more about things—physical diseases but also psychological diseases—that seem to be a part of nature. So, we have a more complex view than the students of the Enlightenment and certainly than the transcendentalists and the romantic philosophers of nature. Thoreau and Emerson looked at nature largely as a positive thing, but our modern view is of something far less certain.

Our view of nature is a part of our view of the uncertainty of life, its complexity. We see human nature very differently also. Knowing what has happened in the twentieth century, the genocide, the Holocaust, the revolutions, the great cost of the revolutions. So, we're not *nearly* as optimistic about people or nature in the modern world. But I think we still have some of that love of the natural world and the environment, the beauty of it and the process, the curiosity to find out more. If I had to use one word to describe the people of those times, I would say it's curiosity. They just want to know what's there. They want to know what's over the next hill. They want to know what kind of plants and animals, what kind of Indian villages. They want to see the interior. They want to go *deep* into the interior of the continent. And I grew up, you know, enough in the backcountry to kind of feel that. The fascination of going deeper, and deeper, and deeper into the mountains, to cross the rivers, to find out what is there.

PB: What do you see as the limits, or the boundaries, of historical fiction?

RM: Well, what I see most are the possibilities, because one of the ways we learn about the past is through narratives, fiction, particularly film. When people learn about history it's because the story of history is well told, whether it's nonfiction or fiction. The burden on fiction writers, I think, is particularly great to illuminate, to be accurate. What most people in the Western world know about the Napoleonic War is from *War and Peace*, and a little bit through Stendhal's *The Charterhouse of Parma*. The burden on a fiction writer, I think, is to try to tell the story as accurately as possible. And this is extremely important in modern times because we tend to feel so isolated in the present.

I believe it's a feature of American culture that we don't feel the connection to the past or the future that some other cultures do. And in our world of computers and shopping malls and expressways and television, I believe, we feel a kind of loneliness. We don't feel a part of the community; we don't see other people, even if they live next door. Often, they're off at work, or in their cars. One of the things that fiction can do is give us a greater sense of community with other people, often people very different from us, different gender, different race, different ethnicity. Storytelling can reach across boundaries of geography and time and language, so that a good historical novel can give the reader a sense of community across time. We see those people are like us. They *are* us. They preceded us. So, we gain a sense of belonging, not just in the present, but to something that has been going on for a long time, particularly in American history and in American culture.

Some of our struggles have been going on a long time; people of the eighteenth century faced many of the same problems, much of the same kind of uncertainty. The phrase I kept coming back to as I was working on *Brave Enemies* was *the moral ambiguity of that time.* Had you been on the ground in 1781, I believe it would have been hard to decide which was the right side. Both were doing such violent things.

PB: Yes. That comes through in the novel quite clearly.

RM: It would *not* have been clear to people that one side was better than the other, necessarily. And one of the reasons Tarleton helped end the Revolution was that he was so bad he persuaded people that the Patriots were on the right side. He tipped the balance. He was so brutal . . . Bloody Tarleton: not taking prisoners, killing everybody, raping women. He really did tip the scales in the war. But I think it was a time that was very confusing to most people, as our own times are to us.

Resa Crane Bizzaro: The point of view is really interesting in the story also, because you have a young woman who tells most of the story, and in a large part of that story she's disguised as a man. What kind of difficulties did this pose for you as the author?

RM: Well, it certainly posed difficulties, you know, particular things . . . like how did she live undetected in a militia? How did she go to the bathroom?

PB: Exactly! A repeated problem there, for her, was how to sneak out!

RM: In fact, that was a great asset for me because most stories of the Revolution are told about the men involved. Here I had a witness who was outside the male hierarchy, the power structure, and therefore, in some ways, had a clearer vision of what was going on. Even though she was close to events, she was seeing them, really, from off to the side, in a way.

PB: She was seeing them maybe more objectively to a certain extent.

RM: And, once I came up with the character of Josie, I just felt . . . I, you know, hit this great stroke of luck.

RCB: How did you come up with that character?

RM: Well, I did the research for this novel twelve years ago. And I studied the Battle of Cowpens so intensively that I thought I knew what was going on on every foot of that battleground, in the forty-five minutes to an hour it lasted, and I wrote the battle scenes then. But I couldn't decide who my main character was. And, of course, novels are not just about historical events but about people, about lives. So, in frustration, I had to give up my project and I wrote *The Hinterlands*, partly narrated by a woman character. I wrote *The Truest Pleasure* narrated by a woman character, wrote *Gap Creek* . . . I wrote *This Rock*, partly narrated by a woman character. The day after I finished *This Rock*, I knew I could go back to my Revolutionary War project because I knew my main character was going to be a sixteen-year-old woman dressed up as a man at the Battle of Cowpens. I thought I could tell that story now. (*Laughs.*)

So, I started writing and dreaming my way into this character who grows up on the Catawba River about where Davidson College is now. She gets in deep trouble; she has an abusive stepfather, has to flee into the wilderness going over toward Gastonia and Shelby when those places were just the woods of western North Carolina. Then, my great stroke of luck was having her find that little church in the wilderness where this tall preacher, John Trethman, was holding a service, and I *knew* they were going to fall in love, and that through Trethman, I could complicate this story. Stories need a contrast and, in this *extremely* brutal place, here was somebody doing something *entirely* different. He was bringing a message of fellowship and peace and love to this backcountry torn by civil war, neighbor killing neighbor, brother killing brother. So I knew this would add immeasurably to the story. Not only would you have a love story, and a romance, a marriage in contrast to this, but you would have somebody who was articulate, who was educated, a witness. Trethman was better educated than Josie, older than Josie. And he is trying to do something other than win battles on the battlefield.

PB: I thought your decisions about when to let Trethman tell the story were really good decisions. As you're reading, you wonder what he's doing. Technically and structurally what was your plan, or did you just trust your instincts about when to let him speak?
RM: I decided that it was mostly Josie's story. Trethman tells about a quarter of it, I guess. But parallel cutting, as they say in film—her point of view, his point of view—was going to be important to the story, partly to get the British perspective, since he's kidnapped by the British, and he can report what Tarleton and the British officers are saying. I felt that it was important to be fair in the story. I decided as I worked that the British soldiers were demoralized by the time they got to Cowpens. They were getting sick of this war.

PB: You said you "decided" . . .
RM: Yes, I decided that.

PB: Is there historical basis for that decision?
RM: It is not something historians talk of. The British certainly were demoralized after Guilford Courthouse. I think even by the time they got to Cowpens they were tired of marching through the swamps and thickets. They were getting farther from the supply lines in this rebellion. It's just logical that as this war goes on and on and on—and something historians have not pointed out, at least no historian I have read—that Tarleton must have been shaken by having lost about fourteen or fifteen men at the Battle of Hammond's Store about two weeks before. He had always won his battles. He had never lost a battle until he got to Cowpens. I think it must have startled him, shaken him. He was very young, only twenty-six years old, to have lost that many men to William Washington's cavalry in the skirmish at Hammond's Store. So he may not have been at the top of his form by the time he got there. As I thought more and more and more about these

events, I became pretty certain that the British were really not in their best shape when they got there. And that partly explains the total defeat. They outnumbered the Americans; they were better trained and yet they were totally defeated at that battle.

And it was through Trethman we find this out in the novel. He was the witness, you know? I was thinking through him. I began to realize that he feels he has really been called upon to be minister to these men. They're in such bad shape.

PB: He does, finally, make a kind of commitment to ministering to them. Whether they're on one side or the other was not his major concern. His concern was their eternal souls, on the one hand, and his calling, on the other.

RM: Yes, he's been called to do what he can. That was all a surprise to me. I had not planned that. And when a novel is going, you know, and the characters come alive they *do* surprise you. You don't know exactly . . . I knew the novel was going to culminate in the Battle of Cowpens and the aftermath. There would be an aftermath. But other than that, I let the storytellers surprise me with what they discovered.

The Authentic Reader: An Interview with Robert Morgan

Tessa Joseph / 2004

From *Carolina Quarterly* 56, no.2–3 (2004): 68–73. Reprinted by permission.

Robert Morgan, internationally renowned poet, novelist, critic, essayist, and teacher, grew up on his family's farm in the Green River valley of North Carolina's Blue Ridge Mountains. Among his many volumes of poetry is his newest collection, 2004's *The Strange Attractor*. His novels include *The Truest Pleasure*, *This Rock*, 2003's *Brave Enemies: A Novel of the American Revolution*, and *Gap Creek*, which in 2000, received the Southern Book Critics Circle Award for Fiction and was a selection of Oprah Winfrey's Book Club, a *New York Times* bestseller, and the Appalachian Writers Association's Book of the Year. He is the recipient of three NEA grants, a Guggenheim Fellowship, and the North Carolina Literature Award.

Morgan's educational career is equally distinguished. He began teaching creative writing at the age of twenty-three at Salem College. Since 1971, he has taught creative writing and literature at Cornell University, where he is now Kappa Alpha Professor of English. He has served as visiting professor at Davidson College, Appalachian State University, and Furman University, and is presently Blackburn Distinguished Visiting Writer at Duke University.

In March of 2004, Morgan sat down with *Carolina Quarterly* to discuss the sometimes-vexed relationship between poetry and pedagogy, the disappearance of poetry into the academy, the phenomenon of the creative writing workshop, and the poetics of popular culture. He is an interviewer's dream: articulate, erudite, patient, warm, and above all, a great teller of stories.

Tessa Joseph: How would you describe your own education?
Robert Morgan: I think the greatest educational advantage I was to be raised in a family of storytellers. My family was not highly educated in the

formal sense, but they loved to read books, and they loved to tell stories. And in the long run, I discovered that I had something that a lot of middle-class fellow students did not have: that is, a sense of how you tell a story, how you keep people interested. I was also exposed to an enormous amount of preaching and Bible reading, and that turned out to be a great advantage to me, because people who do those things love language, they like to play with words, the effects of rhetoric and repetition.

I went off to college first when I was sixteen to study science. I didn't graduate from high school. I wanted to be a rocket scientist! And I was doing well; I transferred to NC State, and was taking advanced calculus, differential equations, physics, mechanics, and really enjoyed it. One day I went in to see my advisor and asked if I could accelerate, and he looked at my records and said, "Well, I know you could do it; you got straight As in your math classes, but you never made up your deficiency in solid geometry. I'm not going to let you accelerate." And I looked at my curriculum and saw that I could sign up for creative writing with Guy Owen, and I took that class. Guy Owen taught me things in the first week or two of that class that I'm still passing on to students, such as learn to listen to the way people talk, get the significant inflections of speech that reveal character. He said, learn the names of things, learn to be accurate in naming flowers and plants and tools, and that sort of thing, extremely good advice.

I wrote a little story for him about my great-grandmother when she was very young. She could remember the Civil War—I actually knew somebody who could remember the Civil War. When she was a little girl she had been taken out of the mountains of North Carolina, because the mountains were overrun by outlaws, and there was no law and order anymore. She lived on the plantation where her mother had grown up. They were safe until Sherman got to Savannah and turned north, in the winter and spring of 1865. She could remember Sherman's army sweeping through and burning and killing; she could remember bodies being heaped up on the porch of their house, dogs climbing up on the bodies. Well, I wrote a little story about her, and Guy Owen brought it into class and said, "When I read this story, I wept." That's when I really got hooked on writing.

But I wouldn't take anything for my studies in science, in physics and mathematics, chemistry, biology, and particularly geology. I have used so much of that in my writing. I recommend to writing students that they take not just creative writing and English but courses in foreign languages, in the sciences, because science gives you a whole new vocabulary for looking at the world, for looking at experience.

TJ: How do you approach the teaching of creative writing yourself?

RM: I've learned a lot from my students over the years, from the things they've written, their questions, and the difficulties often encountered when trying to formulate a response to others' writing and to think of something helpful to say. The first thing I tell writing students is that creative writing cannot be taught, that I as a teacher do something, but I compare it more to coaching than to teaching. The teaching is done when the young writer is sitting at his or her typewriter or computer or yellow legal pad; they teach themselves by doing it. I like the metaphor of coaching because the process is very much like athletics. How do you learn to play tennis? You get on the tennis court and you do it! That's exactly the way you learn to write. It's through the practice of writing. It is a skill; it's all art; it's not a body of information that can be imparted in the classroom. Something important can happen in the classroom, but that has more to do with encouragement, teaching high standards, self-criticism, and a kind of fascination and alertness to the quality of language. That can be imparted in the classroom; and also a kind of articulateness about response to others' writing; that is more what is taught in the workshop than actually the art of writing.

TJ: What kinds of things do you look for when evaluating student writing or attempting to contribute to it?

RM: Well, when I'm teaching fiction, as I am now, I look for all imaginative use of language, but particularly, I'm looking for voice, the voice of the narrator, somebody who has a storytelling sense. You can get away with all kinds of mistakes if there really is a sense of a story unfolding, and then of course a sense of characterization: is it a real character, an interesting character, is it a character in a compelling situation?

TJ: What about when you are teaching poetry?

RM: Well, poetry is similar—you certainly look for somebody with a feeling for language, for the cadence of language, the texture of language, and for a sense of the unfolding-ness of the poem, the flow, the movement of the poem. But there are other elements in poetry that really are not just language. The students I've taught that seem to have the greatest feeling for poetry are those who usually have an interest in music, but also some sort of background, oddly enough, in religion. They have been exposed to liturgical language, to a sense of a spiritual world, not just a material or secular world. Poetry is about seeing several different levels of experience and reality, and often the spiritual. My sense is that the people who develop as poets are not just those who have talent, but those who are driven to do it, who are called to do it, who will just keep on writing and rewriting and trying things until they break through into something that is their own, with a distinctive voice, a distinctive angle of vision. These are people who are willing to strip away the surface and get down to some sort of essence.

I think that writing workshops and writing programs are generally more successful with fiction writers than with poets. There's something so subjective, so personal, so private about poetry that I'm not sure workshops help a great deal. The great poets often—people like Emily Dickinson, Gerard Manley Hopkins, Thomas Hardy, that were off on their own—they go so intensely into their relationship with language and voice and memory that they come up with something very original. I don't know that a workshop is a whole lot of use in doing that. It may have something to do with the nature of American poetry, which Emerson said was going to be a kind of private thing, "deep hidden in nature." That was amazingly prescient about American poetry, that the greatest American poets have been people like Stevens and Frost and Dickinson who really developed in their own odd ways.

TJ: So, why do so many young poets wind up in MFA programs?
RM: What a poet is looking for, what a young poet is looking for, is what I call the essential reader, the authentic reader. This is why poets in history come in pairs and in clusters. In a sense, you can't be a poet until you have somebody who knows how to read you. When you go to an MFA program, or to Greenwich Village, or to Paris, what you're looking for is somebody who can see what you're doing and see what you're capable of. This is why people like Ezra Pound are so important, because he was that kind of reader. It doesn't matter where you encounter that reader, whether you find that reader in an MFA program, or in a PhD program, or somewhere, or in Paris in the cafes. That's why you have an Emerson and a Thoreau, a Wordsworth and a Coleridge, a Goethe and a Schiller. I certainly felt that I had met that reader when I met Fred Chappell, at UNC-Greensboro. He knew how to read what I was doing, and he could sort of see what I was going to do. It's a one-on-one thing.

TJ: What kind of effect has teaching poetry had on your own practice of writing and thinking about poetry?
RM: When I first went to teach at Cornell in 1971, after having lived in real literary isolation for some time, it was such a dramatic change that I actually

stopped writing poetry for about a year. Then when I did start writing again, my poetry was very different: much more conversational, longer, more fluent, more a poetry of voice and less a poetry of imagery. I began as an imagist poet, very much inspired by translations of Chinese poetry, Japanese poetry, and the poetry of Ezra Pound, Robert Bly, James Wright—descriptive, short, evocative poetry. But teaching made me much more aware of voice and being in Cornell's literary community made me much more aware of traditional form, and of the tradition of English poetry. By the mid-1970s, I began to think in terms of rhyme and even meter and syllabics, and particularly as I developed as a poet and as a teacher I became more and more interested in the dimension of sound: poetry as less of a visual medium and much more of a sound medium.

TJ: So, what do you think has happened in the twentieth century to poetry's audience? Has it vanished into the academy?

RM: I don't think there's any doubt that in the twentieth century criticism and what we call modernism took poetry in a direction away from the common reader, away from the general reader. It certainly produced some very interesting poems, but it also pointed poetry in the direction of the universities, and of literary theory and literary criticism, and I think to some extent destroyed the audience for poetry. The poets of the nineteenth century often had vast popular audiences; early twentieth-century poets like Robert Frost and Carl Sandburg had enormous audiences. They thought of poetry as something that any literate person could read and enjoy; poetry delighted everybody. The New Critics, and then the literary theorists, thought of poetry primarily as something for the highly educated few, the cognoscenti. That kind of poetry interests me also, but I think as I got older, I became increasingly interested in the kind of poetry that would appeal to a more general audience. This was especially true as I got more and more interested in fiction. I couldn't see why poets couldn't reach the same audience as fiction writers, if they wrote in a way that would interest more people. I feel like an ordinary person and I want to communicate with general readers! And I don't see why poetry can't again; it did at one time. The kind of poetry I would like to write is the kind that anybody can read, but the more you read it the richer it is.

TJ: Some critics blame the creative writing programs and creative writing jobs for creating a poetry that is either hyperacademic or mediocre or both, for taking poets away from the rest of the world, from a general readership.

RM: I'm not interested in making that accusation against creative writing programs, although I can see why people might feel that way. I know that a lot of mystery writers and science fiction writers feel that universities have destroyed writing, and that the canon should be drawn from the popular genres. Honestly, I'm very interested in the popular genres, but why blame universities? Universities, after all, are doing a lot to preserve the texts and papers of writers, and teach people to read poets they would never read otherwise. A poet is going to do whatever she or he has to do to survive. I think that some of this is based on overoptimistic expectations—assuming that because somebody has studied poetry and is teaching it that that person is going to be writing great poetry.

TJ: When I ask my students why they don't read poetry, they blame television and film for teaching them to receive art passively, as viewers.

RM: We do live in a visual culture, which is a real factor. Television, video, and film are all part of it—and the way poetry is taught as a visual thing. We read a poem on the page—we look at how a poem is shaped on the page as opposed to the sound of it. But I would point a finger just as much at our education system that doesn't teach poetry as much to young children, that does not ask them to memorize it, that doesn't teach poetry as a musical thing, as something to carry around in memory. I went to a school that was so poor and so old-fashioned that we actually memorized poems every year. There's no doubt that that stimulated my interest in poetry, the sense that poetry was something to remember, something to have at the tip of your tongue. And this is true in cultures that have had a lot of poetry, such as Confucian culture. The Confucian education began with memorization of the Book of Odes and different texts, so that all Chinese knew these poems!

But the truth is that some of the most gifted poets in a sense are the advertising people who have to put something that will stick in people's minds into a fifteen-second commercial. We all know these little jingles and turns of phrase. More people know the Pillsbury Doughboy than the poems of Shakespeare. I also think you see this love of memorable language in the way people like to repeat the great lines from movies. I'm sure you've seen people here in Chapel Hill or in other places sit around over coffee, or at a bar, reciting the great lines from *Casablanca*; everybody knows all these lines, *Monty Python* or *Apocalypse Now*. The poetry of the screenwriters gets into the consciousness. And that's where the poetry is, in the memorable language that is so delightful that people want to say it again. Some of the most memorable language of the twentieth century was in screenwriting. Everybody knows "You do know how to whistle, don't you?" or Lauren Bacall describing the kind of racehorse she likes, or looking at Bogart holding the woman and saying, "Are you trying to guess her weight?" Now there's a line! Those were written by Faulkner [in *The Big Sleep*], and they are very fine poetry.

Poetry is not just in literary verse, though that's where we tend to look for it. The poetic imagination is working in many different media. Poetry is the imagination, the imaginative use of words, and *poiesis*, the Greek word for the making of poetry. It's in fiction writing, it's in nonfiction writing, it's in fine editorial writing, it's in speeches, it's in sermons. I do think one of the dangers of workshops is that they turn poetry into something that you study, as opposed to something that you respond to by saying, "Well, it bores me," or "Hey, that's really interesting." You will notice immediately if you teach both poetry and fiction workshops that fiction is the stuff that is to be read and enjoyed and poetry is something to be written. In poetry workshops, you talk about how you're writing, or how it was written, or what the author intended; you don't talk about what poetry does to you as a reader.

Poetry happens where it happens. It can happen in an MFA program, or in a newspaper office, or in the High Sierras, or by Walden Pond. It comes from somewhere else, and we can't take the wonder and the mystery away from it, no matter how much we try. It's not just craft, though craft is very important. It's craft at the service of a vision, or an angle of vision. And somebody who has that is probably going to persist until they develop the craft to express it. The process is mysterious; we still cannot describe it. I don't know that an MFA program could much affect it if somebody is really falling in love with language, with their vision of the world; they'd probably sweep the MFA program up into their enterprise.

An Interview with Robert Morgan

D. G. Martin / 2007

From *Our State* 75, no. 6 (2007): 14–16. Reprinted by permission.

Robert Morgan has taught writing at Cornell University in New York for more than thirty-five years. But his award-winning poetry and fiction still reflect his years growing up on a farm in the North Carolina mountains near Hendersonville. Recently I spoke to him about his latest book, which is about the life of the legendary Daniel Boone, and is Morgan's first biography.

D. G. Martin: Daniel Boone was a person of both history and myth. Since so much has been written about him, what else was there? Why did we need a new biography?

Robert Morgan: I wrote it, I think, first of all, just to please myself. I've always been interested in Daniel Boone and in the frontier period, the Revolutionary War period, which I had written about in *Brave Enemies*, but I have become increasingly interested in the way the white culture, the European culture, met and mingled and fought with and learned from the Indian culture. And Boone is right at that interface. He is probably the main figure in American history, in that story. I think of him, of course, as one of the founding fathers like Franklin, Washington, Hamilton, Jefferson. But he was also a figure of folklore like Johnny Appleseed, almost like Mike Fink and Paul Bunyan. I wanted to look at his life and try to find out what is the real Daniel Boone—and how much is myth, legend, folklore, and how much is real history and biography.

Beyond that I wanted to see if I could tell a story where I really brought him alive as a human being, not just as a legend and even a founding father, but a real person. People as famous as Daniel Boone, Robert E. Lee, and Shakespeare tend to always slip back into myth. We know them best through what other people said about them. They are legends, and I wanted to see if I could nail down the real human being at the source of those legends and also tell what was legend and what was history.

DGM: What were those layers of myth that you found?

RM: Let me give you an example. It takes a lot of bravado for somebody like myself, who has been primarily a poet and fiction writer, to get into biography, especially a biography of somebody as famous as Daniel Boone. There is just so much material to go into. You are competing with some very great scholars and writers of the past. There have been several good biographies of Daniel Boone.

The first thing in my search that led me to believe that I could really do it had to do with the legend that in the summer of 1788, Daniel Boone and his sons in Kentucky, dug fifteen tons of ginseng, put it in a keelboat, poled it up the Ohio [River] to Pittsburgh, and then up the Monongahela [River] to Redstone, West Virginia, put it on packhorses, and took it to Hagerstown, Maryland, to sell. Because some of the ginseng got water-damaged in the Ohio, they only got half price for it. Well, I grew up in North Carolina in a family that had been digging ginseng for generations. One of my uncles not only dug ginseng but also was a trader. He was a kind of dealer in ginseng. He bought it from other diggers.

I got to thinking about that. Fifteen tons of ginseng? When ginseng is dried, it is light as paper, and fifteen tons, or thirty thousand pounds, would be enough to fill a warehouse or a ship. So, I went to the source of that legend, which is an interview that the scholar Lyman Draper did with Boone's youngest son, Nathan, out in Missouri, in 1851. In reading the transcript of that interview, I realized that what Nathan had said to Lyman Draper was fifteen T-U-N-S, meaning barrels or kegs. Almost everything on the frontier—tobacco or flour and everything—was carried in barrels. I knew that is what it was. It wasn't fifteen T-O-N-S.

No Boone scholar that I had come across had ever caught that. They had kept passing on Lyman Draper's mistake. Well, I went to Boone's account books. We actually have his account books. They were gathered up by Draper, and I found an entry from October of 1788 where Boone said he bought "15 caggs of ginseng of Captain Fagan for Hart." That's the merchant in Hagerstown. So, of course, that was right. He had actually not dug most of that; he had bought it. And it was fifteen kegs or barrels.

DGM: So, you exploded that myth?

RM: Well, that made me feel that maybe I could do this project, if I could find the source of this legend.

DGM: What were Daniel Boone's connections to North Carolina?

RM: The Boone family, a large family, moved from Pennsylvania, near Reading, to Virginia in 1750 and then to the Yadkin Valley, close to Salisbury, in 1751. The legend is the family lived in a cave on the Yadkin [River]. In fact, you can visit the cave south of Winston-Salem, where supposedly they lived at first. Then they built a cabin near Dutchman's Creek. They bought land from Lord Granville. You could buy land cheaply there in the Yadkin [Valley]. It was pretty wild country. And then pay a quit rent, a small rent, a few pennies an acre every year. This is back in colonial North Carolina.

Daniel Boone just took to that region. It was still kind of wild. There were lots of deer and beaver and Indians around—Catawba Indians, and you'd go a little farther west, and there were Cherokee Indians. It was really while he was growing up there as a teenager that he became a famous hunter, a commercial hunter and trapper. He really learned the ways of the Indians, learned from the Cherokees and Catawbas. And knew them, was famous among them, as a great hunter. The story is that in that region in the mid-eighteenth century a really good hunter was called "a Boone"—named after him. He was already that well known. He won all the shooting matches.

He met and married the beautiful Rebecca Bryan, who lived just north of the Boones in the Yadkin Valley. And they moved to a community called Sugar Tree, which meant there were sugar maples there. People on the frontier got their sweetening at that time from maple syrup and maple sugar. There were not many bees in western North Carolina at that time, and sorghum had not been introduced. So Boone really grew up and became the man, the hunter he is known for, in North Carolina. He lived in North Carolina for about twenty years and began to explore farther and farther west into the Blue Ridge Mountains.

DGM: Let's talk about you for a little bit. At what point did you know that reading and maybe writing were an important part of your life?

RM: It was a gradual thing. I was always interested in writing. The first story I ever wrote, I wrote in the sixth grade when I was studying with Mr. Ward. Dean Ward was the principle and my teacher. The class took a field trip to the Biltmore House. It cost three dollars to get in the Biltmore House. I didn't have the three dollars, so I stayed in the classroom. Mr. Ward looked over at me sitting there, and he said, "I don't want you to waste the whole day. I know you like to read these books by Jack London and James Oliver Curwood—stories about the Mounties and the Yukon. Why don't you write a story?"

So, he gave me a plot. He said, "A man is lost in the Canadian Rockies. He doesn't have a gun, doesn't have a knife. Tell the story of how he gets back to civilization." So I spent the day working on that story, describing how he sharpened a stick on a rock, rubbed two sticks together to start a fire. I talked about how he took a thorn and used it as fishhook—that kind of thing. I really got into that story. By the time the other students came back from the Biltmore House, I had a story written.

I think that was the first story. But it was reading Thomas Wolfe, when I was fourteen, going on fifteen, that suggested to me that maybe I could be a writer. If Thomas Wolfe could grow up in Asheville and write a famous book [*Look Homeward, Angel*], maybe I could write a book. I just fell in love with it, like most people fifteen, decided that Eugene Gant was me, and his family was my family. I was just intoxicated by that language—"Oh lost, and by the wind grieved, ghost, come back again"—that sort of thing. And I discovered I was born on Thomas Wolfe's birthday, October 3. So, I felt a real kinship with him.

The More Mysterious: An Interview with Robert Morgan

Jesse Graves / 2009–10

From *Georgia Review* 66, no. 1 (2012): 65–87. Reprinted by permission.

Robert Morgan is the author of twenty-four books, including the national bestsellers *Gap Creek* (1999), *This Rock* (2001), and *Boone: A Biography* (2007). In the fall of 2011, two new books appeared, *Lions of the West*, a study of westward expansion in nineteenth-century America, and *Terroir*, a new collection of poems, Morgan's first in a dozen years. This conversation took place in two sessions, the first in Knoxville, Tennessee, in late summer 2009, when Morgan was a visiting lecturer at a one-day conference organized at the University of Tennessee, and the second in Johnson City, Tennessee, in spring 2010, where Morgan was giving a reading at East Tennessee State University.

Morgan has given many interviews over the course of his career as a poet, novelist, essayist, short story writer, and during his forty-year tenure as professor of English at Cornell University. These conversations have covered many topics, and in choosing the set of questions for our discussion I tried to avoid points that he has covered thoroughly in past interviews. My goal was to focus primarily on recent and current work, especially his interest in history and its intersections with literature, as well as the influence of particular writers, such as fellow North Carolina native Thomas Wolfe. I have known Morgan for more than a dozen years, first as my teacher and mentor at Cornell, recently as a subject of my scholarship, and throughout as a good and trusted friend. I believe that friendship allows certain qualities to emerge in our talk, such as Morgan's sense of humor (an underdiscussed quality in his writing) and the intimacy with which he discusses his life and work.

Jesse Graves: For many years you enjoyed a national audience for your poetry and then reached a global readership through your fiction, with several bestselling novels. You followed that success with two nonfiction volumes—can you talk about the relationship between those books?

Robert Morgan: *Lions of the West*, the nonfiction book that followed my biography of Daniel Boone, is a study of the westward expansion from the time of Thomas Jefferson to James K. Polk and the Mexican War. The general outline examines Jefferson's vision of the Republic—it begins with Jefferson writing to André Michaux, the great French botanist, commissioning him in 1793 to explore the Mississippi Valley and hopefully the Missouri, and even to cross the Rockies to the Pacific. It's a beautiful letter, because Jefferson had been working on this idea all his life. It explains what he wanted to know about the West—the navigation of rivers, the soils, the minerals, the climates, the Indians, their practices and languages—and, in fact, came to serve as a draft of his much longer letter to Meriwether Lewis written exactly ten years later in 1803. That's the way Jefferson worked. All of his great writing is essentially revision; the Declaration of Independence is the third draft of something he'd been working on. We know that the art of writing is in revision, and that could not be more true than with Jefferson. In a sense, the story of Boone (who knew Jefferson, by the way) leads to these events.

JG: I understand that you have written a sequel to your most well-known novel, *Gap Creek*. How would you compare the new novel to its predecessor?

RM: When *Lions of the West* was finished I knew I must go back to the lives of Hank and Julie. It had been ten years since *Gap Creek* was published. Throughout that decade I'd assumed I would continue the story in Julie's voice, though I knew it would be difficult to recover and bring to life after so much time had passed. As I began writing I saw Julie had already told *her* story. Her later life should be seen through the eyes and voice of her daughter Annie. And I also saw it was important to have a fresh perspective on the events of Julie's later life—her marriage, her children, the tragedies and satisfactions of middle and old age. Once I began to tell the story in Annie's voice, I knew I'd made the right choice. Rather than going back, I was moving forward, from a new point of view, seeing Hank and Julie and their world from an intimate but different angle. It became a story not so much of looking back to *Gap Creek* and those trials but of looking ahead at the uncertainties of the future, the struggle to define one's self, and, beyond all the grief and unforeseen losses, the discovery of enduring love.

JG: Let me follow with a writing question—about genre. I know that you have been working on a number of things in recent years: you have written new fiction, new poetry, and lecture materials on American writers such as Edgar Allan Poe, along with the historical and biographical writing. How do you keep a coherent approach to the different genres?

RM: I think the genres actually reinforce each other, in that I come across ideas for poems while I'm doing research on historical projects. And poems usually don't take as long to write! The way I work on poetry is that I write a draft, and then I revise in my notebook, and then maybe after a month, or even several months, I type it up and put it on the computer. Then I will revise again that version.

I've found it easier to work on poetry when I'm writing nonfiction than when writing fiction, because poetry and fiction utilize the same kind of verbal imagination. I've always found it refreshing to move among different projects. If you get stale working on fiction, you can reinvigorate yourself by moving to poetry for a while, or turning to nonfiction, or pausing from writing a novel to write a short story. I so far have not had trouble with "writer's block" because when I seem to reach a dead end on one project, I will turn and work on something else. Being an old farm boy, I still feel it's a privilege to be able to work on something like writing, instead of going out and digging postholes.

JG: Yes, it can be easier to revise a sentence than to cut a field of hay.

RM: It still amazes me that I've been able to write as long as I have, and to teach at good schools, and work with good students. When I was a child, work was cutting pulpwood or plowing a cornfield, something you had to sweat at. I went off to college to escape, but I had no idea that I would spend my life writing about that sort of work. One of the things that interests me most as a writer, both of poetry and of fiction, is the way you *do* work—the way to build a log cabin, the way to tan hides, the way a trapper sets a trap.

JG: You have written about physical work in every genre, haven't you?

RM: All those things interest me as a writer of all the genres, though perhaps most of all as a writer of fiction, in which the characters have to mow a meadow, or break new ground, or grub up roots. I guess it's natural that writing about the frontier would interest me because those activities are the essence of establishing a place in the wilderness, of finding your way, of creating a road or a trail. In that sense I feel that my poetry, my fiction, and even my nonfiction are cut from the same cloth. In writing *Boone* and

Lions of the West, I also used a lot of things I've learned as a teacher of literature, what I have taught, discussed, in American literature—in particular Emerson, Whitman, Thoreau, Dickinson. These writers are very relevant to the study of the westward expansion. Boone and Crockett and Kit Carson, like the continent, like the wilderness, were the inspiration for Emerson and the Transcendentalists. The ideas Emerson and Thoreau brought from the Enlightenment, and German Romantics, and religious mystics like Jacob Boehme, as well as from Asian literature, philosophy, Buddhism, and Hinduism, found extremely fertile ground in North America.

The literature of the United States is very closely related to the geography, and to the discovery, of the West. One of the things I've realized as a student of American history is the deep impact not just of the land and wilderness on the American imagination, but the influence of the Native Americans as well, in ways that I had never thought of. There is so much about our culture that is in one way or another derived from American Indian culture, Indian politics, and Indian customs. Obviously, our ancestors learned from the Indians where to find the deer, the buffalo, the bear, the herbs, and the medicinal plants, and most of us literally have Indian blood, through intermarriage. Even if the intermarrying was not literal, it happened in cultural ways, and we see that in the political style of somebody like, say, Lincoln, who was deeply influenced by frontier culture, which itself was deeply influenced by Indian political culture and its ways of doing things. The caginess, the evasiveness, of frontier politicians was very much like that of Indian politicians; for instance, the British found it very hard to make treaties with the Indians because they could never figure out who was in charge or what they were up to. There was great cleverness and strategy in the Indians' methods.

JG: One of the first points David Reynolds makes in his cultural biography *Walt Whitman's America* is how much Whitman had absorbed the native Indian culture there on Long Island. Reynolds suggests that the influence may have been even deeper and more important than has been previously recognized.

RM: Well, the connections are even in the names he uses—Whitman calls Long Island "Paumanok," and New York City he calls "Mannahatta." He was very interested in *both* Indian cultures, the beliefs of Native Americans as well as the mysticism of India he had absorbed through Emerson. So, you have this wonderful combination in the American Renaissance—in Whitman, Emerson, Thoreau, and even in Dickinson and other writers—of the Asian and European mixed along with this fresh soil of the North American cultures. There was wonder in the continent, the sense of possibility, the hyperbolic sense of the New Canaan, the New Jerusalem, this New World that was going to be the hope of the future. The Puritans called it "the city on the hill," but the native influence is very deep.

The irony is that this vision was often pursued with such brutality in the literal expansion of the country, in the extermination of Indians; you have at once people like Whitman and Thoreau, who are so passionately committed—Thoreau says that he was ashamed of his white skin, that he feels like an Indian himself—but at the same time are part of a culture that, in one way or another, is busy exterminating the Indian culture that they so admire. These two sides are present in America from the very beginning and to some extent are still with us today as part of our conflict of loyalties: we love the wilderness and have a tendency to idealize Indian life. Many writers, including myself, have a habit of writing about Indian culture as though it was perfect and there was no torture, cruelty, slavery, and constant warfare among the different nations. Much as we admire them, the Indians were just human beings too.

JG: That is a contradiction we can't seem to escape. In relation to this, I want to ask you about something out of *Boone*, where you use a really compelling phrase, "the Mother World of the Forest." This idea would seem to run counter to the more masculine hunter/trapper image we so commonly see concerning life in the frontier forest. Where did your idea of a more feminine view of the wilderness originate?

RM: I found that Boone spent his youthful summers several miles north of the family homestead in Oley, Pennsylvania, herding cattle and sheep with his mother. He and his mother went into the forest every summer, and thereafter he would claim that that was just about the happiest time in his life. Boone's father, Squire, was a blacksmith, a weaver, a leader in the village and Quaker congregation. But Daniel's favorite world when he was young was the one with his mother in the forest. Of course, that evokes the traditional sense of nature, Mother Nature, which is the opposite of the Father image, which stands for authority, strictness, discipline, business, government. A number of scholars, including Annette Kolodny in *The Land Before Her*, have written about the exploration of the American wilderness as a sexual discovery. Once I got this idea, it was almost inevitable that I would follow it through with Boone's dream that he would live in the Mother World and not the money-driven Father World. For the rest of his life, like the rest of the nation, he was divided between these two worlds—in his loyalties to the Mother World, which was infinitely mysterious, productive, and dangerous, and to the world of settlement and so-called civilization. Actually, I think this is one of the happier ideas I developed in the book, so I'm glad it struck a note with you.

JG: I found it very resonant. Maybe I hadn't seen the argument formed in quite that way before, but it spoke to what seemed a truth about Boone's experience as you presented it, and also a truth I had felt in my own experience of growing up deep in the country.

I'd like to ask you now about poetry—how your ideas about it have changed over the years and what prompted the evolution in your work. I see a significant difference, and I know you do as well, between the early poetry—the imagistic, free-verse writing from *Zirconia Poems* in 1969 and *Red Owl* in 1972—and the later, more formal, and occasionally longer narrative-driven poems of *Topsoil Road* in 2000 and the work in *The Strange Attractor: New and Selected Poems* from 2004. I wonder what prompted those changes, and also if there are particular things that *haven't* changed in the way you write poetry.

RM: I think the subjects of my poems have stayed the same. I came to poetry in a kind of unusual way. When I began to write poems in college, I did not really know much—I knew more about fiction, about prose. I had been in the sciences, in applied mathematics, and the poems I discovered, and began to imitate, were short, imagist ones, translations of Chinese and Japanese poetry done by Ezra Pound, Kenneth Rexroth, and Arthur Waley. I was fascinated by the short poems that had Zen mysticism, a deep resonance, but were very indirect, hard to paraphrase, with concrete images. I was inspired by translations of the Greek epigrams, those very short poems from *The Greek Anthology*. So, I began to write poems that were very concentrated, and I wanted to make language so compact that it was almost explosive and would have deep texture. Every line of one of these short poems would have some "perceptual energy," which is how I defined poetry at that time.

Only later did I become more interested in traditional forms of poetry, and in listening to the voice of the poem. Earlier it was the image and the concept I cared most about. After I left North Carolina and went to Cornell in 1971, I did not write very many poems for about a year, because it was such a big change. I was teaching and listening to people talk about poetry, but I came out of that period with all kinds of new ideas: poetry as narrative;

poems that were dramatic, with fictive characters speaking the poem, not just myself; and also poems about science. Of course, I was reading lots of poetry. I was reading Dickinson, and French poetry, as well as criticism and literary theory. I was also beginning to teach the American Renaissance, particularly Emerson; I guess Emerson's essays had the most influence—when I was younger it was really Thoreau who influenced me, but Emerson more when I got to Cornell. Over the years, I have grown increasingly interested in metrics, in rhyme, in what we call the mnemonic devices in poetry—what makes you remember a poem. I had less sense of that when I was young because I thought primarily of content and imagery. As I read more and thought more about poetry, I began to see that the essence is in the memorability of language. What we think of as poetry is very close to that: the sound, the gesture, the voice that you never forget once you hear it. Though I began writing fiction in college, and even published some stories, I focused almost exclusively on poetry after 1968. But when I began to write fiction again in the 1980s I started thinking about the differences between poetry and poetic prose: what can you do in poetry that you can't do any other way? The rhyme, the meter, and the repetition are the things. There's no way you could write "Do Not Go Gentle into That Good Night" in prose; it couldn't be done, it wouldn't be the same. So, as I've gotten older I've gotten increasingly interested in what makes a poem memorable, what makes someone want to say it again, and hear it again. It's impossible to define that, though it does have to do with devices like metrics, and cadence, and rhyme, but you can write in forms and it's still not memorable, so it has to be more than that. It involves a combination of content and sound and perception all at once. Over the years I have kept my excitement about poetry because I have continued to discover so many new facets and angles. I am as excited about poetry now as I was at twenty years old and just beginning to discover it.

JG: I wonder if you have any feelings about the direction American poetry has taken in the past twenty years, or if there are certain poets whose work you seek out, or make a point to read?

RM: Well, I think there are so many different kinds of poetry now that I don't even have time to keep up. I've been so busy writing fiction and history. I do find that many of the poets I continue to read are in the South. I think this is because many southern poets tell stories, and they write about history, nature, and the physical world—all things that interest me. There are recent British poets I have read very carefully. One of my favorite poets is Philip Larkin, who is just such a great storyteller, and also such a great technician, with his ability to write "in voice" in a very relaxed manner, and in perfect form. It's just amazing how he manages it.

JG: That's the great mystery, isn't it, in Larkin? I've noticed this same thing in your work and have commented in an essay that as your poems take on more formal design they also feel more conversational, or more driven by narrative. They have moved more into telling stories even as they have gotten increasingly structured. That strikes me as something of a paradox in your work.

RM: Yes, poetry is built on paradox. I think it was Cleanth Brooks who wrote that poetry is "the language of paradox." The ideal for me—and I don't say that I've realized it—is to write poems that are in the voice of today and that deal with interesting serious subjects, poems that have a voice as alive as in fiction but at the same time have a formal dimension, a classical dimension, so that they achieve the playful game of poetry, which is formal, in a voice that is contemporary and believable. That is, as I see it, the ideal of poetry, going all the way back to Dante. His treatise on poetry and poetics, which he wrote in Latin, *De vulgari eloquentia* ("on the vernacular eloquence"), expresses the ideal: to write in the vernacular—the language of today—but with the eloquence of classical poetry, be it Greek or Latin or, for us today, Shakespearean. I've always remembered Cezanne's assertion that he wanted to make paintings "as solid as those in the museums." Of course, he was using a very radical and contemporary technique to do that, but the paradox is that you do something fresh to emulate the classical—Pound said that you "make it new," but one of the ways you make it new is to make it very old, the way the poems of the Greeks did, or of the Renaissance. In that sense, poetry doesn't change even as it's evolving and doing fresh, new things. So to understand what Pound meant, you have to look at Pound's own practice: he is urging everybody to make it new, yet he's obsessed with Propertius, with Chinese poetry, with Provencal poetry. . . .

JG: Let's talk about your career in perspective. As an undergraduate, you began as a fiction writer and then primarily wrote poetry for many years after that. Why do you think you returned to fiction writing several years later?

RM: I began to think of writing fiction again in the 1980s for two main reasons: the first was that I had not been able to write poetry in voices other than my own in ways that satisfied me. I wanted to be able to write in fictive voices, dramatic voices. Other poets can write dramatic poems, but I had never been successful at that. The second reason was that I wanted to tell some of the stories I had grown up with, stories I had heard around the fireplace, on the porch, about panthers, bears, and snakes, the Civil War and the Revolution and Indians. I realized more and more that I still had all these stories. I had incorporated some of them into the poems, as in "Mountain Bride," but not as many as I wanted, and I began to feel this urge to explore a larger space—a verbal space, you might call it. For fifteen years I'd been obsessed with lines, with line breaks and with the compact forms of poetry, the economy of poetry, and I wanted to reach out, to stretch out into the field of energy of prose.

I took a long time to really get back into prose—I have said to people, "If there's hope for me, there's hope for anybody!" Because it took me about six years to write stories good enough to publish. After all, I'd published stories when I was very young, and many poems and essays, and I had been teaching fiction writing, but it took a long time to really get the feel of narrative. I remember two things I discovered that really helped me write short fiction. One was that when you start a short story, you grab the attention of the reader and you never let up. I've compared it to a Bach "two-part invention"—you start playing, and you play and you play, and then suddenly it's over. The second thing I learned was that there is no such thing as a good story that goes where you expect it to go, that every good story has a surprise, a turn. Once I learned those two things—which sound very simple, what you might teach college sophomores—they were very important to me.

Once I began to write short stories again, I really got into it. I would write story after story, and go back into them and polish and revise them. I published a couple of collections, but then the stories starting getting longer, and I realized I wanted to create larger fictive worlds, to create characters and live with them, and see what happens next, and what happens next, and so on. The greatest breakthrough I ever made as a fiction writer was to let my characters tell their own stories, to get inside the characters. That breakthrough I made in the novella *The Mountains Won't Remember Us.* I used a woman narrator, and it was so scary writing from that point of view—what did I know about how she would remember things, or talk about her fiancé? I said to myself, "I will try to be like an actor, and try to erase myself, and try to imagine how she would think, how she would talk, what her values are, what her memories are." Once I got about thirty pages into that novella, I realized it was the best thing I'd ever written. I had escaped from myself into my imagination, into the world of the imagination, and that's where the fiction happens. Good fiction is not autobiography; it is the creation of a world one sentence, one detail, at a time. Many young writers have trouble developing as fiction writers because they can't escape from their own world. Now, there are great writers who never escape from autobiography. Thomas Wolfe never grew as a writer beyond *Look Homeward, Angel* because he could never look beyond his own life story, whereas a novelist like Faulkner, like Balzac, could just create story after story, world after world.

JG: I was planning to ask you about Wolfe, and about the use of women's voices in your fiction and how you arrived at that perspective. Isn't *The Mountains Won't Remember Us* based on a family story?

RM: Well, the inspiration came from the death of my Uncle Robert in a B-17 crash in 1943. I knew I wanted to write about him in a novel—a character like him, somebody who grew up on a farm in the Blue Ridge Mountains and had never traveled until World War II. Now he was suddenly in the air force and was sent to Mississippi, and then was sent to Sarasota, Florida, to study mechanics and repairing B-17 engines. Then he was sent to the factory in Massachusetts where they built the engines, and the next thing he knows, he's in Buckinghamshire, England! And then he went to Cambridge and Huntingdon. In preparation, I began studying all the histories I could find of the Eighth Air Force, along with the pilots' manuals, the bombardiers' manuals, the navigators' manuals, and I went to England to find the site of the crash and to talk with people who saw it happen. I found out my uncle was on a top-secret airplane, a Pathfinder. But I had gotten so much into the technical aspect of it that I just got bogged down with information; out of frustration, I thought of writing part of the story from the point of view of the soldier's fiancée, and that's how I came to the woman's voice.

JG: So, did you initially imagine the story from the soldier's perspective?

RM: Yes, I wanted to tell the story of someone who has never really seen anything beyond the Blue Ridge Mountains. Someone who gets to see the world and, for the most part, doesn't know what he's seeing. He doesn't know much about Buckingham Palace, or London, or Cambridge University, not to mention flying out over the Fen country, and up the Wash and across the North Sea, and seeing the Zuiderzee and Amsterdam. The main focus of the Eighth Air Force at that time was to take out the iron industry, which was really the heart of the war industry for Germany. But the happy ending of that frustration is that I came upon the point of view of an older woman looking back at what impacted her youth. I'm still going to write the other book, though!

JG: Did your success telling that story free up your imagination for writing the novels *The Truest Pleasure* and *Gap Creek*, both of which are told from a woman's point of view?

RM: The next thing I wrote was the first two novellas of *The Hinterlands*. The first one was narrated by Petal Jarvis Richards, who tells the story of moving west—you see, that theme was always there, of finding the route to the west. That was a very heady experience, the sense that I could take what I'd discovered and use it for earlier periods, for different characters. I had written, sometime before, a third-person version of the novel that became *The Truest Pleasure*, and one day I realized, "Hey, I can let Ginny tell her own story," and once she started telling her own story, I was so excited that I could hardly wait to get up every day to hear what she would tell me!

JG: That novel seems so dependent—more than any of your other fiction, I would say—on the speaker's voice that it's hard to imagine from another point of view.

RM: Well, there was another version of it, but once I found Ginny I realized I could incorporate into her voice, and into her vision, so many things that I had done in poetry, and in other ways. Her interest in theology, in nature, in history, and her love of language, allowed me to do so much with all the ideas I had worked on in other scenes. So I wrote almost in a state of euphoria. When I did go back with my editor and do some revision, there wasn't all that much to change.

JG: Well, let me ask you more now about Thomas Wolfe, whom you mentioned earlier. I've been looking at your introduction for a recent edition of *Look Homeward, Angel*, published in 2006. I wonder if you could talk about the importance of Wolfe, and any other writers of his generation, to your work.

RM: I first read Wolfe when I was going on fifteen. I got the book from the bookmobile that used to come up to Green River Church, and I just fell in love with *Look Homeward, Angel*, as many fourteen- and fifteen-year-olds do. I was intoxicated by that language—"O Lost, and by the wind grieved, ghost come back again." Since Wolfe had grown up in Asheville and was obviously writing about Asheville, which he called Altamont, I felt that I was Eugene Gant, and his family was my family, and it was that that made me think about being a writer: if Thomas Wolfe could grow up in Asheville, and become a famous writer, maybe I could too. So the influence of Wolfe is very deep in me, and I think in a number of other writers. He inspired me to become a writer, to become an intellectual, to go off and attend college.

One of the ways Wolfe is very special, though he is out of fashion these days, is that more than Faulkner, more than Hemingway, more than Fitzgerald, he really was an intellectual. He was a very well educated man; he knew Greek and Latin, he knew history, and music, and architecture, so he was inspiring in that way. Also, I was born on his birthday, October 3, and felt an even greater kinship with him.

Very soon after I spent this period of intensely reading Wolfe, I discovered his opposite, Ernest Hemingway, and Hemingway's idea of fiction being indirect, implicit, understated, much more revealing in what it doesn't say. So although it was Wolfe who inspired me in becoming a writer, particularly a writer from the southern Appalachian Mountains, years later I realized that Hemingway's style influenced me much more than Wolfe's. Wolfe's rhetorical style, and what I call the "Byronic" posture of Eugene Gant, did not influence me. I was much more interested in finding a humble way of portraying people, realistically and with concision and indirection. On the other hand, years later I read Wolfe's novella, *The Web of Earth*, which was spoken by his mother, and that inspired me to try to write a story told by a woman.

JG: I was thinking about Hemingway as a precursor to your work, but I was also thinking about underappreciated writers and that that term is almost a redundancy in our culture—that a writer could be underappreciated—because it's hard to think of any serious writer who is overappreciated. Can you name some writers, either past or contemporary, whose work you feel has been underread or is still underread?

RM: Well, I think that there are, as you say, very many of them, the writers who were maybe famous at one time and are little read now. One of the short stories that has inspired me over the years is a largely forgotten piece by Walter Van Tilburg Clark called "The Indian Well." That is, as far as I'm concerned, one of the great masterpieces of American literature.

JG: What's the date on that?

RM: It was published in a collection in 1950. *The Watchful Gods* is the title of the book. I can think of no more inspiring and powerful short fiction. To me, it's right up there with "Big Two-Hearted River." Another terrific overlooked work is a novel published in the 1960s by Clancy Sigal, *Going Away*. It's about the McCarthy era and the blacklist and Hollywood and the labor movement. It's just a wonderful book, and as far as I can tell it's almost entirely forgotten. I met Clancy Sigal out in Los Angeles last year. He's now in his eighties and working again as a screenwriter with his wife. One of their best-known movies is *Frida*, the recent film about Frida Kahlo. He also has a book about the labor movement in Britain called *Weekend in Dinlock*. He is a writer I wish was much better known.

There are any number of great writers who are basically forgotten. One I often mention to my students is Robert E. Sherwood. Most of my students have never heard of him. He won three Pulitzer Prizes in drama, a Pulitzer Prize in history for his book on [Franklin] Roosevelt and Harry Hopkins, and an Academy Award for the screenplay of *The Best Years of Our Lives*— and he wrote the screenplay for what I consider to be Alfred Hitchcock's masterpiece, *Rebecca*. He wrote speeches for Franklin Roosevelt, staying up all night on December 7, 1941, writing the speech that Roosevelt would deliver the next day to a joint session of Congress. We all know those phrases: "A day that will live in infamy. We in our righteous might. . . ."

JG: Hah . . . I presumed that was Roosevelt.
RM: That was also Robert E. Sherwood.

JG: Do you think that this sort of dispersion of his writing across so many different genres is why he is not well remembered? It would seem that all that success in drama would have kept his name in circulation.
RM: Well, there are obvious explanations. His style of drama seems old-fashioned now; it was replaced by, you know, Tennessee Williams and a more modern style. Insofar as Sherwood is remembered, he is remembered for his screenwriting, but screenwriters are basically unknown outside the profession. Only people in the field of movies know who the screenwriters are. They are highly paid but quickly forgotten.

JG: So, they get their own kind of compensation. Let me take you in another direction now. You've been at Cornell since 1971. Do you feel at home there in Ithaca as much as in, say, Hendersonville or Chapel Hill, North Carolina? Have you ever felt out of place that far north and with so many of the privileged around you?
RM: Well, I think that I have felt great homesickness for North Carolina. A lot of my writing, I suspect, has been done out of homesickness and nostalgia, to recreate the Blue Ridge Mountains and the language people speak there. In my early years at Cornell, I found myself going to the big library and checking out books on the Cherokee Indians, the geology of the southern Appalachians, the speech of the southern Appalachians, the history of the

settlement of western North Carolina and East Tennessee and far western Virginia. So, in that sense, I did not feel at home. The Welsh are supposed to feel intense longing for home, which is called the *hiraeth*. At the same time, intellectually, I think I came to feel more at home at Cornell, in some ways, than anywhere I had ever been. It was filled with fine students, and people like M. H. Abrams, Robert H. Elias, and Walter Slatoff. The first week I was at Cornell, this old gentleman shuffled by Goldwin Smith Hall—where, as you know, the English department is located—and somebody nudged me and said, "That's Hans Bethe, the great physicist." I thought, "Wow!" because I had been in the sciences when I was younger. Many things about Cornell make it very special: it's an Ivy League university but a very different university from Princeton and Yale and Harvard, with a different culture. It has an engineering school. It's out in the country. (There are very few great universities out in small towns or in rural settings.) It's in the Alleghenies, so it's in northern Appalachia—to which I moved from southern Appalachia. Best of all, they gave me a job when I was young!

JG: Which made it feel a lot like home, right? Once they gave you the job.
RM: It was the only place that gave me a job.

JG: Your Hans Bethe experience reminds me of the second week *I* was at Cornell, when I was working as a reader in the *Epoch* magazine office, and a very elderly gentleman walked by the door and down the hallway of Goldwin Smith. Michael Koch, the editor at *Epoch*, said, "Do you know who that was?" and I said, "Uh, no." He said, "That was M. H. Abrams," and I said, "From the *Norton Anthology*?" He laughed and said, "Yes, among a few other things." As it turned out, the very first paragraph in the introduction to my dissertation has a significant quote from Abrams's essay "Style and Structure in the Greater Romantic Lyric."
RM: You can imagine how intimidating it was, in 1971, when I went to Cornell and sat around the table at the first department meeting, and there's Arthur Mizener, Abrams, Elias, and Slatoff. I was sitting there with my MFA from UNC-Greensboro and my one chapbook from Lillabulero Press.

JG: Not yet thirty years old, right?
RM: I was twenty-six, but they were amazingly hospitable. And, I discovered a great deal in common with these people. That first fall, I began a conversation with Ep Fogel, the Shakespeare scholar, who had been born in the ghetto in Odessa in the Ukraine, taken to Palestine as a child, and then brought to

Brooklyn; he grew up in Brooklyn, but he had kept his Russian, and he was translating Mandelstam, the great Russian poet. Well, I've always been interested in Russian poetry and Russian fiction, and we got into a discussion. I've always been a great fan of Pasternak. In fact, reading Pasternak was one of the great events of my youth. Well, Fogel disliked Pasternak; there's an old rivalry between the Mandelstam people and the Pasternak people. So he and I began a conversation, an argument, which went on for the rest of his life. Really, he would get so angry at me, but we would always patch it up because we were both interested in the same things. One day we were talking about the Futurists, and I said to him, "Well, you know the great theoretician of the Russian Futurists was not Pasternak, it wasn't Mayakovsky, it wasn't even the critic Brik; it was Khlebnikov"—and Fogel said, "You mean you know who Velimir Khlebnikov was?" After that, I was in the club.

JG: That brought you right inside, right in the door, like knowing the secret handshake. I found the same thing to be true of a later generation of Cornell scholars, that they respected you if you could demonstrate knowledge of literature.

Our talk about homesickness makes me think of your parents. I know how important they have been to you, and that you still spend a good deal of time in the house where you were raised. I wonder if you would say something about them and their respective influences on you and your life as a writer.
RM: Well, I have written quite a bit of poetry and an essay about my father, Clyde Morgan, who was a very interesting man, and hard to explain. I've always found it very hard to describe him to people who didn't know him. He was in many ways larger than life. He was a big man, over 6' 2", and he loved to talk, and to read. Had he been educated, I think he might have been a writer or historian, but he only went to the sixth grade. He read a lot of history, he read *National Geographic*, and he knew a lot about science; he loved to talk about it, but he could not work with other people. And he loved to be alone and to mow with an old-fashioned scythe. I have a poem about that called "Mowing."

JG: Those two poems in *Topsoil Road* about him working are wonderful.
RM: About working in the rain and mowing. So, I think he influenced me in many ways: as a storyteller, as somebody who taught me about theology, the Bible, history, and science. I had a much more privileged childhood than people would think. Growing up on a poor farm in the middle of the mountains, we did not have a truck, a tractor, or a car; we plowed

with a horse. But, when I went off to college, I discovered that I had a much better preparation than many of the middle-class students I knew who had not been exposed to discussions of theology, ideas, and history from the time they were children. In many ways, my parents were very different from one another. My mother was a much more practical person who was determined that her children would get an education. Her influence is, in some ways, greater than my dad's, but it doesn't show up in my writing the same way. She, like my dad, was a great storyteller, and in fact *Gap Creek*, to a large extent, is based on the stories about her parents—their early marriage and lives in Gap Creek. I've gotten a lot of my stories from things that she told me. I think her ambition was gratified when I was going off to college; I was going to do something, and I wasn't going to stay on the farm. Oddly enough, my dad did not have very much ambition; he just had a great interest in history. But, somewhat like Daniel Boone, he would return to tramping in the woods, hunting, trapping, and that sort of thing. So I feel that in many ways I had great advantages for a future writer, though we didn't have any money. I saved money to go to college and to a large extent worked my way through school. Luckily, tuition wasn't very much at Chapel Hill.

JG: It was a lot different than now.

RM: I think it was $157 a semester in those days. So the big problem was to pay your board and rent. But I was really lucky in several ways, not just in being exposed to great storytellers but also in growing up out in the country free to roam in the pastures and the woods, learning about animals and plants and agriculture, and taking care of a horse and milking cows; all of these are things I have used in my writing. As a writer, you use what you know, and if you have been exposed to lots of things that other people haven't, you have them there at your fingertips. I know how to pull fodder and cut corn tops; I could hitch up a horse, in the dark, with my eyes closed.

JG: Even still? That's muscle memory, isn't it? You never forget how to do things like that.

RM: I know where the hames go, the collar, the trace chains, the single-tree—and I can say "gee" and "haw" and "giddyup."

JG: You know just what to say to the team.

RM: Because when you're plowing and your hands are busy on the plow, you communicate to the horse mostly by voice. And a good horse is very responsive to the voice.

JG: I think there's a great misperception about families in isolated places, about the kinds of education that those children get. We talked all the time at my house about the past and about current events, and we were taught how to do things.

RM: It's why rural kids, particularly in the South, often have a stronger sense of history, I believe, including family history. I've met any number of highly educated people who know virtually nothing about their family history. I grew up in a world where people talked all the time about what happened in the Civil War—who went here, who was killed there, who the bushwhackers were, who the outlaws were, who stole the corn, who took great-grandpa's pocketknife from him.

James Agee, one of the greatest of American writers, came from right here in Knoxville, in East Tennessee. He acquired his wonderful sense of voice and narrative, to a great extent, from his father's family. I believe his mother was much more upper class than his father, who was from north of here in the hill country. Agee absorbed a lot of that, but at the same time he was being educated at St. Andrew's and Phillips Exeter, and exposed to Anglican ritual.

JG: I'm delighted to hear you mention Agee. He had almost the perfect confluence: the rural sense of storytelling and family history, matched with an educated family on his mother's side who could introduce him to music and art at such a young age.

RM: This circumstance gave him the intimate memories, a native, personal knowledge of having grown up in the region, *and* the larger view of education and the perspective that comes from living for years somewhere else, in Agee's case Cambridge, Massachusetts, and Greenwich Village. *Let Us Now Praise Famous Men* takes its title from an Anglican apocryphal gospel; the language is often Shakespearean and biblical, but the details are so intense, so humble, and so sensual. There's a sensory contact with the world, an immediacy, and I think that's the way art works. Had he known only the hill country, he would never have been the writer he was. Had he known only the upper class Anglican world, he *certainly* would not have been the kind of writer that he was. It's in the combination of those things, the way it's the combination in Emerson and Thoreau of New England piety and zeal coming into contact with the Enlightenment and the world of nature—with respect for the natural world. Or in the case of a great poet like Baudelaire, the combination of a hard classicism with a romantic visionary sense. These are very opposite things. Isn't that the definition of imagination? It is the esemplastic power of putting together disparate things or very different things. I think that's the way Coleridge defined imagination.

JG: You once told me, in your office in Goldwin Smith Hall, that a writer needs to be able to "write where the pain is," which struck me at the time and which I've thought about since. I wonder if you could talk about that idea and maybe share an example of how you have done that in your own work or if it has played out in your own writing.

RM: Well, I was talking probably more about fiction at that time, but I think it applies to all writing. Students say, "Well, how do you find the story; how do you know if you have a story?" And I say, "When you get to the place where it's painful, you know you have a story." You can watch young people who are very gifted circling and circling their subject matter but being unable to really go into it. This could be anything at all; it could be refusing to write about the poverty that you have known in your family or the ignorance or the cruelty underneath in people who seem very decent. But we're all human beings with dark sides and mysterious sides. I think, for me, this meant coming to terms with voice and being willing to go back *under* the educated language that I had acquired in college and as a professor at a university, and to be willing to go back to the diction and the terms that I had been embarrassed by when I went off to be educated. I mean that is just one of many things, but it's an example: my being willing to go back to somebody like Julie Harmon, the narrator in *Gap Creek*, and to write the voice that I knew and remembered. From the very beginning, that was one of the things people picked up on about that novel. Any number of people have come up to me and said, "You know, I didn't think that anybody could ever recreate the voice of my grandmother, but you nailed it." It's an impression; the voice is not scientifically accurate. You know, when you go off to college and you learn to talk about Coleridge and Wittgenstein and Goethe, it takes a while to begin listening to your memory, to really imagine again those other voices.

But of course, even more important is what those voices mean in the personality of the character: the feelings, the fears—to really get into the fears and the contradictions of experience, and to the experience of, say, watching a parent die and being absolutely helpless. The bodily functions—remember, that's one of the things Julie talks about. She's the one who has to clean up her Pa as he's approaching death. But it could be anything that we've learned to avoid. I mean, we're people in society; there are things that are appropriate to talk about and things that are not appropriate. Fiction often comes alive most when you can go back and really look at those things that are inappropriate, and treat them in a context to try to see them as whole as you can. (Sensationalistic writing concentrates *only* on those things, perhaps.)

For me, another example of going to the pain involves religion. I was so embarrassed by memories of attending Pentecostal services. I was really unable to write about that until I was forty when I wrote the poem "The Gift of Tongues." I opened up that difficult area, and then I was able to write, in my fifties, a whole novel, *The Truest Pleasure*. (Actually, I was fifty or about to turn fifty.) But the more you do something the more you are able to do it, the more you are able to recognize what those areas are that are painful and embarrassing, and then to begin to learn how you can go into them. And of course, it is releasing to be able to do that. It's liberating to look at some corner of your memory or imagination that is suppressed or that is inappropriate to talk about, and to be able to dramatize it in a story.

JG: You gave a lecture some years ago called "Nature Is a Stranger Yet," with the title drawn from an Emily Dickinson poem. In that talk, you considered the paradox that the more one observes and studies nature, the more mysterious it appears, even if it is your own native place. That seems to me like an undercurrent maybe to all of your work, even *Boone*. I wonder if you could talk about that mystery.

RM: Well, the world is inexhaustible, and when we know a little bit about something, we feel we know it or understand it. This could be the study of a species of plant, of an ecological system, of DNA, and so on, but the fact is, the more you study something, the more elusive . . . I mean, you never feel like you know the whole thing. This is true with people: the people we know best are often the most mysterious to us; somebody you've been married to for years or some other family member remains essentially mysterious because we know so much about them. There's a wonderful quote from Lytton Strachey—I think it's in the preface to *Eminent Victorians*—"Ignorance is the first requisite of the historian." Because you're going through the process of learning so you can get that process into the history you are writing. If you knew everything about history, you couldn't write a word, because there would be no narrative to pursue. But Dickinson was absolutely right that while you may learn more and more and more and more about anything, it actually becomes more and more mysterious, for you then have a better sense of what you don't know. So the more you know, the larger your ignorance—your sense of ignorance—becomes. That's one of my favorite passages in her poetry and, in fact, in all American poetry.

JG: It's a beautiful concept, and it does put a perspective onto how the scale and the scope broaden once you take on intensive learning.

RM: The first line of that poem is, "What mystery pervades a well!" And the last two quatrains start with the phrase, "But nature is a stranger yet;" and the poem concludes with "That those who know her, know her / Less the nearer her they get."

JG: That's a brilliant opening line, and a brilliant conclusion. Your recitation of that poem, which I can testify that you don't have in front of you and may not have seen in many years, leads me to a sort of tabloid question: Is it true that you have a photographic memory?

RM: By no means. Sometimes I can hardly remember my name. I do remember things that I'm particularly interested in, which helps when you're writing history, but then after I've used them I often forget them. I think that most writers and scholars I know have pretty good memories. Remember, the Greeks call the muses the daughters of memory. It's an old argument—which is more important for writing, for poetry: imagination or memory? The title of M. H. Abrams's most famous book is *The Mirror and the Lamp*: the mirror of memory (mimesis), and the lamp of the imagination. I think memory is very important and should be trained more in school. I went to a school that was so old-fashioned we had to memorize poems and stand up and recite them. We had to memorize the preamble to the Constitution, the Declaration of Independence, and the Gettysburg Address. Contrary to the popular myth, young people love to memorize, and the more they do it, the more they enjoy it. If you memorize when you are young, you have these things you can carry with you all of your life.

JG: We have said a great deal about *Lions of the West*, your book on the American frontier, but we have not discussed your most recent poetry collection, *Terroir*, published in the Penguin Poets series. What can you say about that book? When were the poems written, and do you have particular favorites?

RM: The title is literally the French word for soil, but it is used by contemporary writers to mean a particular vintage or harvest, the product of a specific combination of soil, season, variety, cultivation, and preparation. It reminds me of Hopkins's term *inscape*, meaning individual quality, what philosophers call *haecceity*, or "thisness." The subjects and settings of the poems will be familiar to readers of my previous fiction and poetry, but I think there is a fresh energy and metrical exactness in the poems I've written over the past decade. (Also, two of the poems are from the 1980s and 1990s, never before collected.) A number of poems are about history, the wilderness, and the West. "Prophet," for example, celebrates the bristlecone pine, oldest living thing on earth. "Medicine Circles" meditates on the meaning of the rings of buffalo skulls Indians arranged on the High Plains.

JG: One final question, since we have discussed your early work and your recent work. Are there books that haven't been written, or haven't been finished? In other words, what ideas have you had that you wish you had written about, or still plan to finish?

RM: There are a number of books I have planned but never written or finished. There is a book-length poem I mean to write and a memoir about my first twelve years. And a book of short stories. I have always intended to write a novel about academia and a novel set in upstate New York. And some day I mean to write either a fiction or nonfiction book about the Civil War. So, yes, there are several books I still hope to write.

After the Fighting, the Scars Remain: An Interview with Robert Morgan on His War Literature

Rebecca Godwin / 2012–13

From *North Carolina Literary Review* 23 (2014): 6–17. Reprinted by permission.

My conversation with Morgan about his literature of war began on December 21, 2012, in the stone house that his father built on the square mile of land that Great-Grandpa Pace's father Daniel bought in 1840. Still hanging in the living room is a picture of Morgan's mother's brother Robert, killed in the Second World War. We continued the interview, much of which focuses on his novel of the American Revolution, by e-mail over the next several months, with Morgan editing my transcriptions of tape-recorded discussion and also answering additional questions.

Rebecca Godwin: Several of your works of fiction involve wars that have shaped the American experience. Does your interest in war stem, to some extent, from your Uncle Robert's death in World War II?

Robert Morgan: I think a lot of it comes from my interest in his experience and finding out what happened to him, his career. But it also comes from all the talk I heard when I was a child, by veterans of World War II. We sat around at Christmastime, or Sunday afternoon. So many of my relatives had been soldiers, and they would talk about their experiences in North Africa, Sicily, France, the Pacific. I had that sense that I had been born during the war. Of course, I didn't remember anything about it, but I understood that a cataclysmic event had changed everything, and my relatives had participated in it.

RG: They seemed heroic to you?

RM: Well, somewhat heroic. But I just found it very interesting that they had seen so many places. I can remember long descriptions of going into France and reaching the Rhine and discovering that the Germans had blown up a big dam and flooded everything so that the soldiers had to cross twenty miles instead of half-a-mile of water.

RG: I imagine that world seemed very large, compared to what you knew as a child here in Green River.

RM: Absolutely. I was in this small community and yet knew people who had participated in invasions of Pacific islands. Also, I remember veterans of the Korean War coming back and talking about Korea, saying they were not supposed to be fighting the Chinese but they saw Chinese and Russians.

But a great deal of my interest in warfare came from my dad's talk about the First World War and the Civil War and the American Revolution. He was a kind of amateur historian. You can look around the shelves of the house here and see a lot of his books. When he was twelve years old, he bought a history book. And when he was a little older, maybe thirteen or fourteen, he bought from his teacher a history of the Great War, World War I. It had pictures in it—it's there on the shelf, you can look at it.[1] Daddy talked a lot about the Civil War, too. He could talk for hours about Stonewall Jackson, Robert E. Lee, Sherman's march through Georgia and South Carolina. He also knew a lot about the American Revolution, particularly the Revolution in the South, the Battle of Cowpens, the Battle of Kings Mountain, the Battle of Guilford Courthouse, the great battles that really ended the war, that destroyed Cornwallis's army.

RG: So your father's stories drew you to study and write about the Revolutionary War in the South in *Brave Enemies* (2003)? Why Cowpens and not Kings Mountain?

RM: For years I have lived in the Northeast, and it has often surprised me that even educated people seem to know so little about the American Revolution in the South. Most know only about Lexington and Concord, Saratoga and Valley Forge, Trenton and Princeton. Among other things, I just wanted to call attention to the campaign from Kings Mountain in October 1780 to Yorktown in October 1781 that ended the war. The Battle of Cowpens took place in January 1781.

RG: You say in the "Author's Note" at the end of *Brave Enemies* that at least one relative fought in the Battle of Cowpens. Do you know of more?

RM: Three of my ancestors fought in the battle. William Capps is the one I alluded to there. In addition, there's one named Daniels and one named Bailey. I am also distantly related to General Daniel Morgan, who led the Continentals and militiamen at Cowpens, through a common ancestor, Llewellyn ap Morgan of Bala in North Wales, also an ancestor of Daniel Boone.

RG: Your interest in Cowpens intensified because of your relatives' participation, I imagine.

RM: Yes, but my fascination with Cowpens has many components. One is that it happened very close to Green River. And it is one of the most important and decisive battles in American history. British General Cornwallis lost a large part of his army. He never could replace them as he went into the interior. And although he did not lose the Battle of Guilford Courthouse, he didn't exactly win it, either. Nathanael Greene wreaked so much damage on Cornwallis's army there that he never recovered. A recent article in the *North Carolina Historical Review* describing sickness in Cornwallis's army makes his army seem even smaller than I thought it was. But all this does not change the fact that Cornwallis was an excellent general. He was a resourceful man. He simply was worn out in this campaign and couldn't sustain it. He made major mistakes. One was trusting Lieutenant Colonel Tarleton so much. Tarleton was a bold and reckless fighter, and Daniel Morgan knew that. Morgan countered Tarleton's "down-right fighting" with flanking maneuvers. He simply outsmarted Tarleton. He could do what Lee could do, set the enemy up. That's a classic maneuver. Morgan may not have known that. He probably hadn't studied military history that much. Hannibal knew it. Napoleon knew it. If you have an opponent more powerful than you, you can draw the opponent in and then swing your soldiers in behind. Then your men are fighting in front and behind.

So Cowpens was a more complex and interesting battle than Kings Mountain from the standpoint of tactics. Morgan's forces were considerably outnumbered, and he was confronting one of the finest armies in the world at the time, Tarleton's Green Dragoons, the 71st Highlanders, the 7th Royal Fusilliers. Tarleton had never lost a battle up to that time. Through tactical imagination, some good luck, and skilled leadership, Morgan achieved a total victory, killing or taking prisoner almost all of Tarleton's forces. In contrast, Kings Mountain was mostly a battle of attrition, with the American patriots outnumbering the Loyalist militia under Ferguson.

RG: Why did you decide to make your main character in *Brave Enemies* a woman?

RM: For reasons I can't explain, I've had my best successes as a fiction writer when using female narrators. My breakthrough as a fiction writer came in the spring of 1989 when I found my character Sharon could tell her own story. The result was *The Mountains Won't Remember Us*. Then I wrote *The Hinterlands* (1994), the first section in the voice of a woman character, and *The Truest Pleasure* (1995), again from the point of view of a woman.

The first draft of the novel that became *Brave Enemies* was written in third person, and mostly concerned the Battle of Cowpens itself. I was not satisfied with that draft and put it aside for almost ten years. When I finished *This Rock* (2001), I knew I would return to the Cowpens story, and I knew that my main character and narrator would be a young woman dressed as a man and fighting in the front line with the North Carolina militia. Novels are about people. They're not just about historical events. They're not just about warfare. That was an extremely violent time in the Carolinas, as neighbor fought neighbor, brother fought brother. It was a time of hatred, confusion, and cruelty. Through Josie's eyes and voice I wanted the reader to encounter the awful and exciting civil war, as it really was.

RG: Early in the story Josie murders her stepfather after he raped her. What made you select rape as the instigating event that makes Josie run away from home and begin the journey that leads her to Morgan's troops?

RM: Well, I had two things in mind. I wanted to dramatize the violence of the Carolinas during this period, 1780–1781. In times of war, rape is very common. Women are especially vulnerable in periods of civil unrest and invasion. Also, I had to find a motive for a young woman to be wandering in the wilderness of western North Carolina and end up joining the militia pretending to be a man. Given the circumstances, those acts were choices of necessity. Josie really had to do what she did. I hoped her vulnerability, and courage, would give the reader a sense of just how desperate those times were, and how she was strong and resourceful because she had to be to survive.

RG: Did you find in your research any women who did fight in the American Revolution?

RM: No, but we do know that women fought in the Civil War. The bulk of my research for *Brave Enemies* was the histories of the period, the histories of the American army and the British army, including Banastre Tarleton's memoirs that he wrote with his mistress years after the campaign.

RG: Yes, I thought that an interesting source.

RM: I also read biographies of Daniel Morgan and Nathanael Greene and several histories of campaigns from Charleston (SC) up to Yorktown and went many times to the battlefield at Cowpens as well as to the Pacolet River, the Tyger River, the Broad River, the very places where this campaign occurred. I interviewed people at the Cowpens Museum. The kind of details I was interested in included what kind of uniforms the British soldiers were wearing. Were the First Highlanders wearing kilts, or were they wearing pants? One of the guides at Cowpens said they did wear their kilts for ceremonial purposes but wore pants when they were traveling through brush in the wintertime. That makes sense.

I particularly wanted to know what uniforms Tarleton's Green Dragoons wore. Some sources said they were wearing green jackets. Some said they wore blue and red jackets with a green lapel. Both were probably worn at different times. Paintings of Tarleton often show him wearing a red jacket, the jacket of the British Army in North America. But the people of the time called his cavalry, his Dragoons, Tarleton's Green Horse. He had another cavalry with him wearing red jackets that he sent into battle first. They were the ones picked off by North Carolinians in the first line, the officers. That was the first sign the British were going to lose that battle, when Tarleton lost so many officers during that first charge. Morgan would yell, "hit the epaulets and stripes, boys, hit the epaulets and stripes." They tried to break the chain of command, not to hit privates. Morgan was a backwoodsman. But he knew a well-trained army, like the British, would be seriously damaged if he could break the chain of command because British privates were used to following orders.

RG: Looking at *Brave Enemies* again recently, I was thinking about your decision to start with the prologue that puts Josie on the battlefield. Of course, we find out at the end that she's pregnant.

RM: That's called the memory loop form. You begin close to the climax of the novel. Then you swing back and tell the story up to that point, the story of how she got there in that unlikely situation. I wanted to grab the reader at the beginning as the battle is about to begin. The greatest challenge, finally, in writing *Brave Enemies*, was to tell the story from Josie's point of view, from the point of view of a soldier involved in the battle, and still give the cinematic, eagle-eye view of what was happening.

RG: That's the difference between fiction and history. History gives a broader overview. Fiction narrows. It must be difficult to write a first-person account that enables the reader to understand what is going on all over the field. After all, soldiers are often dazed and confused by the fighting around them.

RM: I wanted the reader to understand what actually happened that day, on all parts of the field. Cowpens was a complex battle, evolving rapidly in several areas. I worked hardest on that, rewriting the scenes several times. The narrative is all in Josie's voice, but she observes actions in the distance as well as close up that enable the reader to grasp the overall unfolding of the battle. To help the reader understand what was happening, I have Josie run back from the second battle line with the South Carolina militia when she gets lost from her own troop. She describes the third line of Continental Regulars at the back of the field, as well as Colonel William Washington's cavalry sweeping in from behind a pine grove on the left flank to rout the Green Dragoons.

RG: When you're writing, do you keep your mind on both the character and the battle equally?

RM: The most important is the character. But when you're writing about a true, important battle, you must give the reader some idea of what really happened. Luckily, the Cowpens battlefield was small enough that I could let Josie give a general view. She was running back with Lieutenant Hughes and General Morgan. Some people never did get back to their troop but stayed lost.

RG: How did you decide to make John Trethman in *Brave Enemies* a preacher?

RM: At the time, I was extremely interested in the evolution of the Anglican Church, which came from the Reformation, with Thomas Cranmer. I wanted to create something to balance the extraordinary violence of this time. Total violence would just sicken the reader. Once I came up with the idea of having this preacher coming in to create congregations and churches, I knew that was the way to go. This very gifted young man wanted to be an Anglican priest. He runs into a follower of Wesley, who was still an Anglican, by the way. His Methodism was a sect of the Anglican Church.

The Wesleyans were some of the most charismatic people who ever set foot in North America. These preachers, creators of congregations, were influential. John is fun: he's literate, he's trying to do something different, and he's a pacifist. He meets Josie, and they have an idyll in the wilderness for two weeks before he's kidnapped. Then the war catches up to them. They're unable to avoid it.

RG: Why have your main characters in historic fiction such as *Brave Enemies* been fictive, while historic figures such as General Daniel Morgan and Banastre Tarleton have been kept in the background of the narrative?

RM: I think it was the playwright Kermit Hunter, author of *Unto These Hills* and other outdoor dramas, who said it's most effective to let fictive characters dominate a story, with major historical figures used as minor characters. It's easier to imagine fictive characters and to follow the imagination with them. The hardest subjects to integrate into fiction are figures such as George Washington or Robert E. Lee. They are, respectively, the Father of His Country and the Marble Man. They resist imaginative attempts to bring them to life as believable characters. Better to let them stay on the margins of the story.

RG: You have a few stories on the Civil War, such as "Little Willie" and "A Brightness New and Welcoming." Do you have any interest in writing more about the Civil War?

RM: My next novel, to be published in 2015, is called *North Star*. Strictly speaking, it is not a war story, but the narratives of two young slaves who escape from plantations in the Carolinas in 1850 and make their way along the Appalachian chain all the way to Ithaca, New York, where they find a home. Later one character does serve as an orderly in the Union army. While not precisely a war novel, it is very much concerned with the events, such as the Fugitive Slave Law, that led to the Civil War ten years later.

RG: In the decades before the Civil War, Revolutionary General Daniel Morgan was a great national hero. Why do you think he is now mostly forgotten? Was he overtaken by Lee?

RM: As the memory of the Revolution faded, the memory of its heroes faded also. Anthony Wayne, Nathanael Greene, Daniel Morgan became names in history books. But it was the cataclysm of the Civil War that wiped out the memory of many earlier heroes. The scale and awfulness of the Civil War replaced the Revolution in the popular mind. Then Stonewall Jackson,

Lee, A. P. Hill, Nathan Bedford Forrest, Joseph Johnston became the heroes in the South. And as far as military brilliance, there probably isn't anybody in American history comparable to Lee. Resourcefulness, making use of materials and men available helped Lee to time and again defeat bigger and better trained armies. And I was once told by someone in Chicago that during the Civil War, historians got so tired of hearing southerners talk about the glorious things that southerners had done during the Revolution that they decided to erase southern glory from the history books.

RG: The Civil War also became tied to the myth of the Old South.

RM: Yes, the Civil War seemed much more romantic, so many novels, plays, biographies, films and television series have been devoted to the Civil War themes. *Birth of a Nation, Gone with the Wind,* Ken Burns's *Civil War* television documentary are just the most famous examples of an ocean of Civil War stories. But recently, there has been a renewed interest in the Founding Fathers and the Revolution, in biographies of figures such as John Adams and Benjamin Franklin, even Daniel Boone.

RG: Are there issues about the Revolutionary period that are especially relevant for our own times?

RM: I think the greatest lesson we can learn from the Revolutionary period is that we must have the courage of our convictions, and act on those convictions. Politics as usual is not enough. The Founding Fathers, and the soldiers who fought the war, staked their lives on their choices. Some now suggest that the war wasn't a revolution at all, but a quarrel among English people over constitutional government. But the courage of the leaders and soldiers who stood up to the mighty British Empire and the most powerful army in the world at that time is hard for us to comprehend. For many different reasons they were willing to confront and challenge overwhelming force, then try to create a new country. They are examples to us all.

RG: You explore the World War II era in several narratives. In "The Welcome," Dutch returns to Green River when the war ends. Forty years after the war, Jones in "Tailgunner" relives crashing into a German cabbage patch. And in the novella *The Mountains Won't Remember Us,* a female character whose fiancé was killed in England remains in love with that lost soldier and abides the hatefulness of a husband who can't compete with a dead man. These stories, as well as your latest novel, *The Road from Gap Creek* (2013), reflect your mother's brother's death in the war, don't they?

Could you share a bit of his story and comment on your decision to treat it in your fiction?

RM: I grew up with the legend of my uncle Robert Levi, my mother's younger brother. I was named after him, and many people compared me to their memories of him. He was killed in a B-17 crash in East Anglia in England on November 10, 1943, almost a year before I was born. So, I never knew him.

Women who had been in love with Robert would stop me in the church yard and say I "favored" him. He had been popular with everybody, a basketball player, tall, with red curly hair, handsome, a lifeguard, a powder man in the Civilian Conservation Corps. He was also an artist, and I grew up surrounded by his watercolors and oil paintings. He wrote poetry too. One of his hobbies had been collecting arrowheads and other Indian artifacts, and I inherited some of those. He was an impossible ideal to measure up to. My poem "Uncle Robert" expresses my admiration and some of my frustration at always being compared to him. For after his death, he had become a martyr.

In 1986 I set out to discover why he had been killed in an airplane crash. He was a mechanic, a crew chief. Why was he flying on the plane? Since they were loaded with bombs, they were on a mission. I traveled to England and found the site of the crash near the village of Eye in Suffolk. I interviewed a farmer who had witnessed the crash. I interviewed pilots, navigators, bombardiers from his 482nd Bombardment Group. I studied B-17 manuals, navigators' logs. I even interviewed Col. Robert K. Morgan, pilot of the Memphis Belle, who lived in Asheville. I studied histories of the Eighth Air Force and strategic bombing in World War II. I found out everything except what Robert was doing on that airplane.

RG: I thought that Sharon's efforts to find out about Troy's war experiences in *The Mountains Won't Remember Us* might parallel your own research into your Uncle Robert's history. She contacts the National Archives, for instance, trying to find out why he was flying on a B-17 when his family in Green River thought he was just a mechanic working on planes on the ground.

RM: Writing *The Mountains Won't Remember Us* was probably the most important breakthrough I've had as a fiction writer, as I mentioned earlier. It was the first fiction I wrote in a woman's voice, from a woman's point of view. That experience taught me that fiction is not about the author's values and opinion, but about the characters' values and opinions. It was scary to try to see the world through Sharon's eyes, and to tell the story in her voice. One way I dealt with the challenge was to let her describe much of the research I had done about Uncle Robert, the contacts with the Air Force archives and the National Archives. She was trying to find out exactly what I had tried to find out. Once I had completed thirty pages, I knew it was the best thing I had written up to that time.

RG: Did you ever discover what you wanted to know about your Uncle Robert's death?

RM: Only in 2012 did one of Robert's closest buddies get in touch with me. His name is Frank O. Conwell, and I talked with him on the phone at his home in Arizona. He told me in a few minutes most of what I had been try-ing to find out. He and Robert were both crew chiefs on sister aircraft in their Pathfinder Group. They oversaw all repairs and maintenance, and they also flew on missions as engineers/gunners. It was their job to check all gauges, do repairs in flight, keep the wing fuel tanks balanced, and when under attack, man the guns in the overhead turret. Conwell also explained to me why the flight log at the airbase recorded their mission as headed to Paris. They were dropping leaflets in France before turning north to drop bombs on the steel-works of the Ruhr valley. They were also experimenting with incendiaries, in this case white phosphorous. Conwell's plane followed Robert's in takeoff, and he saw Robert's plane catch fire and crash and explode.

RG: Do you have plans to write other novels that deal with the drama and trauma of war?

RM: Someday I would like to write a sequel to *Brave Enemies*, about the lives of Josie and John in the aftermath of the war. They move into the mountains and raise a family. But I've done more research on my Uncle Robert's career and death than on any other subject. I still want to write that particular story of the airmen attacking Germany in the dark days of 1943 when the Luftwaffe was at the peak of its power, and Americans were just learning the terrible art of strategic bombing and firebombing.

RG: What novels written in the past inspired you to write about the drama of war and civilians during a time of war?

RM: There is a notable tradition of modern fiction that deals with warfare realistically and unheroically. The greatest war story of all time is probably the *Iliad*, still one of the most violent. But in modern times a new stan-dard was set by Stendhal in *The Charterhouse of Parma*, which begins with a memorable scene at the Battle of Waterloo. I think that novel inspired Tolstoy to write about battles, especially in *War and Peace*. In this country we have *The Red Badge of Courage*, about the Civil War, and James Jones's *The Thin Red Line*, among many others. *All Quiet on the Western Front* by Erich Maria Remarque, about World War I, is especially memorable. Perhaps most impressive of all is Tim O'Brien's Vietnam stories, *The Things They Carried*, one of the best books about warfare of all time.

One of the novels that inspired me very early was *Doctor Zhivago*. It is a love story about a poet and his muse in the terrible days of the Russian Revolution and the even more horrible times of the Civil War. With the two doomed lovers in the foreground, Pasternak creates an intimate story with the cataclysmic history unfolding in the background. In the chapters where Zhivago is forced to serve as a medical officer with the partisans in the taiga country, we get a close-up, first-hand account of the brutal action.

RG: *The Road from Gap Creek* begins and ends with Troy's death, essentially. Government officials bring news of the crash in the first chapter, and late in the novel, the family finally holds a service when his remains are shipped home. Troy's sister Annie, the narrator, reflects that their mother Julie grieved herself to death—she dies just a few days before the war ends. Julie never did talk about her grief but faced life stoically, keeping her sorrow inside. Does that characterization come from family stories about your grandmother's way of dealing with her loss?

RM: Julie of *The Road from Gap Creek* is loosely based on my grandmother Julia Capps Levi, whom I knew when I was a small child. My grandmother would never talk about her grief and depression. She devoted her life to working for others. The death of her youngest son devastated her. She did die of a brain tumor, but in 1948, not 1945 as the character Julie does in the novel.

RG: In your story "Watershed," the narrator, telling his grandson about fighting Indians in the North Carolina mountains about 1800, when he was eleven or twelve years old, reveals what most of your literature about war implies: warring among humans brings less glory than long-lasting suffering and confusion. The narrator sixty-odd years later remains haunted by the face of the young Indian girl he slaughtered. His story reminds me of Annie's reflection at Troy's funeral service near the end of *The Road from Gap Creek*: "smart people . . . would find a better way to settle arguments rather than just killing each other" (308). Does her thinking capture your own judgment of war?

RM: It is one of the mysteries of human life, and human history, that intelligent people, often ethical people, kill each other so often and on such a scale. More people were killed in warfare in the twentieth century than in any other known century before. Annie in *The Road from Gap Creek* is mystified by the paradox. So often people of extraordinary intelligence and culture, the French and the Germans, for example, have slaughtered each other wholesale, and many wars have been fought over issues of religion, which seems on the surface a contradiction. Even in our own time much terrorism is conducted in the name of fundamentalist religion.

Obviously, we have not evolved as far from the killer apes as we like to believe. We still delight in war, in battles, in heroism. We seem unable to think clearly when challenged, when an opportunity for conflict presents itself. Annie's thoughts do reflect my own. Only fools would start wars. Yet we continue to do just that. And when wars are over, the damage to millions of lives lingers. After the fighting the scars remain, the grief among the survivors, the heirs. The South to this day, for example, has never fully recovered from the Civil War.

Notes

1. This book is *America's War for Humanity: A Pictorial History of the World War for Liberty*, published by L. H. Walter in 1919. The frontispiece has the inscription "Clyde R. Morgans Book, Zirconia, NC, 1919. Bought by him from Mrs. Judith Osteen in the month of January 1919 for $2.00."

Interview: Robert Morgan

William Wright / 2013

From *Oxford American* 82 (2013): 34–39. Reprinted by permission.

Robert Morgan is the author of fourteen books of poetry, most recently *Terroir*. He has also published eight volumes of fiction, including *Gap Creek*, a *New York Times* bestseller. A sequel to *Gap Creek*, *The Road from Gap Creek*, will be published in 2013. In addition, he is the author of three nonfiction books, *Good Measure: Essays, Interviews, and Notes on Poetry; Boone: A Biography*; and *Lions of the West: Heroes and Villains of the Westward Expansion*, 2011. He has been awarded the James G. Hanes Poetry Prize by the Fellowship of Southern Writers, and the Academy Award in Literature by the American Academy of Arts and Letters. Recipient of fellowships from the Guggenheim and Rockefeller foundations, the National Endowment for the Arts, and the New York State Arts Council, he has served as visiting writer at Davidson College, Furman, Duke, Appalachian State, and East Carolina universities. A member of the Fellowship of Southern Writers, he was inducted into the North Carolina Literary Hall of Fame in 2010. Born in Hendersonville, North Carolina, October 3, 1944, he has taught since 1971 at Cornell University, where he is Kappa Alpha Professor of English. In 2010 a special issue of *Southern Quarterly*, edited by Jesse Graves, was devoted to essays about his work.

William Wright: Even though you have written eight books of fiction with a ninth forthcoming in the fall of 2013, *The Road from Gap Creek*, you've stated in the past that poetry remains your favorite genre in which to write. Can you speak to why this is the case?

Robert Morgan: For me poetry has been the essential verbal art. No one has ever found a language or a culture that did not include poetry. Poetry is about the cadence of sentences and the textures of words and phrases. Poetry is about repetition, heartbeat and pulse and breath, the rhythm of walking. Through poetry we engage with the sound of words, with language at its most elemental and complex levels. Poetry seems born in our blood and bone and in the synapses of our brains. The truth is we don't know exactly how poetry works, but we recognize it when we experience it. As Yeats famously said, no one can refute "The Song of Sixpence." Once you hear poetry you remember it and want to say it. Poetry must be in our DNA, and we find it like a treasure buried in our everyday speech, waiting to be rediscovered and said. Poetry is a privilege and a legacy; it connects us to all people and all times. It can be both celebration and lament, for those who have gone before, for the passing of the seasons, for the discovery of the things we had forgotten that we know.

WW: Though you started out in college to be a fiction writer, your early books were all poetry collections. Now you have published eight books of fiction and another is forthcoming. You still often identify yourself as a *poet* specifically, as opposed to a *writer*—why is this?

RM: Yes, my first publications as an undergraduate were short stories. But something happened to me in the summer and fall of 1964 as I began my senior year at UNC-Chapel Hill. I started to become aware of words in a new, intimate way. I was fascinated by matching words to things, to emotions, to experience. One day I was working on the loading dock at the GE plant near Hendersonville, North Carolina—a summer job before returning to school— and after a powerful thunderstorm the sun broke through the clouds with a great shaft of light that seemed to be bracing the sky. I wrote a little haiku-like verse about that, and I knew those words had an authenticity of a new kind for me, however modest. It was a small step, but satisfying because it seemed both real and with imaginative reach toward the unexpected.

When I returned to Chapel Hill I kept writing lines and little poems. I was fascinated by compression and economy of language, with implicit metaphors found in the natural world, and with the way words can evoke surprise. I loved translations of Greek epigrams, and Chinese and Japanese poetry.

Two important things happened to me that fall of 1964. I fell in with a group of students, all from the Northeast, who had gone to the finest prep schools in New England and been kicked out for various reasons. They had come to Chapel Hill to be beatniks and poets. They knew far more about poetry than I did. They could talk about metaphor and line breaks, French poetry, and William Butler Yeats. Every day we met and talked about poetry, read poetry aloud, lived and breathed poetry. I read Robert Lowell and Robert Bly, James Wright and Gary Snyder. Because my friends were so much more sophisticated than me, I was reluctant to show them the poems I was trying to write. But the best poet among them, Dudley Carroll, insisted that I show him some of my stuff. One day I gave him a sheaf of the things I'd done, with little confidence in their reception. That night around 2:00 a.m. there was a knock on my door. Dudley and his friend Tim Perkins stood there holding my poems. Dudley said my work as so good, so exciting, he had to come tell me. I don't think any review, any award, any honor I've ever received since has been more thrilling than that. Dudley's praise gave me a new confidence, an energy, that reinforced the momentum already building in me. I wrote a few more short stories, but my real concentration from then on was on poetry.

Another definitive experience that fall occurred while I was reading T. S. Eliot's "Burnt Norton." I read those flowing lines aloud again and again, and suddenly I saw that lines of poetry were made up of firm sentences broken into increments that formed patterns. That may seem an obvious insight, but to me it was a revelation. I had wondered what a line of poetry was, and I saw that lines were just fragments of the perceptual energy of sentences. I incorporated that insight into my own writing and never looked back.

WW: Your northeastern college friends served as catalysts to your confidence in writing but you have said several times many of the finest contemporary poets are associated with the American South. Why do you think that is so?
RM: I know that many of the contemporary poets I read and reread most live in the South or write about the South. As someone who grew up in the Appalachian South I am probably biased. But I believe that southern poetry is cut from the same cloth as southern fiction. Southern poets write about history, about family, about the natural world, about work and struggle. They use the arts of storytelling, the oral tradition, and some of the Gothic tendencies of the fiction writers. Both white and African American poets of the region incorporate a good deal of our vexed history in their work.

Eudora Welty was once asked why there are so many great writers from Mississippi. After a pause she said, "Perhaps we have more to explain." I suspect her insight applies to the whole region. We have a tradition of frontier humor, of comedy and Gothic spectacle. But our legacy also includes tragedy, cruel human imperfection, as well as a passionate quest for spirituality.

WW: Much of your fiction is narrated by women characters and focuses on women's lives. Yet few women appear in your poems. Do you have any explanation for that difference?

RM: To tell the truth I am mystified by this discrepancy myself. My greatest breakthrough as fiction writer occurred in the spring of 1989 when I discovered that I could write fiction in the voice of a woman character. That was when I wrote *The Mountains Won't Remember Us*. I found that fiction is not about me and my experience and opinions, but about my characters, their voices, their world. Since then most of my novels have been narrated by women characters, and I have been surprised and pleased by the response to my fiction by women readers.

I can only speculate on why so few women appear in my poems. For one thing, many of my poems are about natural process, about trees, about time, about tools and instruments. There are not all that many men in the poems either. But a number of my poems have been about my father, grandfather, uncles. It has been said that there is only one plot in fiction: nothing is what it seems. Fiction is rarely heroic in a poetic sense. Fiction is about struggles and intimacy, conflicts of loyalty. One of my teachers used to say poetry is about the heights and fiction about the morass.

Perhaps I unconsciously seek out the heroic in poetry, connecting the humble and everyday with the larger and more lasting, the temporary with the universal, connecting the moment with the everlasting, the near with the far. That is what I call the "reach" in poetry: to see the large in the small, the infinite in the finite, the earthly with the heavenly, the ordinary with the eternal. In his great essay "The Poet" Emerson says, "The ideal shall be real to thee." But the most honest answer to your question is I don't know why I am privileged to write about women characters in fiction but do so rarely in poetry. Perhaps we just write what we are given to write.

WW: More than one reviewer has compared your poetry to the work of William Blake. How does that comparison strike you?

RM: Of course. I am flattered and humbled to be compared to one of our greatest poets, and one of my favorites. I was astonished when a critic first made that comparison. I like to think there is something elemental and dramatic in my poems that may echo some of the drama, the struggle, the contraries, the surprise, in Blake's short poems. I don't know his larger, prophetic poems all that well. Both Blake and myself are deeply influenced by hymns and the language of the King James Bible. And like him I aspire to evoke the natural as a way of seeing beyond the natural. I love rhyme and meter as he did.

WW: If you had to pick one book that influenced you most as a poet what would you choose?

RM: There are so many books that have influenced me over the years that I could get lost in the list. It would be easy to say the Bible, which was read to me every day when I was a kid. Those cadences of the King James Version still ring in my head. And in school we had to memorize poems by Edgar Allan Poe, Sidney Lanier, Wordsworth, and Bryant, and recite them in front of the class. The first book I ever bought with my own money was *Doctor Zhivago*, and I loved the poems at the end of that novel. When my sister Evangeline came home from college after her first year she brought her English text, and in that anthology I read Walt Whitman's "Song of Myself" and Wallace Stevens's "Domination of Black." But if I had to pick only one volume it would be Robert Payne's paperback *The White Pony*, an anthology of Chinese poems in translation from Confucius to Mao. Those poems had a profound effect on me in college. Their compression and concreteness, the surface simplicity with subtle depths, the color and Taoist irony, the implicitness and wisdom, gave me exciting ideas about the nature and possibilities of poetry. I still love the poems and go back to read them in that and other translations from time to time.

WW: Your childhood was spent on a small farm in the Blue Ridge Mountains of North Carolina. Are there advantages to a writer to come from such a background? Disadvantages?

RM: A reporter who once interviewed me on the farm asked me how I could ever have made it to Cornell University from such a humble place. I told him I understood the gist of his question since we were poor and my parents didn't have a lot of formal education. But in fact I had some distinct advantages for a future writer. My parents, my grandpa, my uncles and neighbors, were all great storytellers. They would sit by the fire, or on the porch in summer, and tell yarn after yarn, tale after tale, about the old days, about the Confederate War, about panthers trying to come down chimneys, about maddogs, giant rattlesnakes, bears, ghosts, outlaws, floods, corrupt preachers, witches, babies marked in the womb. When I began writing later I wondered what I had to write about. And little by little I discovered I had this enormous hoard of stories and voices to draw on and choose from. But equally important to me, perhaps, was the freedom I had as a kid to roam in the woods and pastures, and along the creeks and rivers. I climbed trees on the mountaintop and found arrowheads and pieces of Native American pottery in the bottomlands. I felt a close connection to the Native Americans who had lived there on the square mile of land my great-great-grandfather, Daniel Pace, had bought in 1838. I built ponds on the pasture branch and played cowboys and outlaws with my cousins in the gullies of the lower pasture. We dug caves in the walls of the gullies. We used boards to sled down the mountainside on leaves and pine needles.

Besides readings from the Bible and singing hymns, I was exposed every week to dynamic preaching. Those preachers could take a verse from the Bible and spin an hour's sermon from it. The disadvantages of such a rural background are probably obvious. I never traveled farther than Asheville or Greenville, South Carolina. I was not exposed to diverse cultures. And I felt a little afraid of the larger world out there. Watching the big tourist Cadillacs on the highway in summer I felt my poverty and difference. Until I was almost nine my family did not have a car or truck. We had to depend on others to take us to town or to the doctor or carry our produce to the market in summer. We didn't have television. We got our first telephone when I was about ten. I felt a little alien even in the Green River community. In compensation, the larger world was all new to me. It was there to be discovered. I had never seen a movie in a movie theater until I went away to college at the age of sixteen. Believe it or not, the first movie I ever saw in a theater was *La Dolce Vita* at the Peachtree Theater near Georgia Tech, fall 1961. Freeways, fine clothes, educated people, affluent people, restaurants, big libraries, concerts, were all new to me. I was learning fast, and hopefully still learning. The world out here still astonishes me.

WW: Why did you choose a French word like *terroir* as the title of your most recent book of poems?

RM: I like to pick titles that get attention. Perhaps the best title I've ever used for a book of poems is *Sigodlin*, one word with an unusual texture and sound. *Terroir* is a French word meaning literally soil but used by food writers and wine experts to denote the unique quality of a particular vintage or dish, the combination of properties, of soil, sun, rain, cultivation, climate, that make a specific harvest. *Terroir* is closely tied to a sense of place, a specific place, and specific time. For my poems it seemed a relevant term. The fact that the word looks almost like "terror" is interesting too. For we know that terror is an important component of the sublime. I like the combination of the earthiness, the local, and the exotic and refined, in the word *terroir*. And in the title poem, "Terroir," I connect the concept of *terroir* with Gerard Manley Hopkins's term "inscape." Hopkins was very interested in the specific, the individual, the unique, as opposed to categories, types, definitions. He believed he had found confirmation of his idea of inscape in John Duns Scotus's concept of "thisness," *haecceitas* in Latin, in contrast with the Thomist and Aristotelian *quidditas*, or "whatness." So, it seemed to me that Hopkins's inscape was very close to what we mean by *terroir*.

Inscape is the celebration of the individual fact. As Hopkins says, "I have often felt . . . that nothing is so pregnant and straightforward to the truth as simple *yes* and *is*." It is communion with naked being. Thoreau once said that "prayer is the contemplation of facts from the highest point of view."

Another term that comes to mind and is both similar and different from *terroir* is the Spanish *duende*, associated especially with the poet Federico García Lorca. *Duende* is often translated as goblin, demon, evil spirit, and related to the passion, the bravura of Lorca's style. For Lorca *duende* had connotations of "divine spark," magnetism, mesmeric intensity, daimonic energy. I suppose I would say that *duende* could be seen as the force, the inspirational spirit, that perceives, informs, and articulates the experience of poetry, including the experience of *terroir* or inscape. For Lorca *duende* was the irrational spirit of the poetic imagination finding its expression in words and music. The concept of *terroir* has more to do with the perception of uniqueness, oneness, and onceness. Lorca was a very accomplished musician and dramatist, and I suspect there is an element of performance in his concept of *duende*.

WW: Did your experience as a poet help you as a fiction writer?

RM: I'm not sure I would ever have been able to write prose fiction if I had not spent those years from 1964 to 1980 working primarily on poetry. It was writing poetry that taught me about economy, precision, compression of language. It was poetry that taught me to *listen* to words and phrases and sentences. Writing poetry gave me the confidence to try to write prose. As I said before, poetry is the essential verbal art. All other writing derives from it. What poetry did not do was teach me to think like a storyteller. For that I had to go back to the voices and narratives of my childhood, especially the women of my childhood who relished telling of terrible things, scandals, awful storms, the pains of childbirth, the stubbornness of men, snake bites, things that happened a long time ago.

When I began writing stories again in the 1980s I promised myself I would not write "poetic" prose with pretty description. I would strip language down to the essential to dramatize, create dynamic action, and reveal character. I would try to grab the attention of the reader in the first paragraph and not let go until the last sentence. Stories always have to have a surprise. If they just go where you expect they are not satisfying stories. Stories are usually about people in trouble, often with serious conflicts within themselves. Stories are about struggle. Hardest for me was to write dialogue, for good dialogue has to reveal character and move the story forward. I found I could usually cut away about two-thirds of the dialogue I had written, keeping only the lines that were absolutely significant.

WW: What is it about southern Appalachia, and indeed the South in general, that has inspired so many good writers in the past two decades?

RM: The old joke is that when asked why there are so many good writers from the South, the southern writer answers, "Because there ain't nothing else to do down here." And as Eudora Welty said, perhaps we have a lot more to explain, about our history, about our contradictory selves.

But I believe a culture and region going through rapid change inspire writers. In Shakespeare's time insular England was exploding into a world power, absorbing the Renaissance, exploring the New World. In Hawthorne's time traditional New England was disappearing into the industrial age, and he again and again tried to recapture and reveal the Puritan past. So many southern writers of our time have struggled both to understand the past and the extraordinary changes in our region, affected not only by industrialization, then the loss of those industrial jobs overseas, but the mass immigration of Hispanics and now Asians, and the millions of retirees, the gated communities, the loss of agriculture, the homogenization of culture in general. I grew up in a culture where all the men did physical work and hunted in the fall. Now few under the age of sixty will take a rifle and wait in the cold woods for a deer.

My feeling is that the uncertainty about who we are and where we are going stimulates the urge to capture a sense of the past, and to portray the dramatic changes around us. Writing is a way to connect with others, to reassure ourselves we are not alone. And of course we have the great legacy of southern writing, of Thomas Wolfe, Faulkner, O'Connor, Welty, Warren, etc., to draw on also. When I was a student, I felt my teachers, Guy Owen at NC State, Jessie Rehder at UNC-Chapel Hill, and Fred Chappell at UNC-Greensboro, *expected* me to be a writer. I have always been afraid of letting them down.

WW: Do you have any thoughts about how electronic publishing might affect writing in the future?

RM: Well, I have never been a doomsayer. When I was in college "the death of the novel" was discussed all the time. The feeling then seemed to be that the novel was an obsolete literary form. Now fifty years later we've had a golden age of fiction writing. When people talk about the end of publishing and reading, it ain't necessarily so. What is changing is the *way* many people read. My impression is that because e-books can be downloaded so easily, anywhere, any time, people may actually be reading more, at least more fiction and nonfiction. But that doesn't mean that printed books will go away any time soon. Older readers like myself still like to buy books, to hold books and read them, turning pages, and put them on the shelf to read again from time to time. But we seniors are going to have to get used to the idea that a lot of magazines and books will be available primarily online or in digital form. It's mostly a matter of habit, what we are used to. Some of us are lazy about changing our habits. Good writing will always be good writing, whether read on paper or parchment or a clay tablet or computer screen. And for poetry it's still the *sound* of the words that is most important.

WW: In all your writing, poetry and prose, fiction and nonfiction, there has always been a special awareness of history and place. What might have inspired those interests?

RM: Though my dad had only gone to the sixth grade he loved to read history and talk about history. He subscribed to the *National Geographic* magazine and had a surprising grasp of American history and world history, as well as geography. So even though I grew up on a small farm in the mountains I was exposed to discussions from my earliest memory of figures such as George Washington and Lincoln, Teddy Roosevelt, Napoleon, and the World Wars, even Romans such as Julius Caesar and Cicero. History is storytelling, and my dad was a great storyteller. His knowledge of the Bible could make the stories of David and the Apostle Paul come alive for an eager listener.

Also his knowledge of the history of the southern mountains and the Cherokee Indians inspired me. I knew the Indians had lived and hunted right where we lived. My great-grandpa Pace's black hair and dark skin were explained by saying that the family had "Italian blood." But that great-grandpa was a well-known herb doctor, and he took his children when they were gravely ill to an Indian doctor in South Carolina. He was invited to Washington, DC, by the Bureau of Indian Affairs around 1900 to give a deposition on the Treaty of Hopewell, between the government and the Cherokees. He was almost certainly part Indian, though the family would never admit it. As I grew older I loved to read both novels and biographies. I read lives of Bismarck and Lincoln, Jack London, and George Washington Goethals, the engineer who built the Panama Canal.

In the eleventh grade I had a wonderful teacher of American history named Elizabeth Rogers. She made history vivid by describing places she had visited such as Valley Forge and the Gettysburg battlefield. I suspect it was my intimacy with the ground where I grew up that gave me a special sense of place. Until I was sixteen that was the only place I really knew, the streams and gullies, the fields and pine thickets, the riverbank, the mountaintops, and the pits dug by ancestors looking for zircons.

WW: What advice do you give to young fiction writers? To young poets?
RM: Since everyone learns to write in their own way it's hard to give general advice that is useful. Like any art, writing is only learned in the act of doing it, not from any theory or textbook. A good creative writing teacher is more a coach than a teacher in the usual sense of the term. A writer learns to write the way an athlete learns a sport, by doing it and doing it. There is only one word of advice that applies to all aspiring writers: persistence. Those who succeed at any art are those who try and try and try again. Many of the most talented students I have taught over the years have never developed as writers. They were gifted, but the lacked the fire in the belly, the drive, the demon, that would sustain them and enable them to grow in the craft, whatever the setbacks and rejections. Others who have seemed initially less promising have had the tenacity, maybe the madness, that compelled them to keep writing and rewriting until things clicked.

My advice for young poets is pretty much the same as for fiction writers. And I usually say that poets learn a lot from writing prose that can be applied to verse writing, including critical prose. It is no accident that most of the best writing *about* poetry has been done by the poets themselves. And a class in geology, or history, or a foreign language, may be of more use to a poet than another writing workshop. Everything a poet knows will find a way into what he or she writes. Most important, learn to *listen* to language, read poetry aloud and feel it on the tongue. Read whatever you write aloud. The ear is the best editor and critic.

"Music of the Spheres" Heard as "World Opening onto World": An Interview with Robert Morgan

Rebecca Godwin / 2017

From *North Carolina Literary Review Online*, 2017. https://issuu.com
/eastcarolina/docs/2017-nclronline/12. Reprinted by permission.

Robert Morgan calls Thomas Wolfe the "presiding genius of North Carolina literature." At least at first glance, Wolfe's urgent outpouring of words in manuscripts thousands of pages long contrasts with Morgan's own tightly controlled language. In both prose and poetry, this North Carolina native focuses on plain style, with concise, unadorned diction providing easy access to universal mysteries and truths. In reality, Morgan's own outpouring of words rivals Wolfe's: the artist born forty-four years after his predecessor has simply divided his thousands of pages among genres. Morgan has now added drama to his list of literary achievements in fiction, nonfiction, and poetry. In 2014, his play *Homemade Yankees* won the John Cullum Civil War Playwriting Competition sponsored by the East Tennessee Civil War Alliance and the University of Tennessee.

Rebecca Godwin: Your sixteenth poetry collection, *Dark Energy*, came out in 2015, followed by your seventh novel, *Chasing the North Star*, in 2016. You're working now on your fourth book of nonfiction, a book tentatively titled *Women of the West*, a companion to your 2011 sketches of men important to America's westward expansion, *Lions of the West*. How have you managed to keep your hand in both poetry and prose so successfully? How has writing prose fiction and nonfiction influenced your verse writing over the years?

Robert Morgan: Working alternately on poetry and prose has helped sustain me as a writer. When I have finished a project in one genre, or just run out of steam, I have switched to the other form and moved on. But most of my poems and prose are cut from the same cloth, the same preoccupations with memory, family, history, the natural world. While researching history for nonfiction I seem to stumble on many good ideas for poems. Poetry has given me opportunities to explore my interests in science and technology, tools, and the history of science. I do feel that writing prose has helped me evolve as a poet and that writing poetry has influenced the way I write prose, both fiction and nonfiction.

RG: Your poetic style has evolved, from free verse to syllabics. Many of the poems in *Dark Energy* present, for instance, unrhymed tetrameter, eight syllables with four stresses. At what point in your career did you decide to focus on meter? Did particular poets influence that move?

RM: When I began writing poetry I was most influenced by translations of Chinese poetry of the T'ang era, especially the translations by Ezra Pound. It was the images that I concentrated on, images and metaphors, and the compression and economy of language. I sought a clear, natural cadence in the sentences, and tried to make something happen in each line to move the poem forward. It was only after coming to Cornell in 1971 that I became interested in using rhyme, syllable count, and repetition to strengthen the sound of poems. I became more and more aware of the *voice* in poems. And in 1973 I became excited about the use of an incantatory style, which led to the longer poem called "Mockingbird." It's a style I've always meant to go back to, but so far never have.

In the 1980s I began to write poems in syllabics, usually in eight-syllable lines. I found that measure flexible enough to use in longer meditative and narrative poems. Having the consistent syllable count began to free the voice of the poems, relieving the heavy burden on the line breaks in irregular free verse. To add the arbitrary mathematical element to poems was a breakthrough. Gradually I began to realize that the modern axiom that "form is nothing more than an extension of content" was exactly wrong. There is, in fact, no necessary connection between content and form. You can write a good sonnet about any subject, in any voice. Part of the pleasure of a poem may come from the way the natural cadence of a sentence can contrast with the arbitrary form it passes through. That way we have the natural flow of language and the crystalline exactness of the form at once. You don't have that subtle counterpoint in prose. But form can be part of the statement in some cases. When Frost puts "Desert Places" in the form of a terza rima sonnet, the form, associated with the high idealism of Dante and Shelley, adds an ironic element to Frost's tough confession.

RG: Do you usually focus on accents in a line as well as on the number of syllables? I think that the terms might be "syllabic" and "accentual-syllabic."
RM: In the 1990s I began to think more in terms of accents in lines of poetry and gradually wrote more and more in iambic lines of four stresses or tetrameter. We know the four-stress line, common meter, ballad meter, is the norm in poetry of many languages. It has been theorized that the four-stress line is the increment of sound and information the brain can process at once. In my case, I just seemed to find that line worked best for me. Some of my recent poems are written in the more assertive trochaic meter, and a few are in pentameter.

RG: I know that you have a passion for music and allude to it in many poems, for instance "Time's Music," "Tail Music," "Mountain Dulcimer," "Music of the Spheres." Perhaps your ear for music—you do play piano, I understand—influenced your movement to a metered line in your poetry?
RM: As a teenager I wanted to be a composer. I studied piano and some music theory. I wanted to write a symphony or oratorio as grand as the Cicero Mountain across the river from our house. Why would anyone write in words if they could compose music, which is the mother art? The small infant responds to and delights in music. When I discovered that I lacked sufficient talent for music, I turned to the next best thing, poetry, music in language. I'm sure my love of the cadence of sentences and the metrical line is related to my pleasure in classical and baroque music.

RG: You have lived in New York State for forty-five years now. How has living in the Northeast, and perhaps teaching at Cornell, influenced your poetry?
RM: Like most people who have teaching careers, I have learned a good deal from my students. Sometimes it has been a challenge to stay ahead of them. I have had to be a better scholar and thinker because of the opportunity to formulate my thoughts in the classroom and in conferences. And I have had the chance to carry my thoughts further because of the give and take of discussions with colleagues and students. Also, living eight hundred miles from my home in North Carolina caused me to become a student of the southern mountains and their history in a way I might not have had I remained there. Out of homesickness and nostalgia I concentrated on

memory and on the uniqueness (and universality) of that one place. But since I have lived away from my native place, more of my writing is set in the past, and inspired by memory, rather than contemporary Appalachia.

RG: Poetry has never been dominant in popular culture in the United States, but certainly our contemporary era might be seen as an age of prose and film. What do you see as the function of poetry in our time?

RM: It is indeed a challenge for the contemporary poet to gain a sense of his or her audience. Film is the dominant narrative form of our time, and the novel has dominated our literary life. Autobiography, biography, and memoir are also extraordinarily popular. Yet poetry is still the essential literary genre. No one has ever found a language or culture that did not include poetry. Some think that the instinct for poetry is the very source of language itself, our delight in sound, in lyricism, in wordplay such as repetition and onomatopoeia. Children do not have to be taught to delight in nursery rhymes. We are born loving anapests and iambs.

When great national tragedies occur, such as the assassination of President Kennedy, or 9/11, it's the poetry of Walt Whitman or Emily Dickinson that the leaders and memorialists fall back on. The public may not feel the "need" for a lot of poetry, but when the occasion calls for it, they are grateful the significant words are there to draw on to express our grief or sense of unity. For poetry is ceremonial, ritualistic, elevated, in all cultures. What Walt Whitman does in "When Lilacs Last in the Dooryard Bloom'd" can't be done in any other way. Poetry is language that cannot be forgotten, that can be said no other way. People often forget that they need poetry, and then are surprised to discover that they do. My dad was a farmer who had left school after the sixth grade. He loved to read history but was not literary in the least. Yet from time to time, when moved, he loved to recite Tennyson's "Crossing the Bar" or John Burroughs's "Waiting." He was a little embarrassed to do so but could not resist repeating the lines he had learned in his youth.

RG: You see that poetry can accomplish what prose (fiction or nonfiction)— or even film—cannot, then? Poetry carries magical power? Is it essential, or at least useful, for education?

RM: In the schools I attended in the mountains of North Carolina we were required to memorize poems and recite them before the class. Poems you learn in your youth are never forgotten. Remembered poems are a pleasure to call up and recite, even in fragments. Poems become wired into the brain.

It is more difficult to memorize free verse, but we never forget "Whose woods these are I think I know." One test for good poetry is whether it is memorable or not. We don't memorize novels and films, but for the rest of your life you can carry a poem with you. No one can take away from you, "Tyger Tyger, burning bright," or the seventy-third sonnet of Shakespeare.

RG: Do you consider yourself a political poet in any way? I think of your poems that recall the ancients, for example, often implying that we need their wisdom. Many poets suggest that our modern consumer society falls short when compared to earlier civilizations. Your new poem "Urnfield" ends with a strong punch, the imagery of "our age of rust and warming" conveying dismay, certainly consciousness of our negative effects on the world. Would the label eco-poet apply? Your concern for the environment, for instance your worry that Green River soil is going to "decorate the cities" in your poem "Atomic Age," published in *Topsoil Road*, might allow critics to place you in that category?

RM: I am certainly interested in environmental issues, and a number of my poems touch on degradation of land and resources. But prose essays are more effective for direct statements about political and environmental concerns. A poem such as "Jaguar," published in *Dark Energy*, surprised me by questioning the legend that jaguars once roamed the southern mountains and then connecting with the heavy traffic in the Smokies and highways of the region. The poem began as playful speculation and swerved to that conclusion.

I am personally divided about the rapid development of western North Carolina. As someone raised on a struggling subsistence farm, I appreciate the new affluence brought into the region. Still, it saddens me to see the mountains carved out for retirement communities, as family farms disappear, and the rise of crime and drug culture among the young in my native highlands, in the once breathtaking hunting ranges of the Cherokees. When I worked in the fields as a child and turned up arrowheads and pieces of pottery, it seemed to me the very ground was haunted by the Indians who had been there so long.

RG: I wonder whether you're conscious of any connection between your poetry and Ted Kooser's. It seems to me that you share with him a view of the natural world, one perhaps influenced by the Romantics or perhaps by your upbringing. Both of you also write a fairly plain-style verse that is quite accessible. I remember that Kooser selected your poem "Living Tree" for

American Life in Poetry when he was US Poet Laureate and called you one of his "favorite American poets."

RM: I have always admired Ted Kooser's poetry, for its realism and naturalness, and its love of rural life and landscape. His poems are also models of the craft that hides craft, seeming so deceptively plain. As an editor and Poet Laureate of the United States, he has had a significant and healthy influence on contemporary poetry.

RG: Much of your poetic output revolves around science, the mysterious workings of the universe. Can you talk about the influence of scientific knowledge on your poetry? It certainly seems more dominant in your poetry than in your fiction. Do you continue to study science to gather ideas for poems such as "Dark Energy" or "Neutrino," both appearing in your latest collection?

RM: From an early age I loved the articles in the *National Geographic* about science and technology. Through those articles on nuclear energy, rockets, astronomy, geology, I found a thrilling connection to a much larger world, ancient, futuristic, and timeless. Science promised new ideas, beyond the limited world I knew. I went off to college to study science and mathematics, then got sidetracked by writing. I still read everything I can find in *Scientific American* and elsewhere about current discoveries and theories. Many of my poems reflect that interest, but little of the fiction. In many ways science has been our language for understanding who we are. It would be hard to overstate the thrill of discovering Darwin, Einstein, and Newton as a teenager. The more I learned, the more mysterious the world became. It was as though world was opening onto world. I hope my poems show some of that awe and wonder.

RG: A last question involves Thomas Wolfe, North Carolina's famous writer from Asheville. You've credited Wolfe with inspiring you, as a teenager, to think that you, too, might become a writer. You've commented on Wolfe's influence on your fiction—for instance his triggering the idea of writing from a woman's point of view. I see a correlation between his fascination with time and the same concern in your poetry. Have you thought about that connection?

RM: It was reading *Look Homeward, Angel* when I was about fifteen that first made me think seriously about becoming a writer. I was intoxicated by Wolfe's sweeping language and by his ability to make the everyday so vivid and memorable. I never was able to write in his sweeping rhetorical style, but even so he inspired me. And his novella *The Web of Earth* gave me the idea of letting a woman character tell her own story in her own voice. Wolfe is the presiding genius of North Carolina literature. His fascinations with the mystery of time, with the power of memory, are connections I feel with Wolfe, as well as the October 3 birthday we share.

To Connect with That beyond Ourselves: An Interview with Robert Morgan

Robert West / 2017

Robert West's "'To Connect with That beyond Ourselves': An Interview with Robert Morgan" was first published in *Appalachian Journal* 44, no. 1–2 (Fall/Winter 2017): 132–41. Copyright, *Appalachian Journal* & Appalachian State University. Used by permission.

Robert West: This interview will appear alongside a dozen new poems of yours. I'm always amazed at what a prolific and yet consistently fine poet you are. Is your habit still to rise early and write for a couple of hours each day?

Robert Morgan: I do get up around five each morning and work for two or three hours. It's a habit I developed when I was teaching full time and helping to raise three children. I had to have a time when I could work undisturbed, when the house was quiet, before anyone else was up. That's my favorite time of day, when I can live with my sentences and lines of verse and try to make them come out right. But I grew up on a farm where we always rose early, to get the livestock fed, the cows milked, the eggs gathered. So, I was born to the routine. I tell young writers it's essential to have a certain time for your work each day or night, when you let nothing interfere with your writing.

RW: You've been writing strictly metrical poems for some time now. Of the twelve poems in this issue of *Appalachian Journal*, all but three are in iambic tetrameter; the other three are in iambic pentameter. What about the tetrameter line (as opposed to the pentameter) especially appeals to you?

RM: There is a theory that poetry in all languages tends to fall naturally into a four-stress line, as in common meter, ballad meter, hymn meter. A German neuroscientist named Popper has suggested that the four-stress line is about the increment of information the brain can process at once. So longer lines, pentameter, hexameter, are the exception to the more common verse line. The transition from free verse to meter for me was the decade I spent writing syllabic verse, especially the eight-syllable line. I discovered that once I had a consistent line length it freed the imagination to focus on content. From there I progressed to the four-stress metrical line. There is a mathematical dimension to most of the best poetry.

It was writing more prose in the 1980s and 1990s that made me think about the essential differences between prose and verse. I began to be aware of the sound of poetry, the voice of poetry, much more, and I thought about what verse can do that prose cannot. Poetry is about repetition *and* progression, progression of narrative or argument, repetition of line length, of stress pattern, of rhyme and alliteration, anaphora, or repetition of syntactical structures. There is a ceremonial and ritualistic dimension to poetry. You cannot do in prose what Dylan Thomas does in "Do Not Go Gentle into That Good Night."

RW: You've embraced meter, but most of your metrical poems don't rhyme. Once in a while a poem will rhyme throughout; now and then a poem that hasn't rhymed all along will conclude with a rhyme, as scenes in Shakespeare's plays often do. Generally, though, you're writing a kind of blank verse. Do you think you've avoided rhyme so as to keep the poem's composition moving—not letting the need to find a match slow you down—or do you have other reservations about using it?

RM: Blank verse has worked well for me, in pentameter, and especially in shorter tetrameter lines. I do love rhyme and some of my poems are in couplets, or other rhymed forms. But more have irregular rhyme patterns and internal rhymes. I have a special affection for the tag couplet for ending a poem. The tag couplet for me is a kind of tonic chord, a resolution for the poem. I may have avoided regular rhyme patterns at times out of laziness, or expediency. But more often it's because the tone of a poem needs to be conversational in a way where blank verse is most effective. Part of the fun of writing poems is finding the form that works best in each instance.

RW: "Family Bible" is one of my favorite poems from *Topsoil Road*, and now we have "My Father's Bible." As the title suggests, it's a much more personal poem, about a specific object and the place it occupied in a specific person's life. The poem evokes your rediscovery of it: you say at the beginning that it's been "unmoved for twenty years or more," and then proceed to describe how it looks and feels, inside and out, and how thin the pages are. When you announce at the end that tucked in its pages is a photograph of your mother, your sister, and you, that's a touching fact: there are probably several plausible interpretations of it, but my first thought was that he seemed to want to protect you all by wrapping you in Scripture. Do you remember if he had favorite books (of the Bible, that is), or favorite passages? Were there certain verses he liked to quote?

RM: My dad was not a literary person. But there were two poems he had memorized in his youth which he liked to recite on occasion. One was Tennyson's "Crossing the Bar," and the other was John Burroughs's "Waiting." He also loved to read history and the *National Geographic* magazine. I never knew him to read a novel. It was my mother who read fiction.

My dad read the Bible every day, especially in the early morning before the rest of us were up. He made a fire in the stove, boiled some coffee, and pored over the Scripture. After his death in 1991 the Bible lay on a shelf in the bookcase. I never opened it until after my mother's death in 2010, when I inherited the old house. I was moved to see how the pages were worn from thousands of hours of study. He had dozens of favorite passages. In his youth and later he had taken part in Pentecostal Holiness services, as his mother had before him, and participated in the shouting and speaking in tongues. Many of his favorite quotes were ecstatic or evangelical in tenor—for example the first two chapters of Acts, where the disciples meet to pray in the upper room, and are visited on Pentecost by the Holy Spirit, which comes in a whirlwind and inspires them to speak in many tongues. The white-hot rhetoric of Revelation appealed to him, especially the last two chapters. He loved to repeat the phrase "I am Alpha and Omega." Also, the descriptions of the Transfiguration and Ascension in the Gospels thrilled him. No verse pleased him more than the conclusion of Matthew: "Go ye therefore, and teach all nations, baptizing them in the name of the Father, and of the Son, and of the Holy Ghost: Teaching them to observe all things whatsoever I have commanded you: and, lo, I am with you always, even unto the end of the world."

RW: There's a term in the poem that wasn't familiar to me. Lines seven and eight say that "The pages too are stained and foxed / by oil or sweat." What does "foxed" there mean?

RM: "Foxed" is a term perhaps more common in British English than in American English. It means discolored, with a yellowish-brown stain. I like it because the word suggests the color of a fox, and something elusive, old, maybe a little legendary.

RW: "My Father's Bible" is a poem that includes some rhyme, though the effect is fairly subtle. You introduce the photo exactly six lines from the end, and though up to that point the poem hasn't rhymed, those last six lines do—and they do so in a pattern that recalls the sestet concluding an Italian sonnet: "me" rhymes with "three" and "scrutiny," and "gate" slant-rhymes with "white" and "out." One day I'll point that out in the classroom, and a student will raise a hand and ask, "Do you think he did that on purpose?" Would you like to go ahead and answer that question?

RM: I was moved when I found the photograph in my dad's Bible because it was clear he had cherished that picture of his family, keeping it where he could savor it again and again, where he knew it would always be. The picture reminded him of the time when we were all young, when he was young and strong and hopeful. He did not often express affection, but his study of the photograph was an expression of affection. One of my students wrote a paper arguing that when Shakespeare wrote an especially romantic scene, as in *Romeo and Juliet*, he transitioned from blank verse into couplets. The rhyme reinforced the emotion. In "My Father's Bible" I may do the same thing, breaking into rhyme to stress the greater emotional intensity.

RW: "The Knot of Time," another new poem, one about your childhood experience of scarlet fever, reminds me of work by the sixteenth- and seventeenth-century metaphysical poets—I think particularly of George Herbert's "The Pulley." Like Herbert, you announce a central metaphor with the title, you tell a short story, and you conclude by solving that story's central problem in a way that points back to the title: the breaking of your fever delivered you from your sense of knotted time, returning you to "minutes that were linear."

You've said that your poem "Lightning Bug" took years to find its conclusion. Did you discover that last line of "The Knot of Time" when you first drafted the poem? The whole poem sounds seamless. Was it primarily one day's work, or did it take a while to come together?

RM: Having preached revision to my students over the years, it surprised me when I checked my notebooks for dates of composition, while editing my first selected poems, to find that most of the better poems, those I wanted to include in the volume, had been written virtually intact in the first draft. What I had remembered was how I worked on some poems for years, in the case of "Lightning Bug" fifteen years. There are other poems that I have tinkered with again and again also. In the case of "The Knot of Time" I had written a draft of a poem about my memory of the fever delirium and the onion poultice way back in the 1980s. But that poem never worked out, and I left it in the notebook. Over the years since I have thought again and again about that memory. And when I went back to the subject this year I had the advantage of the iambic tetrameter to free my voice and powers of association. The poem was written and revised in a few days. I'm sure I unconsciously incorporated phrases from the earlier discarded poem, though I never went back to look at it. I know the unconscious is a very good editor.

RW: So are the metrical poems coming together differently from the way your earlier poems did, in terms of the writing process?

RM: When I wrote poems in free verse I labored endlessly to get the line breaks right, usually writing dozens of drafts, experimenting with line lengths in short poems. But once I began writing syllabic verse, and then metrical verse, the imagination and voice were freed up to enact and embody experience, memory, meditation. My early poems were short, imagistic, and I revised them hundreds of times because I was trying to discover what a line was. I made up provisional rules such as "a line is an increment of perceptual energy," and "a line is like a pendulum swing, always having the same duration whether long or short. Short lines slow down the pace of a poem; long lines speed it up."

RW: "The Knot of Time" joins a much earlier poem, "Earache," in narrating a childhood episode of serious illness. As prolific as you've been, you've written relatively few poems in which you're the central character, and, of those, most or all (all that come to mind right now) deal with moments from your childhood. So much contemporary poetry features the poet as the star of his or her own poems, over and over (R. S. Gwynn has satirized this tendency in his long poem *The Narcissiad*), but that's not been true of your oeuvre: for you, the autobiographical poem is the exception, not the rule. Did you at some point *decide* that you were going to let the James Merrills and Sharon Oldses go their way while you went yours, or have you just had a natural aversion to stepping into your own spotlight? And is there something about the great distance from childhood that makes it seem more available as subject matter, in those few poems?

RM: Very few of my poems are explicitly autobiographical. More often I try to create, or recreate, the experience of things outside myself, of nature, work, science, and narratives of other people, animals, and history. As poets we write what is given to us. Our subjects choose us. To be able to tap into what is larger than oneself is much of the pleasure of art. This applies to language as well as subjects. All the poems are already immanent in the language. They just have to be discovered and worked free. When we use language, we are accessing the wisdom and genius and experience of the millions who have come before us and given us our language. It is the delight in the playfulness with words and sounds that makes us poets and not philosophers.

RW: You appear as your adult self in "Super Vision," but even there the main character is clearly the red-tailed hawk, not you. You play the object to his subject: it's all about how he perceives you and behaves during your intrusion into "his domain." That's quite different from, say, the relationship between Robert Penn Warren and the same bird in his poem "Red-Tail Hawk and Pyre of Youth," or the way Warren's late sonnet "Mortal Limit" clearly presents the hawk soaring at dusk as a metaphor for himself.

RM: One of the reasons that I enjoy writing poems is that it helps draw me out of my limited self to experience the larger world. So much of the time we are weighed down with ego, selfish concern, with fear, anxiety, tedium. Poetry helps us escape and transcend those boundaries, to connect with that beyond ourselves. That's one reason I fell in love with science as a teenager, along with music and poetry. Science opened up new ways of thinking, new worlds leading to new worlds, after the restricted fundamentalist view I had been raised with. Poetry, both the reading and writing of it, has led to discovery after discovery, of voices and ideas, the pleasures of connection with others, and the satisfaction of work well done.

RW: I'd like to hear you comment on one more of these new poems. "Wise Virgin" reintroduces us to your Aunt Wessie, who appears in at least two earlier poems: "Concert," from your 1976 collection *Land Diving*, and "New Organ," from your 1990 book *Sigodlin*. Both those poems focus on her love of music, but "Wise Virgin" sets that aspect of her life aside and tells us something about "her last days / in [an] expensive nursing home." Right away you tell us that she was restrained, "strapped . . . to the bed / with belts and cords" for her safety's sake. The first seven lines could be the start of a sorrowful meditation on the indignities suffered by a frail family elder. But then the poem turns somewhat comic, inviting us to cheer her as she repeatedly escapes her bonds at night and wanders around the place, "an elderly Houdini." Could you say a few words about that poem?

RM: Aunt Wessie was my mother's older sister. When I was little I spent a great deal of time with her. Sometimes she kept me while my mother worked in the cotton mill, after my grandmother's death. Wessie did love music, and played her piano every day. But she did have very weak eyes, supposedly caused by smoke from poison ash burning on a bonfire when she was a girl. So she played by ear or from memory. Near the end of her life she was placed in an expensive nursing home outside Hendersonville, North Carolina. Whenever I went back home I visited her.

Though she was confused about many things in those final years, she always recognized me. Once she told me, with great conviction, that I must leave Cornell and return home to reopen the old cotton mill in Tuxedo, so local people would have jobs. Clearly she had been pondering this solution to local unemployment for weeks or months. It was flattering to me that she thought me capable of restarting an abandoned textile mill.

It's true that when they strapped Wessie to her bed to prevent her from wandering around the nursing home and falling, she always managed to free herself from the restraints and explore the facility at night from one end to the other. The nursing staff never solved the mystery of her escape from the bonds. And she did dump a pitcher of ice water on her roommate in the dark, apparently thinking she was putting out a threatening fire.

RW: The title refers to one of Jesus's parables, told in Matthew 25:1–13. In some translations it's the parable of the ten bridesmaids, but in the King James Version, the New International Version, and a number of others it's the parable of the ten virgins. For readers familiar with that parable, the poem's title and its conclusion are going to work together to make the whole poem resonate in a different, deeper way than it would otherwise. I think it's ingenious. But titling a poem so allusively is a bit risky: there are going to be readers who don't remember that parable, and of course there will be some who never knew it in the first place. Thinking along these lines leads me to wonder how much, if at all, you make assumptions about your audience and let those dictate what you write, or how you edit what you've written.

RM: "Wise Virgin" because Wessie was always patient, and careful to do the right thing, and because it is almost certain her marriage was never consummated. She did adopt and raise a daughter. She is a figure for whom I feel a great affection.

I think it was Geoffrey Hill who said that difficulty can make poems richer, more significant. Good readers like to work a little to solve mysteries, locate allusions, make connections. In general my poems are quite accessible. But occasionally I like to give the reader something with which to work, to explore. It is one of the pleasures of poetry to find a larger resonance with another text, especially a classic or ancient text, giving the poem a deeper context, a relation to something beyond the immediate narrative and reference. And I prefer to think that my readers are likely smarter and more learned than I am.

RW: I know you've learned a lot about nonhuman nature from your own observation and from family sources, and in interviews and poems as well you've referred to the writings of William Bartram, Alexander Wilson, André Michaux, Lewis and Clark, and James Audubon. Are there any more contemporary sources that have been important to you in this regard? I wonder about that especially with regard to poems about astrophysics and subatomic physics, poems like "Music of the Spheres" and "The Strange Attractor," and several from your latest book of poems, *Dark Energy*: the title poem, for example, and "Dark Matter," "Neutrino" and "Milkomeda."

RM: I have always been interested in the natural world. Having grown up on a farm in the Blue Ridge Mountains of Western North Carolina, I was familiar from an early age with woods and fields, pastures and springs, spring branches, the river bank. I climbed every tree near our house, dug caves in the walls of the gullies, built dams on branches, caught June bugs, jar-flies, crickets, and katydids. I rolled rocks off mountaintops, and played baseball in the pasture. There was about a square mile of land I knew intimately.

As we hoed corn in the river fields I found arrowheads and pieces of Indian pottery. It seemed the soil was haunted by the Cherokees and the other indigenous people who had been there. From my earliest memory I felt a connection to the native people. My dad loved to tell stories about the Indians, about Daniel Boone, and the American frontier. He subscribed to the *National Geographic* magazine, and I pored over the pictures and stories that stimulated my interest in history and geography. Among my favorite books found at the bookmobile were biographies of Buffalo Bill, David Crockett, and the *Little House on the Prairie* series, Jack London's stories of the Klondike.

In my teens I began to discover science, which opened doors to new worlds, and new ways of thinking about history, and our place in history. In college I studied mathematics and science and engineering, before switching to English. But I have kept up my interest, reading *Scientific American* and many other publications over the years. Articles about astronomy, atomic physics, geology, and ecology are like poetry to me. Many of my poems are inspired by that reading.

After moving to Cornell in 1971, I became more and more interested in studying the place where I had grown up, western North Carolina and the southern Appalachian Mountains. I read the accounts of the early explorers such as James Adair and John Lawson, many histories of the Cherokees and first settlers. I read Jefferson's *Notes on the State of Virginia*, and Revolutionary War histories. Those accounts inspired poems also.

RW: Over the last decade you've brought out two fine prose books related to the exploration and settlement of the West—*Boone: A Biography* (2007) and *Lions of the West: Heroes and Villains of the Westward Expansion* (2011)—and I know you're working on a third. There are also poems in *Dark Energy* that deal in one way or another with the West: "Big Bone Lick," "Endowments," "Canebrake," and "Ancient Talk," the last of which tells of Thomas Wolfe's travel out west. There's also "Going West," which describes your childhood longing to "walk to the horizon, / go all the way," and so "be free." If that was the boy's ambition, I'll ask this of the man, who's often labeled as an Appalachian or a southern author: *has* your embrace of the West (as subject matter) been in some sense liberating? Or does it seem to you just a natural extension of your work set in the southern mountains?

RM: Our culture has always looked toward the West, and been drawn to the West, from the time of the Romans and before. Celts and Germanic people moved west into Europe, Romans conquered Gaul and Britain, Vikings invaded Iceland and Greenland and North America. Europeans invaded all the Americas after Columbus. The English-speaking settlers finally crossed the Appalachian chain after the American Revolution. My study of the westward expansion of the United States grew naturally out of my study of the Appalachian region. For the settlements just kept moving west, through the Cumberland Gap, down the Ohio River. The crossroads and heart of the continent was Missouri, and from there people launched out on the Oregon Trail, the California Trail, and the Santa Fe Trail. Those trails were just extensions of Boone's trails into Kentucky and then into Missouri. My interest in the West is a continuation of my study of Appalachian settlement. There is no more interesting history than that of California, the Indians, the missions, the presidios, the Hawaiians who worked there, and the Americans who plunged across the Sierra into the great valley.

RW: Though you've lived in Ithaca for nearly fifty years, you've stayed in touch with your home country of Henderson County, in western North Carolina. That county has changed a great deal over the last few decades: the population has doubled, many retirees from the northeast and elsewhere have moved there, a large number of Spanish-speaking families have done the same, and many farms have been replaced with subdivisions. The area's full of chain restaurants and shopping centers. What are some of your thoughts about the changes that have taken place there since you moved north? Do you think those changes have had any effect on the way you think about the area and engage with it in your poems and/or your fiction?

RM: Henderson County and western North Carolina have changed utterly since I left there in 1971. Having been relatively poor in my childhood, I'm pleased to see more affluence in the area now. There are better schools, more jobs, more opportunities, and far more cultural events. And the retirees and Hispanic people have enriched the culture. When I lived there, there were no Mexican restaurants; now there are dozens. But of course much of what was most distinctive about the region has been erased as it entered the American mainstream. There is always compensation, a trade-off, in change. I'm sure much of my writing in both verse and prose has been inspired by a desire to preserve a sense of the past, to save for our children and grandchildren an appreciation of a culture now gone. You will notice that most of my writing is set in the past, often based on memory. Others are better qualified to write about contemporary Appalachia, the meth culture, the suburbs, the new poor, the overwhelming traffic, and the retirement communities. I have never sought to idealize the past, but to present it realistically.

And yet the vast hunting and haunting ranges of the Cherokees are still there, and the waterfalls, Devil's Courthouse, the hidden coves in some areas. Deer and wild turkeys have returned, and people see the occasional bear. There are even rumors of panthers sighted.

RW: We first met over twenty years ago, and you seem to have hardly aged since. You've recently faced some serious health challenges, but you've just brought out a cinematic new novel, *Chasing the North Star*, and of course too *Dark Energy*, which I think is one of your best books of poetry. *Dark Energy* includes a poem titled "MRI," and it's not hard to imagine where that poem came from. More broadly, though, what effect, if any, do you think your recent experience of illness has had on your writing? Or has the writing served as an escape from such concerns?

RM: In 2013 I was diagnosed with CML, chronic myeloid leukemia. In former times that would have been a dire diagnosis. But now there are drugs such as Gleevec that completely control the disease. That same year a benign meningioma was found on my brain, but it has given me no problems so far. And in that same year I was struck by Lyme disease, which made me very ill indeed because it was not diagnosed for months. Once I began taking antibiotics I recovered and I have felt fine since. I'm not sure I've ever felt better in my adult life.

That experience with Lyme disease gave me a much greater appreciation of health. I have had dozens of MRIs to monitor the meningioma, and I visit the hematologist every few weeks as he keeps an eye on the CML. To tell you the truth, I have kind of enjoyed it. The hematologist has become a friend and the neurosurgeon in Rochester is a history buff, so he and I spend more time talking about American history than discussing brain tumors. I have never worked harder, or enjoyed life more. A serious illness can put things into perspective. You realize what a privilege it is to have your health and to be able to work. The sense of a job well done is one of the most important and lasting satisfactions we know.

Additional Resources and Selected Bibliography

Ashburn, Gwen McNeill. "Working without Nets: Early Twentieth-Century Mountain Women in Fiction." *Journal of Kentucky Studies* 24 (2007): 133–40.

Baker, David. "Heaven and Earth: On Ellen Bryant Voight and Robert Morgan." In *Show Me Your Environment: Essays on Poetry, Poets, and Poems*, 144–49. Ann Arbor: University of Michigan Press, 2014.

Banks, Russell. "Bob Morgan at Chapel Hill." *Pembroke Magazine* 35 (2003): 82–84.

Bherwani, Bhisham. "The Elegiac Strain in Robert Morgan's Poetry." *Yale Review* 105, no. 1 (2017): 80–106.

Bizzaro, Patrick. "Food as Commodity and Metaphor in *Gap Creek*: The Making of Julie." *Appalachian Heritage* 32, no. 3 (2004): 29–35.

Booker-Canfield, Suzanne. "'Middle Sea': Robert Morgan and a New American Romanticism." *Pembroke Magazine* 35 (2003): 71–76.

Booker-Canfield, Suzanne. "The 'Rush Toward the Horizon': The Geography of Land and Language in Robert Morgan's Recent Poetry." *Southern Quarterly* 47, no. 3 (2010): 36–44.

Bourne, Louis M. "On Metaphor and Its Use in the Poetry of Robert Morgan." *The Small Farm* 3 (1976): 63–79.

Chappell, Fred. "Morgan's Things." *Appalachian Heritage* 32, no. 3 (2004): 19–26.

Chappell, Fred. "A Prospect Newly Necessary." *The Small Farm* 3 (1976): 49–53.

Conway, Cecelia. "Robert Morgan's Mountain Voice and Lucid Prose." *Appalachian Journal* 29 (2001–2002): 180–99. Rpt. in *An American Vein: Critical Readings in Appalachian Literature*, edited by Danny L. Miller, Sharon Hatfield, and Gurney Norman, 275–95. Athens: Ohio University Press, 2005.

Denham, Robert D. "'Service Is Also Praise': Recognition in Robert Morgan's *The Truest Pleasure*." *Southern Quarterly* 47, no. 3 (2010): 129–41.

Drewitz-Crockett, Nicole. "Authority, Details, and Intimacy: Southern Appalachian Women in Robert Morgan's Family Novels." *Southern Quarterly* 47, no. 3 (2010): 117–28.

Gilbert, Roger. "Sea and Mountains, Motion and Measure: The Complementary Poetics of A. R. Ammons and Robert Morgan." *Southern Quarterly* 47 no. 3 (2010): 71–90.

Godwin, Rebecca. "Thomas Wolfe and Robert Morgan: Influence and Correspondences." *Thomas Wolfe Review* 38, no. 1 (2014): 54–70.

Graves, Jesse. "Editor's Introduction." Robert Morgan Special Issue of *Southern Quarterly* 47, no. 3 (2010): 6–11.

Graves, Jesse. "Formal Tendencies in the Poetry of Robert Morgan and Ron Rash." *Southern Quarterly* 45, no. 1 (2007): 78–86.

Grimes, Larry. "Echoes and Influences: A Comparative Study of Short Fiction by Ernest Hemingway and Robert Morgan." *Southern Quarterly* 47, no. 3 (2010): 98–116.

Harmon, William. "Robert Morgan's 'Mockingbird' in Company." *Southern Quarterly* 47, no. 3 (2010): 61–70.

Harmon, William. "Robert Morgan's Pelagian Georgics: Twelve Essays." *Parnassus* 9, no. 2 (1981): 5–30.

Johnson, Don. "Robert Morgan's Alchemy: Listening to Time and Space." *Southern Quarterly* 47, no. 3 (2010): 45–52.

Lang, John. "Coming out from under Calvinism: Religious Motifs in Robert Morgan's Poetry." *Shenandoah* 42, no. 2 (1992): 46–60.

Lang, John. "'He Hoes Forever': Robert Morgan and the Pleasures of Work." *Pembroke Magazine* 31 (1999): 221–27.

Lang, John. "Speaking Charmed Syllables: The Two-Fold Vision of *Topsoil Road*." *Pembroke Magazine* 35 (2003): 16–21.

Liotta, P. H. "Robert Morgan: Genius as Music." *Southern Quarterly* 47, no. 3 (2010): 182–88.

Liotta, P. H. "Pieces of the Morgenland: The Recent Achievements in Robert Morgan's Poetry." *Southern Literary Journal* 22 (1989): 32–40.

McFee, Michael. "'The Witness of Many Writings': Robert Morgan's Poetic Career." *Iron Mountain Review* 6, no. 1 (1990): 17–23.

Merod, J. B. "Robert Morgan's 'Wisdom-Lighted Islands.'" *The Small Farm* 3 (1976): 54–62.

Perry, Lori A. Davis. "Becoming America." [On Morgan's novel *Brave Enemies*.] *War, Literature, and the Arts* 16 (2004): 274–80.

Rash, Tom. "The Poetry of Robert Morgan: An Appreciation." *Southern Quarterly* 47, no. 3 (2010): 53–60.

Schultz, Robert. "Recovering Pieces of the Morgenland." *Virginia Quarterly Review* 64 (1988): 176–88.

Shurbutt, Sylvia Bailey. "Robert Morgan's Peripheral Vision: 'The Point Beside the Point' in *The Hinterlands*." *North Carolina Literary Review* 19 (2010): 30–43.

Smith, Newton. "Going Back to the Mountains from 'Topsoil Road': A Retrospective Look at Robert Morgan's Poetry." *Pembroke Magazine* 35 (2003): 55–64.

Smith, Rebecca. "The Elemental in *The Truest Pleasure* and *Gap Creek*: Nature as Physical Force and Spiritual Metaphor." *Pembroke Magazine* 35 (2003): 37–46.

Villiers, Regina. "Women in Robert Morgan's Short Fiction: A Study of *The Blue Valleys* and *The Mountains Won't Remember Us*." *Pembroke Magazine* 35 (2003): 65–70.

Waage, Fred. "In the Non-Euclidean Mountains of Robert Morgan's Poetry." *Pembroke Magazine* 35 (2003): 47–53.

West, Robert. "'Here's the Church, Here's the Steeple': Robert Morgan, Philip Larkin, and the Emptiness of Sacred Space." *Southern Quarterly* 47, no. 3 (2010): 91–97.

West, Robert. "A Study in Sharpening Contrast: Robert Morgan and the Distinction between Poetry and Prose." *Pembroke Magazine* 35 (2003): 77–81.

West, Robert. "Toward 'Crystal-Tight Arrays': Teaching the Evolving Art of Robert Morgan's Poetry." In *Appalachia in the Classroom: Teaching the Region*, edited by Theresa L. Burriss and Patricia M. Gantt, 252–64. Athens: Ohio University Press, 2013.

Wilhelm, Randall. "Bricking the Text: The Builder in Robert Morgan's Mountain World." *Southern Quarterly* 47, no. 3 (2010): 142–50.

Williams, Mary C., and Parks Lanier. "Inside-Outside in Robert Morgan's Poetry." In *The Poetics of Appalachian Space*, edited by Parks Lanier, 149–60. Knoxville: University of Tennessee Press, 1991.

Williams, Mary C. "The Toolshed, the Feed Room, and the Potato Hole: Place in Robert Morgan's Poetry." *Iron Mountain Review* 6, no. 1 (1990): 26–30.

Index

About the Editors

Randall Wilhelm is editor of *The Ron Rash Reader* (2014) and coeditor, with Zackary Vernon, of *Summoning the Dead: Essays on Ron Rash* (2018). He teaches at Anderson University as assistant professor of English.

Jesse Graves is author of three poetry collections and a recipient of the James Still Award for Writing About the Appalachian South from the Fellowship of Southern Writers. He teaches at East Tennessee State University as associate professor of English and poet-in-residence.

www.ingramcontent.com/pod-product-compliance
Lightning Source LLC
Chambersburg PA
CBHW020653030726
47498CB00002B/495